THE DILEMMA OF

LAODICEA

"He Who Has An Ear, Let Him Hear"
"Woe to those who are at ease in Zion" (Amos 6:1)

by James Jacob Prasch

Cover Art by Carrie Nelson

First Edition   August, 2010

THE DILEMMA OF LAODICEA

Publishing Rights: "True Light" on behalf of James Jacob Prasch

Library of Congress Control Number 2010931988
Trade Edition ISBN 978-0-9828599-0-2

Contents

Contents

Contents

Foreword
by Dr. David L. Hocking

James Jacob Prasch is my friend. I have been involved with him in prophecy conferences throughout the United States and other countries. I have heard many unusual and different messages from him that have always stimulated my interest and increased my understandings of Bible passages.

Jacob is a true scholar, especially in areas of Jewish history and understanding. You will find this book to be a "refreshing" look at the Seven Churches of Revelation, and one that will provide you with a greater understanding of historical backgrounds that affect the interpretation of these final messages of our Lord Yeshua (Jesus Christ) to the churches of Asia Minor. After hearing one of his presentations on these matters, I immediately encouraged him to do some writing and make his teachings known to a wider audience.

I am quite familiar with the Book of Revelation, having written a commentary on it several years ago, and preaching messages on the book and its warnings and promises for many years now. I have also taught the book in college and graduate school settings. In that respect, I found this work by Jacob to be exceptional in every way. The Jewish understandings that he brings to the reader will open up many passages concerning the Seven Churches. His historical backgrounds and the details presented in them are indeed excellent and very informative.

9

The Dilemma of Laodicea

Jacob takes the time to help the reader understand the four basic ways to interpret the Book of Revelation, and why each view contributes something to one's final conclusions.

Jacob lives in England, but travels extensively around the world. He is fluent in Biblical languages and history. Because he has continued to confront churches about compromise, deception, and false teaching, some have misunderstood him and his motives. I know him well. He is most sincere and dedicated to our Lord and the infallibility of His written Word. Jacob is bold and confrontational, but never unaware of what he is attacking. His fear of the Lord far exceeds any attempts to criticize and avoid His analysis and insights. His messages are greatly needed among believers today.

His expertise in Jewish Messianic teachings and practices is outstanding, and the reader will greatly appreciative his wisdom about these matters. His explanation of the methods of "midrash" in the interpretation of the Bible is also very helpful.

Jacob takes a strong position in this unique book on the historical interpretation of these church messages, seeing them as a panorama of church history from the Day of Pentecost in Acts 2 until the present day. He also believes that all seven of these churches can exist in any moment of time within the historical framework that he presents so well.

One may not agree with all the positions that Jacob takes in this book, but every reader will thank the Lord for the depth and impact that this book will make upon the body of Christ today. I believe that so far in his incredible ministry Jacob has given us a resource that present and future scholars of all interpretative beliefs will not only appreciate, but also gain much help in the teaching and preaching of these wonderful and powerful messages from the lips of our blessed Lord Yeshua!

It is a joy and privilege for me personally to recommend this outstanding book to all who will take the time to read carefully its comments and admonitions. Thank you, Jacob, for giving us such a wonderful legacy of your ministry and your love of our Lord!

Dr. David L. Hocking
HOPE for TODAY Ministries

Introduction
Nothing New Under The Sun

This book examines the history of the church in the light of the letters of Jesus Christ to the seven churches in Asia, as recorded by John in his Revelations.

The age of some of the most common errors held regarding the seven churches is surprising. Unless learning can be achieved from the errors of the past it is a sure thing that those errors will be repeated. Indeed, as the teacher King Solomon wrote:

> *That which has been is that which will be,*
> *And that which has been done is that which will be done.*
> *So **there is nothing new under the sun**.*
> *Is there anything of which one might say,*
> *"See this, it is new"?*
> *Already it has existed for ages*
> *Which were before us.*
> *There is no remembrance of earlier things;*
> *And also of the later things which will occur,*
> *There will be for them no remembrance*
> *Among those who will come later still. (Ecc. 1:9-11)*

The Significance of the Names of the Seven Churches

The Greek names reveal something about each church. Each church also seems to represent an approximation of a certain period of history, but the types of each church and the periods they each represent overlap. Although this is the predominant characteristic of the church overall within any given period of history, churches bearing characteristics of all seven are found to exist to one degree or another.

Ephesus: "Not lasting," "short lived." Represents the apostolic church of the first-century Apostles.

Smyrna: "Anointed for burial," "bitterness," "myrrh," "mourning." Represents the Pre-Nicean church during the 2nd and 3rd centuries.

Pergamum: "Divorced," "spiritual idolatry." Also "tower" or "worldly strength." Represents the church from the 4th through 16th centuries from Constantine to the Reformation during the height of the "Holy Roman Empire."

Thyatira: "Continuing sacrifice." Represents the Church from the 11th through 16th centuries at the height of the Dark Ages.

Sardis: "Incomplete" or "of the flesh" or "renewal." Represents the church during the period commonly referred to as the Reformation beginning in the 16th century onward.

Philadelphia: "Brotherly love." Represents the Evangelical missionary movements and Great Awakening from the 18th century onward.

Laodicea: "People's opinions." Represents the final church in the Last Days before Jesus returns, thought to have begun post World War II and continuing today.

Application to Actual Churches

"Therefore write the things which you have seen, and the things which are, and the things which will take place after these things. (Rev. 1:19)

So there are *"things which you have seen," "things which are,"* and *"things which will take place."*

These seven churches, which actually existed in the first century (*"things which you have seen"*), also represent seven broad types of churches that can exist at any time in history (*"things which are"*), and seven generally overlapping periods of church history (*"things which will take place"*). These letters to the seven churches of Asia can be applied in four main ways:

• They existed literally and historically at the end of the first century A.D.

• They are seven types of church which exist at any time throughout history.

• They represent seven types of church that will exist at the end of the age.

• They correspond quite well to seven periods of church history.

Interpretation by "Midrash"

"Midrash" is a term meaning "enquire into." Jews read the Scriptures with a completely different approach from the manner the Western mind reads them. The meaning of a word and the context are important, but the Jewish approach looks for a consistent theme or pattern to explain it.

The subject of exegesis in the Early Church generally, and more specifically New Testament uses of Midrash by the Apostles as a hermeneutic (method of biblical interpretation), is an involved subject beyond the purposes of this book. Hence we only address it in brief, relative to the contents at hand. A more exhaustive treatment of this important aspect of understanding holy writ would require a separate work dedicated to that purpose. Biblically-based Evangelical theologians dating back to the 17th century have contended for a necessity of the church to revert back to understanding the hermeneutics of the early Jewish church that produced the New Testament.

This was a common feature among the Puritans such as John Robinson , but was later developed by early dispensational expositors, particularly among the Plymouth Brethren in the 19th and early 20th Centuries. In the first century a resurgence of interest in the subject of Midrash and midrashic methodology being employed in the composition of the New Testament has re-emerged as a result of the increased numbers of Jews accepting Christ as the Messiah and looking for what St. Paul called the "reza" or "Hebrew root" of the church as it is defined in Romans 11.

Much of this so-called Messianic scholarship has focused on a rediscovery of the "Sitz im Leben" of the Second Temple Period Judaism from which the original Christianity of Jesus and His apostles sprung. The pioneer of much of this scholarship was without doubt Alfred Edersheim, followed by David Baron, Rachmiel Fryland, and the late Dr. Louis Goldberg. Today it continues with Dallas Seminary graduate Dr. Arnold Fruchtenbaum, Dr. Michael Rydelnik of Moody Bible Institute and other Dispensational (but also some Reformed) scholars.

The Dilemma of Laodecia

Much Messianic scholarship has also been pursued by non-Jews versed in Judaic studies. Centers of this have been the Caspari Library and Holy Land Institute, both located in Jerusalem. The essence of this area of scholarship has been Messianic apologetics with the focus on the evangelization of Jews. The noted Finnish scholar Dr. Risto Santala has probably been at the forefront of an advanced level of Messianic apologetics for the messiahship of Christ based on rabbinic sources. Curiously, if not remarkably, there has been an upsurge in rabbinic scholarship by unbelieving Jewish academics and scholarly rabbis into the Jewish background of the New Testament.

After the late Anglican scholar J.A.T. Robinson abandoned the liberal higher critical presupposition that the Gospels were a product of a Gentile church authored centuries after the time of Jesus as implausible in large part due to the familiarity of the texts with first-century Judaism (supplemented by the discovery of a key first-century Gospel fragment and the crucial Thiessen text), rabbinic interest independently began to surface. Ivy League Professor Jacob Neusner labeled the Gospels as the pivotal ancient Jewish literature between the Apocrypha and the early midrashim. Oxford professor Gezer Vermes, Rabbi and professor Pinchas Lipade, the late Rabbi and professor David Flusser, and British rabbinic scholar Hayim Macobee, among others, endorsed the Jewish origin of the Gospel narratives.

All of this renewed scholarship and the Renaissance of interest in the Judaic origins of the New Testament and Christian faith however, have not been positive. The Jerusalem School of Synoptic Research in the absence of solid manuscript evidence has conjectured an original Hebrew authorship of the Gospels, when in fact even the earliest existing Syriac texts were translated from Greek and, apart from a single patristic reference for a Hebrew authorship of Matthew from Papias and Hegesippus (which may have been the Hebrew dialect in Aramaic), no real evidence exists for their contentions.

Additionally, most of the popular Messianic Movement has degenerated into a Judaized legalism, even seeking to place non-Jews under rabbinic custom and Torah observance, and is generally devoid of serious Judaic scholarship. However, the rediscovery of the Hebraic nature of the Christian faith and Judaic nature of New Testament narratives and certain of the Epistles addressed to Jews, such as James, Hebrews, Jude, and Peter, is once again much in vogue. This articulates well with propositions for a fresh assessment of biblical hermeneutics pressed for by such renowned scholars as Moisés Silva. This includes a focus on the midrashic hermeneutics that increased numbers of New Testament scholars are finding unavoidable.

Introduction

A good introduction to the use of Jewish exegesis, including Midrash by the New Testament authors, can be found in the works of a plethora of conservative Evangelical (and some other) scholars, including R.N. Longenecker, David Daube, T.S. Doherty, and John Lightfoot. The classic academic treatment is to be found in the extensive research of Bilderbeck and Strauss. Again, this massive area of theology lies outside the scope of this book, and we shall therefore limit our uses of it to the theme.

It is imperative that we watch out for false rules of exegesis, of interpreting meaning *out* of Scripture. "When the plain sense makes sense, seek no other sense" is a rule that has guided most Western techniques of study. Notably this is not found in the Bible. When Jesus said to give food to the hungry, He certainly meant that food should be given to Somalia or to the Sudanese, but He *also* meant that the Gospel, the bread of life, should be given to those who hunger for it, to all who will listen. It is not a case of "either/or"; it is a case of "both/and." *Both* interpretations are correct.

Thus to a Jew the Exodus ("coming out") of Egypt with its worldly riches, away from Pharaoh, across the Red Sea and into freedom, is a pattern or a foretaste of how Yeshua (Jesus) leads followers out of the world with its riches, away from the Devil, through the water of baptism in His name, and into the Kingdom of Heaven. Similarly, when Moses went up a mountain, made a covenant with the people and sprinkled them with blood, it was a pattern of Yeshua going up to Jerusalem and bringing in the New Covenant with His own blood.

The theme of midrash also links Joshua to Revelation. At Jericho there was silence for seven days, and on the seventh day the seven trumpets were sounded seven times. At the last trumpet there was a great shout, the kingdom of this world (Jericho and its walls) fell down, and God's people rushed in with divine justice. (Make no mistake, the Canaanites were very evil people. Sodom and Gomorrah were no better. That is why God destroyed them except for a few righteous people.) In Revelation is found the same thing. Within the seven seals are seven trumpets and seven plagues, a subset of seven coming out of seven coming out of seven. At the last trumpet there will be a great shout and the kingdom of this world will fall down at the coming of the King of Kings and Lord of Lords with the armies of heaven following Him at a place called Armageddon. Then the new Kingdom of our God and His Messiah will begin on earth.

Genesis and John fit together in this same manner. Both begin with "*In the beginning ...*" The fig tree has long been taught in Judaism to be a metaphor for the Tree of Life since the Intertestamental Period (0 - 400 BC). When

Jesus said He saw Nathaniel under the fig tree (Jn. 1:48), it must be understood that this related not simply to a literal fig tree where it seems Jesus had seen him in a vision, but that He also saw him under the Tree of Life in the Garden of Eden. Jesus, in the Jewish way of interpreting Scripture, was saying that He saw Nathaniel from the very beginning, from the creation of the world.

Abel was the first martyr according to Jesus, and his blood cried out (Lk. 11:51). In Revelation the martyrs cried out (Rev. 6:9-10). The beginning teaches about the end. God inspired the Book of Revelation, also the Gospel of John, and Genesis. They recapitulate and parallel each other. To understand the *new* creation, examine the account of the *first* creation.

Midrash as recorded in the original Hebrew text of The Old Testament (2 Chr. 13:22), and as used in the New Testament, never violates the principles of context and co-text and depends on first recognizing the literal straightforward meaning (the *Peshet*) as essential to discovering the further meaning (the *Pesher*).

Note that there is one rule that is most important to follow: Never, ever, *ever* base doctrine on a "type" or an allegory. The Bible never does that. What the Bible does do, and therefore what its adherents should do, is *illustrate* doctrine with allegory.

For example, consider the Passover meal. The Bible never bases atonement on the Passover lamb and its symbolism. But it does use symbolism to illustrate doctrine, to explain how Jesus died *like* a Passover lamb in place of all who believe in Him, just as the blood of the Passover lambs set free all the Jews who believed in Moses.

Consider also Daniel and Revelation:

> *"But as for you, Daniel, conceal these words and* **seal up** *the book until the end of time; many will go back and forth, and knowledge will increase." (Dan. 12:4)*

> *And he said to me, "* **Do not seal up** *the words of the prophecy of this book, for the time is near. (Rev. 22:10)*

The Holy Spirit encoded these things, and in the Last Days the Holy Spirit will decode them for the faithful. That decoding requires re-reading Scripture in the original context God provided, which was according to a Jewish mind-set.

Genesis also fits with Revelation. God declared the end from the beginning (Is. 46:10). Man's relationship with God began in the Garden of Eden. It continued in the Garden of Gethsemane followed by the cross and the garden tomb. Three days later Mary Magdalene saw the resurrected Jesus and thought He was the gardener. She was not entirely wrong – remember in Genesis 2 that God took Adam and "put him in the garden to work" (Gen.2:8). In a sense Jesus was a second Adam, but He ascended into heaven.

And it all ends in Revelation when Jesus returns. The Garden of Eden will be restored with the river of the water of life and the Tree of Life and man walking again with God. The curse that came in with sin and the fall of man in Genesis 3 is broken and "There will no longer be any curse" (Rev. 22:3). Nor, of course, any sin. The whole story is symmetrical, with Jesus and the cross at the center. In the *beginning* everything was very good, and in the *end* everything will be very good.

These are all examples of Midrash – theme, or pattern. The Bible usually interprets itself.

In dealing with the seven churches of Revelation, including Laodicea, we will applicatively explore how a literal church at one period of history is figurative of other churches at a different time and place. This is a key component in the way the New Testament midrashically handles other Scripture.

In Matthew's Nativity narratives we have four formula citations where Old Testament passages are cited and applied to Christ where the considerations that met the circumstances of one situation co-equally applied to another. (The classic example of this is Hosea 11:1 where the Exodus motif is applied to the return of the infant Christ from Egypt.) Thus we see that in the seven churches such Old Testament texts as the teaching of Balaam (Num. 31:16) is applied to events in Pergamum (Rev. 2:14), or where the epic of Jezebel is applied to the church at Thyatira (Rev. 2:20). Davidic motifs are likewise applied to Christ (Rev. 3:7, etc.).

Although we do not subscribe to an unqualified acceptance of Dispensationalism (as the Scriptures plainly teach only two dispensations, not multiple as most Dispensationalists assert), we do hold to the basic Dispensationalism conveyed in the New Testament, and we reject most of the tenets of Covenant Theology as it has no overt scriptural basis, and many of its tenets and adjuncts are contrary to truths specifically stated in Scripture. In exegeting the seven churches we affirm, but do not limit ourselves to, the dispensational interpretation which views the actual seven churches as typologically corresponding prophetically to seven somewhat overlapping church ages. Again, the viability of this argument would depend on a midrashic hermeneutic where what is true of one circumstance has dual application to another. However, lest we be found guilty of eisegetical argumentation (or deductive, as opposed to inductive, conclusion), we do exegetically cite Revelation 4:1, *"After these things,"* where John's transfiguration and witness to the heavenly vision sequentially follows seven churches. These seven churches are sandwiched between Revelation 1:19 and 4:1, where Jesus prefaces His dictation of the seven short epistles to John by stating that the things are, yet are also to come. Thus the seven churches literally existed at one time, yet still had a future meaning before the primary revelation to John commenced in Revelation 4:2.

Therefore in examining each church we shall open with a historical prologue of the actual church in the Roman province of Asia at the end of the first century, but thereafter move to the things which *"are to come"* in future church ages in the character of each of the original seven churches.

Do Not Add or Take Away

All doctrinal error either adds to Scripture or takes away from Scripture. Either way, it always takes away from the truth about the Lord Jesus. Consider the consistent theme of these eight Scriptures:

"Now, O Israel, listen to the statutes and the judgments which I am teaching you to perform, so that you may live and go in and take possession of the land which the LORD, the God of your fathers, is giving you. **You shall not add to the word which I am commanding you, nor take away from it,** that you may keep the commandments of the LORD your God which I command you." (Deut. 4:1-2)

"These words the LORD spoke to all your assembly at the mountain from the midst of the fire, of the cloud and of the thick gloom, with a great voice, and **He added no more.** He wrote them on two tablets of stone and gave them to me." (Deut. 5:22)

"Whatever I command you, you shall be careful to do; **you shall not add to nor take away from it.**" (Deut. 12:32)

As for God, His way is blameless; **The word of the LORD is tested**... (2 Sam. 22:31; Ps. 12:6; 18:30; Prov. 30:5)

Do not add to His words Or He will reprove you, and you will be proved a liar. (Prov.30:6)

The words of wise men are like goads, and masters of these collections are like well-driven nails; they are given by one Shepherd. **But beyond this, my son, be warned:** the writing of many books is endless, and excessive devotion to books is wearying to the body. (Ecc. 12:11-12)

Introduction

*Now these things, brethren, I have figuratively applied to myself and Apollos for your sakes, so that in us you may learn **not to exceed what is written**... (1 Co. 4:6)*

*"I testify to everyone who hears the words of the prophecy of this book: if anyone **adds to them**, God will add to him the plagues which are written in this book; and if anyone **takes away from the words of the book** of this prophecy, God will take away his part from the tree of life and from the holy city, which are written in this book." (Rev. 22:18-19)*

Classical Interpretations of End-Times Prophecies

There are four primary ways to interpret Revelation and approach biblical eschatology, the formal study of the End Times. Each way is correct and they are not necessarily mutually exclusive. The problem comes when one is taken exclusively and all others subsequently dismissed.

The first is called "***Preterism***" and is favored most by liberal scholars. They believe that the Bible is primarily intended to teach moral principles and they therefore assert that these things have already happened. They acknowledge the events have been captured in Scripture in the future tense as if they were still going to happen, but assert this is literary license describing events **after** they happened as if they had been predicted in advance.

Believe it or not this is not entirely wrong. Remember, Jewish prophecy is pattern: one Scripture interprets another; it must all fit together. Revelation 13 presents the Antichrist and his image. Antiochus Epiphanes partially fulfilled this is 168 BC when he sacrificed pigs on the altar in the Temple, and Judas Maccabeus overcame him in a great victory remembered to this day at the Feast of Hanukkah or "Dedication," held on the 25th of the month of Kislev in winter, which Jesus celebrated in John 10:22. But later, in Matthew 24, Jesus said that it was **going** to happen **again**. So Preterism is not wrong. He spoke of something that already happened in the course of explaining how it would happen yet again. What is wrong is what the liberals do with it!

Even more ludicrous than the liberal higher critical Preteristic approach to eschatology is the Preterism of self-defined Evangelicals often holding to a Reconstructionist-Reformed position among certain Calvinists, or a Dominion Theology position among hyper-Charismatics. The contentions of these voices that the Olivet Discourse (Mt. 24-25; Lk. 21; Mk. 13) were totally fulfilled in AD 70 along with the prophetic predictions of the Book

19

of Revelation is dismissed by the context and plain teaching of Jesus. Not only did Christ not return to give people their eternal rewards based on what they did with their talents in AD 70, but He made it clear that nothing as bad as the Great Tribulation would ever happen again. The traumatic events of AD 70, while a prophetic foreshadowing of the Great Tribulation and "Time of Jacob's Trouble," could not possibly have been the coming Great Tribulation because historically far worse events have happened both to Israel and the Jews and to the church since that time. To hold to this kind of Preterism is therefore prima facie pure folly as it is inconsistent with both biblical indication and historical record.

The second is called "*Historicism.*" This approach asserts that these were events predicted for the future, but they have already been completely fulfilled during the early church era. Luther rejected the Book of Revelation. (He also rejected the Epistle of James.) Calvin and Zwingli believed in Historicism. So when the emperor demanded to be worshipped, he was deemed the fulfillment of the Antichrist. When the Emperor Constantine moved to Constantinople the popes took the place of the Emperor as the Antichrist, and the Reformers thought of them this same way.

It is important to note that Historicism is also not wrong. These prophecies all had a *partial* fulfillment in the early church. Jesus spoke about events in the Last Days in the same breath as He spoke about the events soon to come in AD 70. He said, "*When you see Jerusalem surrounded...flee*" (Lk. 21:20-22). Somehow this will happen again, but it also *literally* happened in AD 70. To the Jewish way of thinking, it can be fulfilled more than once—a series of partial fulfillment leading up to a final, ultimate fulfillment.

Historicism has its obvious problems, one of which is that not everything predicted happened in the early church. Certainly Jesus did not set up His kingdom on earth with all government on His shoulders. There is a special blessing in Revelation 1:3: "*Blessed* (continuously in Greek) *is he who reads* (continuously) *...the words of the prophecy.*" If it all happened already then there can be no blessing! This book is a blessing throughout history. Historicism is true only as far as it goes—a pattern of partial fulfillment until the ultimate, final fulfillment.

Then there is "*Poemicism,*" from a Greek word meaning "war" or "controversy." This approach asserts that prophecy is designed to encourage Christians at any time in history, particularly during times of persecution. Once again, this is perfectly valid. The problem is when it is claimed that this is all there is and nothing else.

Introduction

Finally there is "**Futurism**." The Futurist says it is **all** about things yet to be fulfilled in the future, and **only** about things of the future. According to such a view, this book will mean nothing until the Last Days. The problem with that approach is that these seven churches existed in the first century and lasted another 500 years. No, the blessing is for **any** believer who reads Revelation at **any** time, so it cannot be **wholly** futuristic. When it is seen how all these things were largely fulfilled in the early church it provides the example of how they will be ultimately fulfilled at the end.

These are the four ways one can interpret End-Times prophecy. The Western mind often sees them as "either/or" and believes only one approach can be true, rendering all other approaches invalid. The Jewish way of looking at the Scriptures allows for all four approaches to be true simultaneously and as complementing each other.

A Warning from Jesus

As He was sitting on the Mount of Olives, the disciples came to Him privately, saying, "Tell us, when will these things happen, and what will be the sign of Your coming, and of the end of the age?" And Jesus answered and said to them, "See to it that no one misleads you. For many will come in My name, saying, 'I am the Christ,' and will mislead many...'"..."Many false prophets will arise and will mislead many"..."For false Christs and false prophets will arise and will show great signs and wonders, so as to mislead, if possible, even the elect. Behold, I have told you in advance." (Mt. 24:3-5, 11, 24-25)

Earlier, during the Sermon on the Mount, Jesus warned,

"Beware of the false prophets, who come to you in sheep's clothing, but inwardly are ravenous wolves. (Mt. 7:15)

"In sheep's clothing" – so they will look like Christians! If they did not, they would be unlikely to deceive. It takes only one false direction in a set of directions to cause someone to get lost.

It is so easy to think that the trained, professional and paid preacher must know best. Scripture commands us, *"Examine everything carefully"* (1 Th. 5:21). Always remember, it was the Lord Jesus who said, *"Watch out for false prophets... See to it that no one deceives you."*

Chapter 1

Ephesus: "Not Lasting"
First Century

1st	2nd	3rd	4th	5th	6th	7th	8th	9th	10th	11th	12th	13th	14th	15th	16th	17th	18th	19th	20th
Apostolic Church																			
Pre-Nicean Church																			
					Rise of the Institutional Church														
										The Dark Ages									
																The Reformation			
															Great Awakening				
																Apostate Church			

"To the angel of the church in Ephesus write:

"'The One who holds the seven stars in His right hand, the One who walks among the seven golden lampstands, says this:

"'"I know your deeds and your toil and perseverance, and that you cannot tolerate evil men, and you put to the test those who call themselves apostles, and they are not, and you found them to be false; and you have perseverance and have endured for My name's sake, and have not grown weary. But I have this against you, that you have left your first love.

Therefore remember from where you have fallen, and repent and do the deeds you did at first; or else I am coming to you and will remove your lampstand out of its place—unless you repent. Yet this you do have, that you hate the deeds of the Nicolaitans, which I also hate.'"

"He who has an ear, let him hear what the Spirit says to the churches. To him who overcomes, I will grant to eat of the tree of life which is in the Paradise of God." (Rev. 2:1-7)

The Ephesian Age

Ephesus differs from the other six of the seven churches in that it refers to the Apostolic or Ephesian age of the church up to the close of the first century AD. Hence, unlike the other six churches, it has no future application to another age in any primary sense prophetically although the principles for which Christ both commends and admonishes it apply to churches of all ages. The original time frame of Ephesus is the age in which the church existed at the time of John's vision. (The author holds to a classical Johannine authorship – but the reasons for holding this position are found beyond the scope of this work).

Ephesus, a Great City

Today Ephesus is a Muslim village called Selsuk, which is a popular place to visit. According to tradition it was the burial site of John after he returned from prison on the island of Patmos, and one can stand where some Evangelical archaeologists from the United States say he is buried. Ephesus is described in its letter as having a special lamp among the seven golden lamp stands that no other church had (Rev. 2:5). Because of its apostolic associations, and because of its Jewish roots and its ability to understand Scripture from the original Jewish perspective, it was able to see things that other churches were not. But that lamp was removed.

When visiting Ephesus today (the village of Selsuk), one will hardly even find a nominal Christian, let alone a born again Christian. Visitors can explore the ruins of the Temple of Artemis where the riot occurred during Paul's ministry (Acts 19:23-41). There is a place called "Mary's House" which, according to the tradition of the Greek Orthodox Church, was the place to which Mary retired with the apostle John. For about £20 a personal tour will be provided. However, although this is a place that was associated with Peter, Paul, Barnabas, John and later Polycarp—all pillars of the church—today it is completely devoid of **any** form of Christianity. It is amazing how that can happen, how a place can be the center of so much of God's truth and history and yet practically turn to nothing overnight.

John wrote the Book of Revelation around AD 96, and in those days Ephesus was the greatest port in Asia. Although Pergamum was the capital city of the Province of Asia, Ephesus was much larger with a population of around 250,000. It was considered to be the fourth largest city in the Empire after Rome, Alexandria and Antioch. Roads from Colossae, Laodicea and Galatia reached the Mediterranean at Ephesus via Sardis. Thus Ephesus was on the highway to Rome. It boasted fabulous architecture and impressive roads, including a seventy-foot-wide tree-lined road running down to the harbor.

Ephesus was home to a 25,000-seat theater and the Temple of Diana (also known as Artemis) which is considered one of the seven wonders of the ancient world. Built entirely of marble, it was the largest building in the entire Greek world. 36 of its 127 pillars, each sixty feet high, were overlaid with gold so that it was hugely extravagant and impressive to people of the time. The image of Artemis in the center was a squat, black, multi-breasted figure, an excavated statue of which is on display in the Vatican Museum. It bears a startling resemblance to icons of Mary the mother of Christ. In fact it was at the Council of Ephesus in the fifth century that Mary was later proclaimed "Queen of Heaven" and "Mother of God" in imitation of the pagan worship of Diana (or Artemis) of Ephesus, even though the Greek term "Theotikos" − or "mother of god" − is nowhere found in the New Testament. One need only read Acts 19 to see how precious Artemis was to the Ephesians.

This same city identified so closely with the apostolic church became foundational to the later paganizing that saw mainstream Christianity transformed into a paganized and politicized Christendom. There were also temples to the Emperors Claudius, Nero and Domitian, the latter housing a statue of the Emperor four times larger than life-size, depicting Domitian as Zeus, the ruler of the gods. A huge forearm survives in a museum.

Later, when Christians were brought from Asia to be flung to the lions in the arena in Rome, Ignatius (c. 35 – c. 110), the third "Bishop of Antioch" who was himself martyred, called Ephesus "the Highway of the Martyrs."

The Time of Emperor Domitian

Pliny (c. 61 – c. 113) complained about Domitian's practice of being addressed as "Dominus et Deus Noster."—that is, "Our Lord and our God." The poet Statius called him "the morning star," a title the Bible gives to Jesus, although Lucifer wanted to be that morning star. Therefore Domitian, who introduced a terrible persecution of Christians, is seen as a type of antichrist, the devil personified. Significantly, as if to correct Domitian's claim, John records in his Gospel that Thomas acclaimed Jesus as "*My Lord and my God*" (Jn. 20:28). Furthermore, in His Revelation the final words of Jesus are, "*I am the root and descendant of David, the bright morning star.*" (Rev. 22:16).

There were many signs of the end of the age in the first century. When James was martyred, a man called Simeon became the senior pastor of the church in Jerusalem. He remembered what Jesus said and led the believers in Jerusalem to a place called Pella. (See *The Jewish War* by Josephus.) All the believers were rescued because when they saw the fulfillment of all the signs, they took advantage of a temporary withdrawal by Roman forces and fled Jerusalem. But the Jews who remained through the siege of Jerusalem by Titus in AD 70 suffered great tribulation and even ate their babies, fulfilling the terrible warnings of Deuteronomy 28. This happened before when Jerusalem was besieged by Nebuchadnezzar (Ez.5:10). This prefigures what will happen again before Armageddon.

Persecution

The Emperor demanded to be worshipped on the Lord's Day (Rev. 1:10) one day a year. Many Christians refused to bow down to a false god. Peter and Paul were killed and Rome was burned. This prefigures the death of the two martyrs of Revelation 11, a word which also means "witnesses." Those events which actually happened will be replayed at the end of the age. They are a shadow of the final fulfillment to come.

Ephesus as a center of Pagan worship furnishes a high definition image of the persecution in the Last Days. The promenade leading to the *Agorra* (market) was decked with a gate containing the overhead inscription hailing Caesar as the son of god. Hence, in order to buy or sell, there had to be de facto recognition of the claimed deity of the emperor. The Christians refusing to do so found themselves excluded from commercial life of the city and were unable to buy or sell. Moreover, they were tied to poles on either side of the promenade and set alight as human street lamps to illuminate the way into the market. This is a foreshadowing of what Antichrist will attempt to do, linking one's capacity to engage in commerce with an implicit recognition of his claimed deity.

Before the establishment of denominations there was a degree of unity in the church which was brought about by persecution. It will be the same in the Last Days. In the early church there existed the repeated teaching about the Last Days. "When is He coming?" was a common concern, so when Jesus did not reappear people began to get discouraged. So Jesus appeared via his angel to say,

> "He who overcomes...until the end..." (Rev. 2:26)
>
> But, "How long, O Lord, holy and true?" (Rev. 6:10)
>
> "Until the number of their fellow servants and their brethren who were to be killed even as they had been, would be completed also." (Rev. 6:11).

It is a fearful thought, but just as there was strong persecution in the early church, so there will be again in the Last Days. Look at what is happening today in China or North Korea to born again Christians. Rome under Emperor Nero burned Christians—citizens of his own kingdom—and in the 16th century the Church of Rome burned its own members for reading the Bible. The Last Days will indeed call for patient endurance on the part of the saints (Rev. 13:10)!

Jesus the High Priest

"The Revelation of Jesus Christ, which God gave Him..." (Rev. 1:1)

God gave it to Jesus.

"Then I turned to see the voice that was speaking with me. And having turned I saw seven golden lampstands; and in the middle of the lampstands I saw one like a son of man, clothed in a robe reaching to the feet, and girded across His chest with a golden sash. His head and His hair were white like white wool, like snow; and His eyes were like a flame of fire. His feet were like burnished bronze, when it has been made to glow in a furnace, and His voice was like the sound of many waters. In His right hand He held seven stars, and out of His mouth came a sharp two-edged sword; and His face was like the sun shining in its strength." (Rev. 1:12-16)

Notice that Jesus appears dressed as the new High Priest, replacing the Jewish High Priest of Exodus 29. The High Priest was consecrated by blood and had special garments, but his blessings and calling were passed on to his sons. Remember, Jesus is now the High Priest. And just as the sons of Aaron were the priests who carried on the ministry of Aaron, so all followers of Jesus are priests who are to carry on the ministry of Jesus who is the High Priest.

Specifically, it is the ministry of priests to bring sacrifices and intercede for the people. As it says in 1 Peter 2:9, *all* believers are priests. There is no such thing as a Christian who is not a priest. Anyone who is not a priest is not a Christian or minister; anyone who is a Christian is also a priest and a minister, a word meaning "servant." The idea of an ordained "priest" under the New Covenant is entirely a human invention. Therefore the whole debate about female "priests" is utter nonsense. How an entire institution can split over something which has no basis to begin with defies logic!

> *...and in the middle of the lampstands I saw one like a son of man, clothed in a robe reaching to the feet, and girded across His chest with a golden sash. (Rev. 1:13)*

But the appearance of Jesus in Revelation 1 typifies the High Priest's garments. He had to wear a form of breastplate on His shoulders, and a tunic that He must not remove. This tunic represents the garment of salvation. The Mormons wear a kind of underwear that they never take off, and the pope wears a scapular, a form of apron or vest. It sounds absurd, but this is where they get the idea. On top of this, Aaron wore a breastplate with twelve plates on his chest representing the twelve tribes.

When a priest prays for someone's toothache, the prayer is said and done and the task is completed. However, the breastplate represented a burden, the burden of intercession which the High Priest did not take off, day or night, until the battle was won. If someone is an intercessor, that burden is going to be on his heart until it is answered and the battle won. That is what Jesus is doing now; He is carrying the burden of Israel and those adopted into her by His work on the cross as the High Priest of the New Covenant. But notice that Aaron had to pass these garments on to his sons.

All believers have been given a measure of faith by God and "*without faith it is impossible to please Him*" (Heb. 11:6). But not everyone has the gift of faith. There is a special gift of faith (1 Co. 12:9) and people who are intercessors have this God-given gift and carry a burden for a particular issue just as the Lord Jesus did. But every believer should still, in a sense, carry the burden that is on their shoulders and on their heart, not only for Israel but also, by extension, for the church—and for the lost.

Slain in the Spirit

> *When I saw Him, I fell at His feet like a dead man. And He placed His right hand on me, saying, "Do not be afraid; I am the first and the last, (Rev. 1:17)*

Contrast this to Zechariah 4:

> *Then the angel who was speaking with me returned and roused me, as a man who is awakened from his sleep. (Zech. 4:1)*

Ephesus

The phenomenon of being "slain in the Spirit" occurs many times in both Testaments. They fell down in God's presence. But the term comes from Revelation 1:17 where John says he *"fell at His feet as a dead man."* It happened to Daniel as recorded in Daniel 10.

George Whitefield was very disturbed when he saw people being "slain in the Spirit" at John Wesley's meetings, but a few days later it happened in his own meetings. Granted a lot of it found today is just nonsense, pushing people down or people getting stirred up emotionally by a hypnotic and manipulative speaker. Of course it may be counterfeited, but the real thing is scriptural—it does happen.

"He said to me, "What do you see?" And I said, "I see, and behold, a lampstand all of gold with its bowl on the top of it, and its seven lamps on it with seven spouts belonging to each of the lamps which are on the top of it; also two olive trees by it, one on the right side of the bowl and the other on its left side." Then I said to the angel who was speaking with me saying, "What are these, my lord?" So the angel who was speaking with me answered and said to me, "Do you not know what these are?" And I said, "No, my lord." Then he said to me, "This is the word of the LORD to Zerubbabel saying, 'Not by might nor by power, but by My Spirit,' says the LORD of hosts. 'What are you, O great mountain? Before Zerubbabel you will become a plain; and he will bring forth the top stone with shouts of "Grace, grace to it!" ' "

Also the word of the LORD came to me, saying, "The hands of Zerubbabel have laid the foundation of this house, and his hands will finish it. Then you will know that the LORD of hosts has sent me to you. For who has despised the day of small things? But these seven will be glad when they see the plumb line in the hand of Zerubbabel—these are the eyes of the LORD which range to and fro throughout the earth."

Then I said to him, "What are these two olive trees on the right of the lampstand and on its left?" And I answered the second time and said to him, "What are the two olive branches which are beside the two golden pipes, which empty the golden oil from themselves?" So he answered me, saying, "Do you not know what these are?" And I said, "No, my lord." Then he said, "These are the two anointed ones who are standing by the LORD of the whole earth." (Zech. 4:2-14)

Somehow the architecture of the physical temple reflects the truth of heaven, and somehow it reflects certain truths about the church. That is what Revelation tries to bring together, reflecting Zechariah Chapter 4: the seven lamp stands in Revelation are the seven churches, and the two anointed ones appear again in Revelation 11. Some say they represent Moses and Elijah whose bodies were taken up by God; others say they represent Moses and Enoch, for Enoch also walked into heaven.

It is interesting that the phrase "*son of man*" appears in Revelation 1:13 . Whenever it occurs in the Old Testament it is teaching something about Jesus. Daniel and Ezekiel are types of Jesus. Ezekiel is a major type of Jesus. And in Daniel 10:9 he says, "*I fell into a deep sleep on my face, with my face to the ground.*" Daniel evidently also fell down like one slain.

Paul writes:

> "*Boasting is necessary, though it is not profitable; but I will go on to visions and revelations of the Lord. I know a man in Christ who fourteen years ago—whether in the body I do not know, or out of the body I do not know, God knows—such a man was caught up to the third heaven. And I know how such a man—whether in the body or apart from the body I do not know, God knows— was caught up into Paradise and heard inexpressible words, which a man is not permitted to speak. On behalf of such a man I will boast; but on my own behalf I will not boast, except in regard to my weaknesses. For if I do wish to boast I will not be foolish, for I will be speaking the truth; but I refrain from this, so that no one will credit me with more than he sees in me or hears from me. Because of the surpassing greatness of the revelations, for this reason, to keep me from exalting myself, there was given me a thorn in the flesh, a messenger of Satan to torment me—to keep me from exalting myself!*" (2 Co. 12:1-7)*

Paul was obviously talking about himself, probably when "*they stoned Paul and dragged him outside of the city, supposing him to be dead*" (Acts 14:19). It was a form of rapture; he was somehow caught up into heaven. And it also happened to Zechariah, Elijah, Ezekiel and Enoch. Every one of those passages says something about what is going to happen when "*the dead in Christ shall rise first. Then we who are alive and remain shall be caught up* (in Latin, "*rapturo,*" hence the word "raptured" in the AV) *together with them in the clouds to meet the Lord in the air, and so we shall always be with the Lord.*" (1 Th. 4:16-17).

When Jesus was transfigured on the mountain (Mt. 17), suddenly there appeared Elijah who never died, and Moses who died but his grave could not be found. But they all had this same glorious splendor, this white radiance. Whether believers die or not, they shall all appear the same. What is going to happen to them when they die? That is the big question which Revelation explains. Somehow, perhaps after "sleeping" for centuries, believers will all be caught up to be with the Lord forever. People like Paul and John had a glimpse of these things ahead of time—"things inexpressible" (2 Co. 12:4).

The Faithful Witness with a New Body

Next comes the concept of the faithful witness.

...and from Jesus Christ, the faithful witness, the firstborn of the dead, and the ruler of the kings of the earth. To Him who loves us and released us from our sins by His blood. (Rev. 1:5)

Jesus is described as "*the faithful witness.*" But in the Psalms...

"His (David's) descendants will endure forever
And his throne as the sun before Me
It shall be established forever like the moon,
And **the witness** *in the sky* **is faithful***.*
But You have cast off and rejected,
You have been full of wrath against Your anointed (your Messiah)."
(Ps. 89:36-38)

Hence in Revelation is described the faithful witness Jesus who was rejected but is alive forevermore. Looking at the heavenly court in Revelation it can be seen how God uses heavenly or spiritual things to describe physical things.

His feet were like burnished bronze, when it has been made to glow in a furnace, and His voice was like the sound of many waters. (Rev. 1:15)

Note that bronze has to do with judgment.

Therefore from now on we recognize no one according to the flesh; even though we have known Christ according to the flesh, yet now we know Him in this way no longer. (2 Co. 5:16)

Paul is saying what John said. They knew Him in His glorified form. John knew Jesus intimately, better than any other disciple; he rested his head on Him at the Last Supper. Yet when John saw Jesus in His glorified form it was like the difference between a caterpillar and a butterfly. After a life climaxing in death in the cocoon, which represents the grave, the caterpillar undergoes a change which brings forth this beautiful new creation. Believers are destined to follow Him. One day all believers will be beautiful like the butterfly risen from the larva. When they get to heaven and look in the mirror they are not going to recognize themselves!

Salvation, Saved and Born Again

Notice that there are three aspects of salvation:
- I *have been* saved,
- I am *being* saved, and
- I am *going to be* saved.

Similarly,
- I *have been* born again,
- I *am being* born again, and
- I *am going to be* born again.

The past aspect of salvation is called "justification." Everyone has sinned by stealing, lying, etc. but they have been justified—they have been saved—because Jesus paid the price for their sins, and they have repented and thanked Him and stopped doing those things.

But at present, believers are *still* being saved and are *still* being sanctified—continuously, every day.

> And He was saying to them all, "If anyone wishes to come after Me, he must deny himself, and take up his cross daily and follow Me. (Lk. 9:23)

> "I have been crucified with Christ; and it is no longer I who live, but Christ lives in me; and the life which I now live in the flesh I live by faith in the Son of God (by the faith of the Son of God - AV), who loved me, and gave Himself up for me." (Gal. 2:20).

Every day in the life they *now* live they are *still* being saved. The present aspect of salvation is "sanctification."

And in the future they are *going* to be saved.

> "But the one who endures to the end, he will be saved." (Mt. 24:13)

That is redemption. It will be at the end of the age, still to come in the future.

> "But when these things begin to take place, straighten up and lift up your heads, because your redemption is drawing near." (Lk. 21:28)

Revisit the connection between Genesis, John and Revelation discussed previously, and the repeated appearance of both the garden and the Tree of Life. This is why the Tree of Life appears in the letter to Ephesus.

> "To him who overcomes, I will grant to eat of the tree of life, which is in the Paradise of God." (Rev. 2:7b)

What was lost in the Garden will be given back. There is a three-way parallelism occurring here:

Ephesus

- Creation – that was Genesis;
- New Creation – that is the Gospel, new life in Christ now;
- Re-creation – what will take place according to Revelation.

The three go together. That is why the same figures, the same symbols, the same language is repeatedly employed throughout Scripture. For example, what is seen in Revelation 6:9? The martyrs crying out from under the altar, slain because of the Word of God and the testimony they had maintained. And what is under the altar? It is where the blood runs down into the ground. What is portrayed in Genesis? Able's blood cries out from the ground. And in John? The blood of Jesus gushes out onto the ground.

Or again, God separated the light from the darkness in creation as recorded in Genesis. God came to separate the light from the darkness in the new creation. In John's gospel Jesus came as the Light of the world, but men preferred darkness because their deeds were evil (Jn. 3:19). Unrepentant sinners still prefer darkness, and much sin still goes on under cover of darkness. But God can see in the dark. He knows everything. And all repented sins are blotted out. Believers must learn to walk in the light always.

And finally, in the re-creation in Revelation, the Lamb is the lamp, and the glory of the Lord is the light (Rev. 21:23).

What Jesus Said to the Ephesians

There are three particular things in this letter to Ephesus which require special attention:

- First, false apostles;
- Second, the loss of their first love;
- Third, the practices of the Nicolaitans.

Jesus was described to each church with some aspect of the vision of the deified Jesus given to John in Chapter 1. To Ephesus, the church whose name meant "not lasting," He was described as "*the One who walks among the seven golden lampstands*," and Revelation 1:20 specifies these are the seven churches. So Jesus is in some way walking among all of these churches. This is important because Ephesus was a church that had lost its first love. They had subscribed to the Greek mentality that heaven is above and earth is below and separated from heaven, so man is separated from Jesus. Ephesus needed to be reminded that He continually walks among the lamp stands, among the churches. He is continually with believers even though He cannot be seen.

It is noteworthy that Jesus always began with praise. (Paul did this in his letters, and everyone would do well to follow his example.)

The Dilemma of Laodicea

"'I know your deeds and your toil and perseverance, and that you cannot tolerate evil men, and you put to the test those who call themselves apostles, and they are not, and you found them to be false; and you have perseverance and have endured for My name's sake, and have not grown weary.'" (Rev. 2:2-3)

Jesus points out their faithfulness and the fact that they could not tolerate false apostles. Notice how He *commends* them for having put such to the test.

For I am jealous for you with a godly jealousy; for I betrothed you to one husband, so that to Christ I might present you as a pure virgin...

A true apostle is going to have as his central goal the presentation to the bridegroom of a pure, spotless, virgin bride.

...But I am afraid that, as the serpent deceived Eve by his craftiness, your minds will be led astray from the simplicity and purity of devotion to Christ...

Note that in Revelation there is the serpent and the dragon—Satan's two forms. The dragon persecutes the church, the serpent seduces it. Paul is warning about being seduced.

...For if one comes and preaches another Jesus whom we have not preached, or you receive a different spirit which you have not received, or a different gospel which you have not accepted, you bear this beautifully. For I consider myself not in the least inferior to the most eminent apostles. But even if I am unskilled in speech, yet I am not so in knowledge; in fact, in every way we have made this evident to you in all things. (2 Co. 11:2-6)

Look what Paul said: "If one comes and preaches a different gospel..." But what is a "different" gospel? Notice that it will be largely correct. It will even appear correct at first glance. If it did not, it would not deceive. But it will always distort the one essential truth upon which all other Christian truth is based:

- Christ crucified,
- Christ resurrected,
- Christ coming again.

Christ died, Christ rose, Christ is coming again. This is the essential truth. All other truth has to be based on that truth. Jesus is the truth. We have:

- The truth of the cross,
- The truth of the empty tomb, and
- The truth of the Mount of Olives where He will return.

All other truth has to be built on that threefold truth. If somebody takes any other truth, even though it may be *a* truth and makes it central, then it distorts this threefold central truth of Christ and Him crucified, Christ and Him resurrected, Christ and Him returning. It not only distorts, it obscures, and that which is obscured is put out of the picture.

Those propounding the false Faith-Prosperity gospel got hold of *a* truth. But that truth is only valid if you look at it in the light of the main truth: the crucifixion, resurrection and promised return of Jesus. These people do not emphasize the crucified life; they do not lay it down. Instead they take millions for themselves! So the central truth is replaced by another truth and that alternative truth becomes distorted into a lie.

There are those who have taken hold of God's End-Times purpose for Israel and the Jews, which is indeed a truth, but have made Israel, and not Jesus, the central truth. And so what happens? The message of the cross gets obscured. There are organizations whose ministry has prioritized the task of carrying the Jews back to Israel, loving them and blessing them as best they can, but they have promised not to proselytize. Can you imagine Peter, John or Paul making such a promise?

False Apostles

But what I am doing I will continue to do, so that I may cut off opportunity from those who desire an opportunity to be regarded just as we are in the matter about which they are boasting...

In other words, people who want to be considered apostles. Jesus tells those with ears to hear at Ephesus, "*I know ... you put to the test those who call themselves apostles, and they are not, and you found them to be false.*" (Rev. 2:2) Paul continues...

...For such men are false apostles, deceitful workers, disguising themselves as apostles of Christ. No wonder, for even Satan disguises himself as an angel of light. Therefore it is not surprising if his servants also disguise themselves as servants of righteousness, whose end will be according to their deeds. (2 Co. 11:12-15)

And what is the context in which Paul is speaking? "Another gospel." They take their eyes off Jesus, off the cross, off the central message, and it begins to go wrong. Every false apostle makes that mistake in some way. They take their eyes off the essential truth of Christ and Him crucified, resurrected and coming again, and begin to emphasize some other truth, making it central. It always happens that way.

True Apostles

There are at least four kinds of apostles in the New Testament. First and foremost there is Jesus himself.

> *"Therefore, holy brethren, partakers of a heavenly calling, consider Jesus,* **the** *Apostle and High Priest of our confession;"* (Heb. 3:1)

Jesus is called the High Priest in Hebrews and He is identified as, and appears as, the High Priest in Revelation 1. But in the Greek in Hebrews 3:1 it is the definite article—Jesus is "*the*" Apostle. All other apostles must derive their apostolic authority from Jesus, "*the Apostle and High Priest.*"

But there are three other types of apostles. First there were the original twelve. He appointed (ordained) twelve, designating them apostles.

> *And when day came, He called His disciples to Him and chose twelve of them, whom He also named as apostles:* (Lk. 6:13)

Then there was Paul. He was not one of the original twelve, and some people teach that the apostles acted presumptuously in selecting Matthias instead of waiting for Paul, but that would be a mistake. Carefully examine Acts 1:21. When Judas committed suicide they looked for someone to replace him from among the men who had been with them the whole time that the Lord Jesus went in and out among them since the baptism of John. The other apostles were disciples of John the Baptist and were probably baptized by him before they were disciples of Jesus. Paul was not.

So there was Jesus "*the*" Apostle, the twelve, the almost unique case of Paul, and finally there were men such as Apollos and Barnabas. Barnabas was called an apostle in Acts 14:14. The word "apostle" simply means "away from post" or "one who is sent." The only kind of apostle that can exist today are church-planting missionaries sent out by their home church.

Where can the biblical model for church-planting missionaries be seen? Acts 13. Paul knew he was an apostle. God told him through Ananias in Damascus, "*he is a chosen instrument of Mine, to bear My name before the Gentiles*" (Acts 9:15). He was called to be an apostle to the Gentiles. But notice what happened. He did not embark on that ministry until seventeen years later when it was confirmed to the church by the Holy Spirit. Then, and not until then, the **church** sent him.

A lot of people today who are claiming to be apostles ("God said to me" types) should learn from Acts 13. Paul did not go out as an apostle until it was confirmed *to* the church and he was confirmed *by* the church, and sent **together** with Barnabas. Did God send out only Paul? No, the Holy Spirit said, "*Set apart for Me Barnabas and Saul.*" The basic New Testament model is for plurality of leaders. Even as a church-planting missionary, Paul was yoked and in submission.

Some of the people claiming to be apostles today are autocrats on an ego trip. They may have started out right, but pride has overtaken them. Too many churches are known as so-and-so's church. That is not biblical. They are not subordinate to anybody. Paul was always reporting back to Antioch. On issues of doctrine, in Acts 15, he submitted to the joint authority of the elders and the other apostles. And he always had Barnabas or Luke with him. That is the way it was. There are many church-planting ministries and ministers, but if they are legitimate, they will be scriptural.

So whenever people are encountered who call themselves "apostles," the biblical requirement is to test them to see if they are true apostles. Jesus commended the church at Ephesus because they tested such people.

Forsaken Your First Love

The second thing Jesus said to Ephesus was that they had lost their first love. That happens. When first "saved" the people around new believers think they are crazy. There is the case where a believer had been busted for drugs, burned his draft card, and was thrown out of private school, which was alright with his Dad. But when he gave his life to Jesus, his father pulled a gun on him!

When first saved, some new believers might think they are the next Paul. They may be clumsy, but they have a zeal. The church should be run on the wisdom of the old sheep but on the zeal of the newly born-again lambs!

Sadly, the lukewarm church so often takes a zealous, newly born again Christian and makes him a lukewarm one! They lose their first love. Yet people who still have that enthusiastic first love intimidate and convict others by the power, sheer joy and passion of the Holy Spirit that is in them.

The first-century apostolic church is often regarded as the ideal church, and in some ways it is. But believers then had their problems, too! Yet they were not so very different to problems facing the church today. Hyper-charismatic extremists in Corinth, people with crazy ideas about the Last Days in Thessalonica, legalistic Christians in Galatia who wanted to add rules to the Gospel—it is what happened then and it still happens now. There is nothing new under the sun. But how did their problems commence? The way every problem commences. What happens in marriage? The loss of one's first love.

When my wife gets on my nerves, I just think back to walking along the shore of the Dead Sea holding hands with this Israeli girl from whom I could not take my eyes off—this girl I led to a confession of faith in Christ on the streets of Jerusalem. I remember walking with her by the Sea of Galilee explaining to her the basic truths of the Bible. That is the person I fell in love with, and that is the person who, in my heart of hearts, I am still in love with. If you are married, think back to that time and, husbands, just love her. There is a natural tendency to forget one's first love. But everyone is supposed to remember that first love for Jesus. He told the Ephesians to remember it.

When genuine revival comes to a church everybody is full of life and awe at the holiness of God. But over time that first love is lost and eventually what happens? There are two things that happen when people begin to lose this first love:

- The quality and quantity of their prayer life begins to decrease.
- They lose their evangelistic zeal.

They do not have the same desire to tell everybody what Jesus did for them. They get into the excuse, "I am not an evangelist." Not everyone is an evangelist, but everyone is a witness. Jesus declared, *"You shall be my witnesses"* (Acts 1:8). There is nobody who cannot give out tracts, knock on doors, talk to people one-on-one and establish relationships. This is not to say that everyone should all give out tracts or knock on doors, but Jesus has a ministry as a witness for every believer. Ask Jesus to show you what to do. There is no Christian who is not called to be Christ's witness.

Hate the Practices of the Nicolaitans

'Yet this you do have, that you hate the deeds of the Nicolaitans, which I also hate. (Rev. 2:6)

Finally, Jesus actually **commended** the Ephesian church because they hated the practices of the Nicolaitans which He Himself hates. The Bible usually interprets itself, and the words "nico" and "laity" together mean "suppression of the people" or "rulers of the laity." This implies a clergy class like the Levitical priests who ruled or lorded it over their brothers.

Before Satan succeeded in introducing pagan practices into the church he tried to Judaize it. What happened in Galatia? They were trying to circumcise the Greek converts. They taught the Gospel of Jesus and then added, "But you must be circumcised as well." Similarly today there are Seventh-day Adventists who believe that you must not work on Saturday. They add part of the Law.

So instead of a priesthood of all believers, the Nicolaitans introduced a separate priesthood, a ruling class. It came in part from a Gnostic influence, from the idea that there is some special, secret knowledge or power given only to certain specially-ordained people. Yes there are leaders; yes there are elders, apostles, prophets, evangelists, teachers; yes there are pastors, guardians of our souls, and thank God there are. But a special "priesthood"? Rulers over the laity? And should such people be tolerated? For anyone not under such people is there really no salvation for them as they would have them believe?

Once people claim some kind of apostolic authority and ability to control others lives, test them. Do they fit the pattern of biblical apostolic authority? Are they yoked and under authority themselves the way that Paul and Barnabas were? Are they reporting back to Antioch or meeting the other apostles and elders in Jerusalem to check out their Gospel? Or are they Nicolaitans? Jesus hate their deeds; He says so directly.

Whenever there arises a Nicolaitan priesthood or priestcraft, people are ultimately excluded or hurt spiritually and psychologically. Ireland has a priest in every village, yet Ireland has the highest rates of alcoholism and schizophrenia in the world. But this is also seen in new churches. What they call "apostolic authority"—whether from a pope or from a local heavy-handed pastor—could also be the mark of a Nicolaitan.

Conclusion

It should be each believer's utmost desire and prayer, beginning with miserable excuses of Christians like themselves, that the church today would return to its first love. When Jesus is continuously loved the way He was loved the day He was first recognized and believed upon, nothing can go wrong. And He is going to take care of those who do love Him.

Chapter 2

Smyrna – From "Myrrh": "Anointed for Burial"
2nd & 3rd Centuries

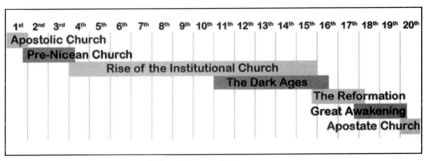

The City of Smyrna

Smyrna (today called "Izmir") was a beautiful jewel of a place known as *To Agalma tes Asias*—"The Delight of Asia." Smyrna was and still is a deep-water port, and was a keen rival to Ephesus thirty-five miles to the south. In about 600 BC it was destroyed by an earthquake and was not rebuilt until the fourth century BC. With a population of some 100,000 people, it was home to the Temple of Cybele by the sea with further impressive temples dedicated to Apollo, Asclepius, Aphrodite and Zeus. It enjoyed a flourishing trade in wines and was also famous for its science and, like Laodicea, medicine.

The Dilemma of Laodicea

"And to the angel of the church in Smyrna write:

"'The first and the last, who was dead, and has come to life, says this:

"''I know your tribulation and your poverty (but you are rich), and the blasphemy by those who say they are Jews and are not, but are a synagogue of Satan. Do not fear what you are about to suffer. Behold, the devil is about to cast some of you into prison, so that you will be tested, and you will have tribulation for ten days. Be faithful until death, and I will give you the crown of life.'"

"He who has an ear, let him hear what the Spirit says to the churches. He who overcomes will not be hurt by the second death." (Rev. 2:8-11)

It is important to bear in mind that the name is derived from the Greek word for "myrrh" which was used essentially for anointing dead bodies for burial. In John 19:39 it states that Nicodemus brought myrrh to anoint the body of Jesus. Myrrh is alluded to in the typology of Song of Songs where the bridegroom is depicted as going up to the mountain of myrrh.

"Until the cool of the day
When the shadows flee away,
I will go my way to the mountain of myrrh
And to the hill of frankincense." (SS 4:6)

Frankincense is what was burned in sacrificial offerings, and the hill, of course, pointed to Calvary, the hill where Jesus would be executed.

Smyrna relates approximately to the pre-Nicean period of history after the Apostles in the 2nd and 3rd centuries until the time of Constantine (AD 321) and the Council of Nicea (AD 325).

Jesus reminds each church about one aspect of the description of Himself from Revelation 1 that they need to remember. Smyrna needed to be reminded that, although He had died, which was not at all unique, He had come to life, which was. In other words, He reminded them about the resurrection. Persecution is not the end; there is eternal life afterward.

"I know your tribulation." As to all the churches, Jesus appeals first to what is right before He deals with what is wrong. Smyrna (along with Philadelphia) is a church in which He found no fault, no fault at all. The reason was that it was a church that was being persecuted. It is very difficult to criticize a church that is being literally, and terribly, persecuted and yet keeps faith.

The area of Soho in London was settled by people from France called Huguenots—Bible-believing Christians who were terribly persecuted at the hands of the Roman Catholic Church. On St. Bartholomew's Day people remember the St. Bartholomew's Day Massacre. The authorities invited the

Smyrna

Huguenots to meet openly, promising them peace and security. When they presented themselves, the Roman clergy had them exterminated. This was genocide. As a result of much persecution of this sort the survivors fled to Britain. Some went to Northern Ireland where they began the millinery trade, the textile trade, and the fabric and lace trades. Others settled in the East end of London in the area around Whitechapel.

As a result, Soho became the "Bible Belt" of Britain, as it were. It probably had more born-again Christians per square mile, or per street, than anywhere else in the world at that time. They had daily prayer meetings and Bible studies. The Huguenots went house-to-house. Today, Soho is the red-light district of London. The same places where the Lord was lifted up, where God's Word was studied, where the Gospel was preached and Christians met for prayer and worship daily have become houses of pornography and prostitution. It does not take long for things to go astray, and that is very much what can be seen happening in the Western world today.

Future Historical Prophetic Antitype

The "*ten days*" of Satan imprisoning the church in the local persecution of Smyrna is normally related to the ten primary periods of persecution under a string of emperors inimical to Christianity, who frequently also held an anti-Semitic disposition toward Jews. This relates back to the prophecies of Genesis 3:15, an enmity between the serpent and the woman. From Imperial Rome to Papal Rome and the Inquisitions, to Sovietism in the age of the Iron Curtain, to contemporary fundamentalist Islam, those who opposed the *theological* descendants of Abraham, Isaac, and Jacob also opposed the *anthropological* descendants of the Hebrew patriarchs. Both the true church and the Israelites are the covenant people of God upon which God's agenda for the salvation of man prophetically depends. Hence the true church and the Jews have been the recurrent targets of the same persecutors.

The same satanic spirit bent on the extermination of the Jews is likewise bent on the extermination of the true church. Beginning with Rome, any nation that turned against the church has largely also turned against the Jews. The traumatic events of AD 70 by Titus against the Jews in Jerusalem followed persecutions by Nero of the church. Similar trends were evident in the imperial reigns of Claudius. By the second century, when the post-Apostolic church commenced, the Second Jewish Revolt under Simon Bar Kochba saw a removal of Jews from Jerusalem and a scattering of the Jews from biblical Israel into the Diaspora which prevailed through the reign of

Hadrian. This was concurrent with the horrific series of persecutions of the church by a consecutive list of mad emperors, all of whom were polytheistic pagans, and most of whom were bisexual.

It is astounding how the same allegations made against Christians, faulting them for the self-inflicted calamities of a morally decadent society, were likewise leveled against the Jews, blaming them for *everything*. The difference is that these kinds of accusations, made to justify pogroms against Christians, ended when Constantine pseudo-Christianized the Roman Empire, but continued against the Jews. Only they were no longer perpetrated by Imperial Rome, but by the Roman papacy which not only replaced it, but continued its debauchery under the so-called Holy Roman Empire. This process had its rudiments however, with Nero and Titus, but took shape in the second to fourth centuries in an age that was in the character of the church of Smyrna. What was faced locally by the Christians in Smyrna was a foretaste and a microcosm of what would plague the church throughout the Roman Empire for over two hundred years.

Domitian, Marcus Aurelius, Septimus Severitus, Caligula, Decius, and Diocletian were chief among the emperors who orchestrated ten major periods of intense persecution. They constructed the template by which the pontiffs of Papal Rome would slaughter more Christians and Jews than even the pontiffs of Pagan Rome. Indeed, as we have already discussed, the true church became *Religio Illicita*, operating outside of the pontifical pantheon. Once again, in the modern world, we have witnessed the same thing in the papacy of Pope John Paul II (Karol Wojtyla) and Benedict XVI (Joseph Radzinger); both fancying themselves as "bridge builders" between *any* two faiths and Rome, but denouncing born-again, scriptural Evangelicism. Such men are not the heirs of Peter but of the original pontiffs, the Antichrist emperors of Imperial Rome.

Turning from God Leads to Political and Moral Decline

No doubt the political, economic and social decline we are observing in the Western democracies is a reflection of their moral and spiritual decline. Around the British Parliament are posted the words in Latin, *Pater Noster Qui Es Caelis*—"Our Father who art in Heaven." Today, according to a poll recently announced on television, most Parliamentarians have no religious affiliation whatsoever. The largest number would be nominal Anglicans. This is followed by quite a number of atheists and agnostics, then Muslims, Buddhists, Hindus, Jews (that is, unsaved Jews; Disraeli was a Jewish Christian), Catholics and so on. These are the people who, under the

Smyrna

Erastrian system of church government practiced in Great Britain, appoint Bishops by vote. (Erastus, 1524 - 1583, was a Heidelberg physician who held that ecclesiastical power should be subordinated to secular government.) These people in the British Parliament, some of whom do not even believe in God, are appointing the hierarchy of the Church of England!

Watch Out That No One Deceives You

Eve represents in type Israel and the church, and she was seduced by the serpent. The serpent in Scripture represents deception, whereas the dragon represents persecution. At Smyrna, the serpent and the dragon are attacking the church simultaneously.

Matthew 7:15, 24:24, Acts 19 and 2 Peter 2 all warn of false prophets and false teachers. The early church was challenged by false prophets not merely from without, but from within, which is far more deadly. In the early church there were Arians, people named after Arius (c. 250 - c. 336) who believed that Jesus was a created being and who denied His divinity. Today they have resurfaced as Jehovah's Witnesses. *"There is nothing new under the sun."* Conversely, there are also "Jesus-only" people who ignore the Father.

The Archbishop of Canterbury, Rowan Williams, is so multi-faith and liberal that he sees nothing wrong with participating in a Druid ceremony. He is apparently committed to the sanctification of same-sex marriages and the ordination of homosexuals. Williams was appointed by the same Blair government that is determined to forfeit more of the democratic powers of Parliament to the unelected Eurocracy of Brussels. They want to take the economic destiny of Britain and the British pound out of the hands of the elected government and the Bank of England and place it into the hands of Frankfurt's European Central Bank, the de facto heir of the German Bundesbank. How did the Queen ever give her royal assent to the European Communities Act in 1972 which signed away her sovereignty, something every monarch pledges to keep?

A personal conversation recently took place with the Parliamentary Correspondent of the BBC. His position is that replacing Parliamentary democracy by the European bureaucracy was essentially a turning away from the Parliamentary principle as it has been known. A non-elected commission makes proposals and only consults the European Parliament. The Parliament is primarily becoming nothing more than a consultative body.

For all of their mistakes, faults and problems, it should be remembered that the Puritans went a long way towards establishing democratic tradition. The democratic institutions inherited at present were closely associated with the emergence of religious freedom and freedom of conscience, freedom to believe and to preach the Gospel. The Puritans and their forerunners suffered tremendously both at the hands of the Church of Rome and at the hands of the Church of England. They established the present democratic tradition based on biblical principles. When digressing from biblical Judeo-Christian moral principles, the institutions that are built on those principles are going to crack and disappear along with them. And that is basically what is happening. It does not take long for things to go from good to bad, and from bad to worse.

The federal republics of Eastern Europe such as the Soviet Union, Czechoslovakia and Yugoslavia have disintegrated and turned from being governed by an unelected, highly-centralized socialist elite. Meanwhile Western Europe is turning towards the very system of overly centralized control that brought catastrophe to those federal republics. This is what the present government is pushing Britain into. The departure from biblical Christianity leads to the departure from parliamentary democracy which biblical Christianity helped shape.

Rowan Williams participated in a Druid festival where he took the ceremonial name of the son of a Celtic god represented by a dragon in Welsh mythology. It seems to be of little interest today that in the book of Revelation the dragon represents the Antichrist. Thus it is little wonder that Williams is quoted in the *Daily Telegraph* of 6th January 2002 as describing what he called "the wilder passages" of the Book of Revelation as:

> *"tightly written pen driving into cheap paper, page after page of paranoid fantasy and malice, like the letters clergymen so frequently get from the wretched and disturbed."*

To the Archbishop of Canterbury the Revelation of John which Jesus gave him, God's Holy Word no less, is "paranoid fantasy and malice"!

Preparation for Persecution

Jesus warns the church in Smyrna about impending persecution.

> *"Surely the Lord GOD does nothing.*
> *Unless He reveals His secret counsel*
> *To His servants the prophets." (Amos 3:7)*

Throughout most of history in most countries, most genuine born again Christians were persecuted for things taken for granted which ought not be taken for granted. This has been the case in Eastern Europe, in Roman Catholic countries, Muslim countries, Communist countries, etc. The reason freedom is possessed which is taken for granted is because it was purchased by the blood of Bible-believing Christians in the 16th and 17th Centuries. But as soon as one's back is turned on that biblical heritage and away from the Lord and His commands, personal freedom is going to go away with it. And that is what is beginning to happen. There can be no doubt that Jesus is warning the church in the Western world to prepare for persecution. It is the same as He warned the church in Smyrna.

The faith of the early Christians is found in the Epistle to the Hebrews.

"... and others were tortured, not accepting their release, so that they might obtain a better resurrection;"

They did not believe that Jesus died to make them prosperous in *this* life or in *this* world. They believed that Jesus died to make them prosperous in a kingdom *to come.*

"...and others experienced mockings and scourgings, yes, also chains and imprisonment. They were stoned, they were sawn in two, they were tempted, they were put to death with the sword; they went about in sheepskins, in goatskins..."

Not in Mercedes Benz® and Cadillacs®.

"...being destitute, afflicted, ill-treated (men of whom the world was not worthy)..."

Staying in five-star hotels like so many of the big, prosperity preachers today? No way!

"...wandering in deserts and mountains and caves and holes in the ground. And all these, having gained approval through their faith..." (Heb. 11:35-39)

That was the faith of the early church. They did not believe that Jesus died to give them a rich lifestyle in *this* world; they believed that Jesus died to give them a much, much better life in a much, much *better* world.

Kingdom Now Theology

Married to such false doctrine is "Dominionism," also called "Kingdom Now" theology. This has become very, very prolific in much of the charismatic and Pentecostal world today. Basically it propounds that the church is going to conquer the entire world for Jesus before He comes, and the church is going to set up His kingdom for Him. The church is the kingdom-*now*! It is also called "over-realized eschatology." It is a big movement and it has the tacit endorsement of many major Evangelical leaders in Britain and in America today. In its popular expression, it combines the false elements of the heretical Latter Rain/Manifest Sons beliefs, condemned by mainstream Pentecostalism of the 1940's, with hyper-Calvinistic Reconstructionism. Its hyper-charismatic proponents have included American anti-Israel preacher Rick Godwin (famous for the highly publicized financial scandals in his Eagle's Nest church in San Antonio) while the Reformed Reconstructionist counterparts have included theonomists living and dead such as Rousas J. Rushdoony, Gary North, and David Chilton. These unscriptural doctrines are very unfortunate, very false, and potentially very dangerous to the Body of Christ. Ultimately it is not biblical , and simply wishful thinking. Jesus Himself reveals,

> "And just as it happened in the days of Noah, so it will be also in the days of the Son of Man: they were eating, they were drinking, they were marrying, they were being given in marriage, until the day that Noah entered the ark, and the flood came and destroyed them all.

> "It was the same as happened in the days of Lot: they were eating, they were drinking, they were buying, they were selling, they were planting, they were building; but on the day that Lot went out from Sodom it rained fire and brimstone from heaven and destroyed them all.

> "It will be just the same on the day that the Son of Man is revealed."
> (Lk. 17:26-30)

Life in Smyrna under Pax Romana and Internationalization

There were negative aspects of Colonialism, exploitation of people in poor countries, but there were also positive aspects. For example, under the more recent *Pax Britannica*, Great Britain kept far more dangerous empires at bay: Russia in the East, the French and Spanish Roman Catholic empires in the West. In Israel everyone knows the bad things the British government did against the early Zionists when they revoked the Balfour Declaration and let Jews perish in concentration camps instead of coming to the land had actually been promised them. And yet in Israel today is the system of roads, the port of Haifa, and the airports. Most of the infrastructure of the country was built by the British.

There are places where people genuinely want colonialism. Try to tell the people in Gibraltar that they should be Spanish, or the people of the Falkland Islands that they should be Argentine, or the people of Hong Kong that they should be Chinese. They would much rather be British. There are two sides to the coin. And look what has happened to so many countries in Asia and Africa after the British left.

Smyrna

There is no defense for exploitative colonialism and imperialism. But the there is another side to the coin. Under *Pax Britannica*, Britain brought relative stability and prosperity to a world that would have been extremely troubled otherwise. Many believe that God blessed Britain at that time because of the biblical influence on its society. It sent the most missionaries to the most countries for 200 years. Remember William Carey, Hudson Taylor and many more. Today there is *Operation Mobilization, Youth with a Mission* and *Christ for the Nations*, merely obscure shadows of the true, biblical missions organizations that at one time operated out of Britain.

Pax Americana came in after the Second World War. There was the Soviet threat, but the United States, in association with Great Britain under NATO, basically brought peace to Europe. Far from occupying and exploiting the countries it had conquered, the Americans turned Germany and Japan into Western democracies with free-market economies bringing prosperity and affluence. It is not a defense for everything, but just as God blessed Britain when it was the most Christian and the most prolific missionary-sending country, so God has blessed America for the same reasons. Firstly America has blessed and defended Israel better than any other country, and secondly America now sends the most missionaries and the most mission dollars to the most countries. Today three out of every four dollars spent on missions comes from the United States. Otherwise God's judgment would have fallen on America a long time ago, if only for the abortion rate.

But in the days of Smyrna it was *Pax Romana* which prevailed. The Romans kept other powers in check while drawing their philosophy from various schools of thought. From the Phoenicians they took trade routes and they built a system of roads everywhere, some of which still survive. In Israel can be seen remnants of the *Via Maris*, the "Way of the Sea." South of Rome is the *Via Apia*, the "Apian Way" near the catacombs. They built a system of courts for social justice. They made not Latin, their own language, but Greek the international language, the *lingua franca*. And by so doing the Gospel was able to spread. There was a very large Jewish Diaspora after the Babylonian Captivity. So throughout the major cities of the Roman Empire there were established Jewish communities. Not only that, but there was also the Septuagint, the Greek translation of the Hebrew Scriptures (the *Tanak*) which was now available in the international language. The stage was set for the Gospel to prosper among the Gentiles during *Pax Romana* and God actually used it. On the other side of the coin, *Pax Romana* would only provide peace and prosperity to those who put their trust in it, followed it, and submitted to it.

The Dilemma of Laodicea

The Antichrist will reinstitute the emperor worship of pagan Rome. This is seen in the typology of the Nativity. When Jesus was born the emperor undertook a headcount in order to gain economic control of the world. That is what was going on then, and somehow that alludes to what is going to happen when Jesus comes back. Rome went from being a republic to a dictatorship. During times of war the Senate would elect a dictator and his word became law. But when someone is in constant war they have constant dictatorships. The other thing that happened was hyper-inflation which has always historically produced dictators. Napoleon, Hitler, Mao Zedong—even in modern times most dictators came to power following periods of hyper-inflation. And this is what happened back in ancient Rome.

Something like it will happen again when the Antichrist is revealed. In times of trouble he will promise the world peace and safety just like every other false prophet and would-be prime minister and president. And just as people had to bow the knee to the emperor on the Lord's Day one day a year, so it will be under the Antichrist. Everyone will be forced to worship his image or be killed (Rev. 13:15).

Rumors abound that Brussels is already drafting legislation to make illegal any religion that does not respect all other religions as its equal. Thus the *Treaty of Rome* would put true Christians and the Taliban in the same boat: *religio illicita*! The pope will declare all religions to be equally valid as long as he is the spiritual head of all religion, and no one will be able to contest his claim without in turn claiming a superior knowledge—which would be illegal!

So what Rome did in the second and third centuries teaches something about what is going to happen at the end of the world. Remember that the early Christians identified Rome with Babylon. The early Christians, being Jews, knew that the mystery religions, the false religious system of the world which began with Nimrod in Babylon (Gen. 10:10), found its way to the city of Pergamum in Asia Minor in the Greek world, and from there to the Roman world. The Greeks called him "Zeus," the Romans called him "Jupiter," but that is how it came about. Early Christians associated Rome with Babylon, particularly as a confederation of the false religions and corrupt politics of a fallen world. That is how they understood Rome, as Babylon. When the early Christians looked at the Book of Revelation and saw a woman on seven hills who represented a most evil city, they immediately thought of the Capitolina. To them Rome was certainly Babylon.

Keep in mind that the Romans had found a way to give people not only relative peace and prosperity, but also autonomy and their own identity and religion by imposing just one condition: they bowed the knee to the emperor once a year.

Look at the way the whole world is going now. Today the nation-state is collapsing; countries are re-confederating. One can go practically anywhere in the world and see General Motors, Barclays Bank, Pepsi Cola, Mitsubishi— the same multi-national corporations predominating in the economies of every country. Labor unions are international. It is a world in which economic problems and internationalization of the economy can no longer be solved autonomously by one country. Neither can any one country solve its environmental problems autonomously. Polluted air permeates trans-nationally. The Danube flows through about fifteen countries. Yet at the same time countries are dividing, such as the Czech Republic and Slovakia, and also Yugoslavia, and nobody knows what to do about it. That is exactly the kind of situation at the end of the Roman Empire.

Today some people think they know what to do about it. Trust the dictator, the strong man, or the state; it will take care of everything. Nearly twenty-five years ago the prime minister of Belgium actually said this:

"If somebody can come along and bring economic stability out of this chaos we don't care if he is God or the devil, we will follow him."

That is what happened in pagan Rome, and that is what is happening now.

Whether or not the mark of the beast will be a credit card chip implanted on a person's right hand, the people who receive the mark of the beast on their hands will have already received it in their hearts. They have a materialistic world view and their hope is in this life and this world. Somebody will come along and say, "You can have your identity, your autonomy, control of your region, and I will make it harmonize with the international scenario – just trust me."

Look how presidential campaigns are orchestrated in the United States and are beginning to be orchestrated in Britain. It is all done by media hype, manipulation and consumer psychology. In the political sphere this finds its equivalent in what is popularly called "spin-doctoring." There is very little attention devoted to substantive issues. It is all done by the way people are portrayed manipulatively through what is basically advertising psychology. It is even getting into the churches. That is what the Roman emperors did.

Today's politicians are going to find a way to harmonize these two problems, localization and internationalization. One should have no doubt that the way the world is evolving now is exactly the way the world evolved when it produced emperor worship. This is what the early church was up against. At that time, as will be seen when discussing the church at Pergamum, in the Pantheon of Rome all gods were deified and worshipped. As long as the people also bowed down to the emperor it did not matter what other god they had.

Today, what is happening? Even in Church of England schools they are teaching Hinduism, Islam, Buddhism, etc. New Age philosophy is beginning permeating Western society. This is exactly the kind of thing the early Christians were up against.

False Jews, a Synagogue of Satan

"I know ... the blasphemy by those who say they are Jews and are not, but are a synagogue of Satan" (Rev. 2:9).

After the Apostles, the church drifted progressively further and further from its Jewish roots. As more and more Gentiles became believers, it stood to reason that this would happen demographically and even culturally. But Paul warns in Romans 11 that it should never happen theologically. By the time of people such as John Chrysostom (AD 345 - 407, Bishop of Constantinople in 398) it began to happen theologically as well. The church not only got away from its Jewish roots, it began to turn *against* them and even to take on a strongly anti-Semitic character. Nonetheless, it cannot be forgotten that long, long before Christian anti-Semitism the unsaved Jews were persecuting Jewish Christians. (*Religio licita* and *religio illicita*—legal or licensed religion, and illegal or unlicensed religion. Judaism was licensed, Christianity was not, until Constantine about AD 321.)

Under *Pax Romana* any religion was permissible as long as you the people also bowed their knees to the emperor. The Jews had a problem with this because the Hebrew word "to worship"—*hishtahavout*, meant to bow the knee in an act of worship, so they would not do it. But they made a deal: they would sacrifice *for* the emperor instead of *to* the Emperor.

In the beginning the Jewish Christians were protected because they were seen as nothing other than Messianic Jews, a sect within Judaism. But after they had been excommunicated from the synagogues because of their faith in Yeshua (Jesus) as the Jewish Messiah, they lost their status as *religio licita* and they became *religio illicita*, an unlicensed and unlawful religion which would not bow to Rome. Hence the rabbinic establishment gave Jewish Christians over to persecution at the hands of the pagan Romans, as well as frequently persecuting them themselves.

"Those who say they are Jews but are not" (Rev. 2:9). Paul wrote about this at the end of Romans 2:

Smyrna

For he is not a Jew who is one outwardly, nor is circumcision that which is outward in the flesh. But he is a Jew who is one inwardly; and circumcision is that which is of the heart, by the Spirit, not by the letter; and his praise is not from men, but from God. (Rom. 2:28-29)

This was nothing new; Paul was trying to explain that this was what God had been intending all along. It has always been His desire to separate the true from the false. This is especially true in the spiritual realm, and it can be accomplished only through much tribulation.

Thus says the Lord GOD, 'No foreigner, uncircumcised in heart and uncircumcised in flesh, of all the foreigners who are among the sons of Israel, shall enter My sanctuary. (Ez. 44:9)

A distinction was made between physical circumcision and being uncircumcised in heart. This is a recurrent theme in the book of the prophet Jeremiah.

Thus says the LORD, "Let not a wise man boast of his wisdom, and let not the mighty man boast of his might, let not a rich man boast of his riches; but let him who boasts boast of this, that he understands and knows Me, that I am the LORD who exercises lovingkindness, justice and righteousness on earth; for I delight in these things," declares the LORD. "Behold, the days are coming," declares the LORD, "that I will punish all who are circumcised and yet uncircumcised. (Jer. 9:23-25)

They were **physically** circumcised but **unconverted** in their hearts. And then he goes on to say:

"'Egypt and Judah, and Edom and the sons of Ammon, and Moab and all those inhabiting the desert who clip the hair on their temples; for all the nations are uncircumcised, and all the house of Israel are uncircumcised of heart.' (Jer. 9:23-26)

God was not so much concerned with the ethnicity of an Israelite as with whether or not he was circumcised in heart. When Israel was uncircumcised in heart, God just buried them right in with all the Gentile nations! They were just as bad and, in a sense, even worse because they had the Torah and should have known better. That is what Paul was getting at. Jesus called them *"a synagogue of Satan."*

Remember what Jesus said in John's Gospel:

"For if you believed Moses, you would believe Me...Do not think that I will accuse you before the Father, the one who accuses you is Moses..." (Jn. 4:45-46)

The Dilemma of Laodicea

It was not Jesus who condemned; it was the Torah. The problem with unsaved Jewish people is not that they do not believe that Yeshua (Jesus) is the Messiah; that is the *result* of the problem. The problem is that they do not believe the Torah; they do not believe Moses and the Prophets. If they really were circumcised in heart, if they really believed the Tanak, if they really believed Moses and the prophets, they would see Jesus as the Messiah. The fact that they do not recognize Him as the Messiah is not the problem; it is the tragic consequence of not knowing the Torah.

But then again, what about the church? There were Jews who were nominally Jews, anthropologically Jews, sociologically Jews, genetically Jews, even religiously Jews—they were Jews in every way except the way that matters most: they were not Jews at heart. The world of Christendom is no different. There are people who are sociologically Christian, culturally Christian, even religiously Christian, wearing Christian symbols, going to church services—Christians in every way except the way that really matters: they are not circumcised of heart; they are not born again. That is what was happening in Smyrna, and this is what happens again in the Last Days.

Paul says if someone is circumcised in heart and born Jewish there exists an advantage because to them belong the oracles of God—the original culture and language of the Bible (Rom. 3:2). Of course it is a practical advantage, but it all depends on faith in Yeshua, in Jesus. Without faith in Yeshua, being Jewish is nothing.

There are so many Christians who have a love and a heart for Israel yet mistake a love and a heart for Jesus with some kind of an infatuation for Israelis. They will see little children born in Galilee, speaking Hebrew, and they marvel at this. But they do not marvel how wonderful it would be if these children were being brought up to believe that Jesus, Yeshua, is the Messiah as the Bible says. If they did, they would be marveling at something worth marveling at. But this child is Chinese, that child is African. It does not mean anything to be Jewish unless one is Jewish in *heart!*

There are Rumanian Jews who now live in Israel. First they went through the Holocaust and survived. Then they were Refuseniks under the Communists for eleven years before Ceausescu secured a bribe and let them go to Israel. Then, living in Galilee, putting on gas masks, going down to the bomb shelters, their main problem was not that they were living in a country that is constantly under the shadow of war. Their main problem was, and remains, that they do not have Yeshua as their Messiah. That is their *main* problem.

There are volumes of literature which almost makes Judaism a holy religion. Actually, there are two kinds of Judaism that truly are biblically correct:

Smyrna

- One is the original Judaism of the Torah that has not existed since AD 70 when the temple was destroyed, putting an end to sacrifice.
- The other is Messianic Judaism fulfilled in Yeshua, the Messiah.

In contrast, the Judaism of the rabbis of today is a false Judaism; it is a false religion. Not only that, but according to Scripture it is the worst kind of false religion...

> "Who is the liar but the one who denies that Jesus is the Christ? This is the antichrist, the one who denies the Father and the Son. Whoever denies the Son does not have the Father; the one who confesses the Son has the Father also." (1 Jn. 2:22-23)

Today, inscribed on the Mosque of Omar on the Temple Mount is a quotation from a sura in the Quran. It says, "God has no son." Right on the Temple Mount! This demonstrates that Islam is an Antichrist religion. But so is today's Rabbinic Judaism! **Both** deny that Yeshua is the Messiah openly and deny the Father and Son relationship. The New Testament, these words of John the Apostle, state that this is of the Antichrist, sar ha moshiach in Hebrew, antichristos in Greek.

There is something that the Ultra-Orthodox Jews read in their synagogues every Saturday called Ha birkhat ha minim. There are eighteen benedictions or blessings called Hashmona Asra. But they add a nineteenth which is called Birkat Ha-Minim meaning "blessed are...," only it is not a blessing but a curse. Every Sabbath they pray that the names of Jewish believers in Yeshua will be blotted out of the Book of Life. The Ultra-Orthodox still pray this way, and have done so for centuries. Significantly, they call Jesus not Yeshua but Yeshu, an acronym for "May his name be blotted out."

Just as the Jews persecuted Jewish believers in the first century, so they are persecuting Jewish believers today. St. Paul's, a Christian congregation in Jerusalem, has been fire bombed five times by Orthodox Jews. The Baptist House in Jerusalem was burned down by Orthodox Jews. The Messianic Congregation in Tiberius was burned down after the believers had run upstairs. Then they stoned the children of the Jewish believers. This happened again in Ashdod. Yes, the synagogue of Satan still does this.

One's love for the Jews must be the love of Jesus who died for them. Paul showed this love most clearly when he said, "My heart's desire...for them is for their salvation" (Rom. 10:1; also Rom. 9:13). This is **biblical** love. But Rabbinic Judaism is not "holy"; it is just as perverted and false as any other false religion of Satan. It curses its Messiah, it turns its own people against their own holy Scriptures, it perverts the Torah. It prays that the names of Jewish Christians will be blotted out. And it is setting the Jewish people up for the final deception by the Antichrist. That is what unbiblical Judaism is in reality.

There are many claiming that Judaism and Christianity are somehow allies against Islam. ALL religion is against Jesus! ALL religion. Jesus never taught a religion; He taught a relationship with God through a relationship with Himself. Jesus taught the *opposite* of religion. ALL religion is man trying to reach God. But the Gospel, the good news of the Kingdom of Heaven, is that God came down from heaven to reach man.

Messiah Has Come

In Daniel 9:25-26 the prophet spoke of the temple being rebuilt and then destroyed. In the rabbinic writings, the Talmud, Rabbi Yolkut explains that the Messiah (the Anointed One) would have to come and die before Jerusalem was destroyed. This can actually be read in the Talmud! The Sanhedrin wept "*oy veh oy lanu* – "woe upon woe to us, for the temple has been destroyed and you are not come." They knew it!

There was a famous rabbi called Rabbi Leopold Cohen who was perplexed when he read the book of the prophet Daniel because he could not understand it. So he went to the Talmud and tried to understand what Daniel 9 was talking about. He found one place in the Talmud where it said there is a curse on anybody who reads Daniel because it tells of the time of the end and Messiah's coming. He went to another place in the Talmud that comments on Daniel, Chapter 9, and it confirmed that Messiah had already come! Yes, their Talmud says He has already come—they just do not know who He was! Well, Rabbi Cohen had a big problem. He did not know what to do about it at first, but he said, "The Talmud says there is a curse on anybody who reads this book, but I understand it is about the Messiah and His coming. What shall I do?"

What Rabbi Cohen did was become a Baptist minister, but that is another story! He was the founder of the American Board of Missions to the Jews.

In summary, there are essentially three categories of Judaism. The first is the Judaism of Moses and the Torah, which was fulfilled by the Lord Jesus. The second is the Messianic Judaism of the New Testament (later known as Christianity) for those who believed that Jesus had fulfilled it. And the third is the false Talmudic Judaism of the rabbis which Jeremiah predicted would be established after the rejection of the Messiah, the fountain of living water (Jer. 2:13).

Jesus picked up on this in Matthew 24 and Luke 21, the Olivet Discourse. He began echoing the prophecies of Daniel, "*Not one stone will be left upon another, which will not be torn down,*" prophesying that the temple would be destroyed, but only after the Messiah had come and had been cut off—that is, killed for the sake of the people. So the rabbis had a big problem. The prophecies of Daniel were fulfilled, the predictions of Jesus had actually happened, the temple was destroyed after the Messiah came and died. It had plainly happened.

A Tale of Two Rabbis

There was a very famous rabbi called Rabbi Gemaliel (Acts 22:3; also Acts 5:34) and rabbinical literature documents that when Rabbi Gemaliel died "righteousness perished from the earth with him." That is how great Rabbi Gemaliel was considered to have been. And it can be seen in Acts 5:34 that he defended Christianity. He said that if Jesus was not the Messiah then His sect would disappear just like all the other false sects; but if it was of God then no man could stop it.

Rabbi Gemaliel was the grandson of Rabbi Hillel. Rabbi Hillel was the founder of the Hillel School, or Hillel Rabbinic Academy. There were two main schools of the Pharisees, the School of Shamai and the School of Hillel. The School of Hillel was much more benevolent and had a kind of universalist idea that God also loved Gentiles. This was where Rabbi Shaul of Tarsus was groomed.

An interesting classmate of Rabbi Shaul was Rabbi Johannan Ben Zakai. He is called "The Mighty Hammer." After AD 70 when the Temple was destroyed, they convened a council in Yavna and asked what to do. How could they carry on their religion with nowhere to sacrifice animals? Rabbi Johannan Ben Zakai led the rabbis into deciding that the rabbis would replace the Kohanim and the Levim, the priests and the Levites. Furthermore the synagogue would replace the Temple. Other rituals of human invention such as doing good works would replace the sacrificial system.

When Leviticus and Deuteronomy is read it is clearly seen that the largest single portion of the Law of Moses had to do with sacrifice and Temple rituals. But they could not keep it any longer with no Temple, so they invented another religion based on the synagogue. They still follow this man-made religion.

According to the Talmud, at the end of his life Rabbi Johannan Ben Zakai was weeping, and his disciples came and said to him, "O Mighty Hammer, why are you weeping?"

Rabbi Johannan Ben Zakai replied, "I am about to meet *Ha Shem*, the Great God, blessed be his Name, and there are two roads before me, one leading to Gehenna, and one leading to Paradise. And I do not know to which of these two roads He will sentence me."

He had no confidence of salvation. In fact he did not know if God was going to send him to hell for inventing this religion. That is why he was weeping at his death according to the rabbinic literature. In contrast, his classmate, Rabbi Shaul of Tarsus, better known as "Saint Paul the Apostle," said as death approached:

> *For I am already being poured out as a drink offering, and the time of my departure has come. I have fought the good fight, I have finished the course, I have kept the faith; in the future there is laid up for me the crown of righteousness, which the Lord, the righteous Judge, will award to me on that day; and not only to me, but also to all who have loved His appearing.* (2 Ti. 4:6-8)

So they had reached a point in history where every Jew would follow one of these two rabbis. Either they would follow Rabbi Shaul of Tarsus, who found the fulfillment of the Torah in Yeshua Messiah, or they would follow Rabbi Johannan Ben Zakai. Rabbinic Judaism later evolved through Rabbi Akiva and so on down through the centuries, but that is how it unfortunately began. So this is the origin of the synagogue of Satan, of false Judaism, which persecuted Jewish Christians, particularly at Smyrna.

Early Commentators

A significant document for anyone interested in understanding the first- and second-century church is the *Didache*. Also there is the *Shepherd of Hermes* and the *Epistle of Barnabas* (which was almost certainly not written by the original Barnabas). Unfortunately it all began to become anti-Jewish. However, it also shows us how the early church understood biblical typology and the midrashic method of understanding Scripture held by the early church.

For instance, Jews could not eat swine. Swine had to do with people who did not care about the truth and would only mock it. When Jesus said, "*Do not throw your pearls before swine*" (Mt. 7:6), He was not referring to pearls or to pigs but to the Word of God and to unclean people who would only mock those who brought that Word to them. In the tradition of the kosher laws that formed the basis for the dietary laws, swine represented mockers. This was their rationale.

Smyrna

Similarly, when Jesus said, "*I will make you fishers of men*" (Mt. 4:19), He was using the act of fishing to represent evangelism. The sea represents the nations, boats represent the Body of Christ. Jesus told the apostles where to cast their nets to catch the fish in order to show them that He would enable them to become evangelists. They could not catch anything until Jesus directed them where to lower their nets or their lure. In the same way, no one is going to catch anything unless Jesus through the Holy Spirit directs their evangelism. Shellfish live on the seabed. They represent fish that are buried too far into the world to be caught. Therefore shellfish are not kosher. There was a logic and a validity to this interpretation; it was not wrong. The problem was that it became anti-Jewish to the point where people added to it, saying, "God never intended the Jews to be caught in the net."

Other writings include something called *Contra Heresium*, (*Against all Heresies*), written by Irenaeus who became Bishop of Lyon in about AD 199. Irenaeus had been a student of Polycarp, Bishop of Smyrna, who was martyred under the reign of Marcus Aurelius in AD 155. Polycarp had been a student of the Apostle John himself. These three authors became very significant for the future of Christianity.

The principal Greek apologist who wrote to defend the church against persecution was Justin Martyr who was born in Palestine and wrote sometime around AD 165. The fact that he was so early and was from Palestine makes him an important source of what the early church believed. The principal Latin apologist was Tertullian (c. 160 - c. 220).

There are two kinds of people known as church fathers, and their literature is called the patristic literature. They are pre-Nicean; that is, before the Council of Nicea, and pre-Constantine. The pre-Nicean ones were closer to the Apostles. Their writings were much more biblical and much more in tune with what the early church actually believed. One thing known for certain is that all the pre-Nicean fathers believed there had to be a literal millennial reign of Jesus on earth for a thousand years. The idea of Post-Millennialism was invented by Augustine (354 - 430) and those influenced by him. But every pre-Nicean writer said that the Apostles taught and believed that there had to be a literal Millennium to fulfill Revelation 20.

Ignatius of Antioch

Ignatius (c. 35 - c. 110), Bishop of Antioch, refused to deny his faith in the Lord Jesus and was taken to Rome to be martyred during the reign of Trajan (98 - 117) by being fed to wild beasts in the arena. Our knowledge of him is derived from seven letters written while he was being taken to Rome. His single crime was that he would not say, "Caesar is Lord," and thus deny Jesus as his supreme Lord. From Smyrna, while en route to Rome, Ignatius wrote letters to the churches of Ephesus, Magnesia, Tralles and Rome. From Troas he wrote to the church at Philadelphia and also back to his church at Smyrna and to its bishop, the future martyr Polycarp. He was certainly an encourager in the face of terrifying choices.

Recurrent themes in these letters were insistence on obedience to the bishop and the presbyters and deacons under him. He also taught, "No Eucharist is valid unless celebrated by the bishop or a presbyter delegated by him." He also spoke of "the church which ... in the land of the Romans, has the presidency," thus probably acknowledging the leadership of the Bishop of Rome. It started back then, but that does not make it right. He called this idea "Monoepiscopy"—one bishop, a singular head.

In contrast to Ignatius, the biblical church, as best we can tell from the Scriptures, believed in and practiced a plurality of leadership. In Acts 15 we see that it was an assembly of the apostles and elders who made doctrinal decisions. Paul and Barnabas, when they planted churches, ordained "elders"—plural. *Presbuteroi* (Greek: "elders") occurs five times in the New Testament and always in the plural. Ignatius had this idea that to defend the church against error every city should have only one overall leader, particularly in churches that had been planted by the Apostles.

Having said that, it should be noted that the Brethren and the Jehovah's Witnesses have a plurality of elders to govern them, and yet they are the most controlling of all sects. They might even be called cults. But in Acts 15 the Apostles submitted to one another and concluded that their answer "*seemed good to the Holy Spirit and to us*" as Luke put it. At the end of the day all one can ensure is that they honestly submitted their thoughts to God and sought His answers. The good kings always inquired of the Lord. It is for man to inquire and it is for God to answer. Man should not invent God's answers.

Not to denigrate Ignatius, he was a martyr. But it must be noted that although his faith is not in question, his teaching certainly is. At least some of it. Ignatius played a very important role in organizing the church. But he was up against this problem of the serpent and the dragon: deception from within and persecution from without. And he tried to cope with this problem the way that seemed right to him. Possibly he knew the bishops in question were trustworthy and he may not have had all the New Testament, so his model may have been the High Priest of the Old Covenant. But Ignatius did not deny his Lord.

Ignatius also had a strange idea about a martyr's crown. He believed, and taught others to believe, that if they put a believer in an arena with the lions, the lions would be afraid of them because of the anointing of the Holy Spirit. And that sometimes actually happened; the lions were afraid of the Christians because of the *Shekinah* glory on them. What a church! But he also taught people to yearn for martyrdom. He said that if the lions did not attack him he would attack them because he was not going to be deprived of his martyr's crown. So people began following his ideas and got themselves killed as a result. This was suicide, kamikaze, a faulty and dangerous precedent, albeit with the best of intentions.

Later these people became known as "fathers," and the senior ones as patriarchs in the East and popes in the West. They claimed that since, for example, Ephesus was founded by apostles, therefore the true teaching of the apostles must still be in Ephesus. So they began looking for lines of descent. John discipled Polycarp, Polycarp discipled Irenaeus, and they began looking for lineage. But this is not the biblical model. Ignatius may never have intended these singular bishops to lead to any kind of popery resulting in torture and bloodshed if anyone did not follow their teaching. But it did set the stage for that to evolve, and evolve it did.

The difference was that during this period, pre-Nicea and pre-Constantine, if a Christian would not say "Caesar is Lord" it was Caesar, the Roman Emperor, the Latin-speaking *Pontificus Maximus* who killed him. And post-Nicea, post-Constantine, when the popes gained control, if a Christian would not obey the pope it was (guess who) the pope of the Roman Empire, the Latin-speaking *Pontificus Maximus* who killed him. It harkens to the fourth empire of Daniel. It keeps going until the end with its rule of iron, and will eventually cover the whole earth.

Joseph – A Type of Jesus, and David – A Type of Jesus

From a Jewish perspective there are two pictures of the Messiah: *Ha Mashiach Ben Yosef*, and *Ha Mashiach Ben David*: "Messiah the son of Joseph," and "Messiah the son of David." All the Law and the Prophets point to Jesus as Messiah in some way or another, including the characters of Joseph and David.

When in Genesis 37 Joseph was betrayed by his brothers into Gentile hands, God turned it around and made it into a way for all Israel to be saved. Similarly, midrashically, Yeshua was betrayed by His Jewish brothers into the hands of Gentiles and God turned it around to make it a way for all Israel (and all Gentiles) to be saved. There are numerous parallels between the life of Joseph and the life of Jesus. Consider also the two thieves, one a baker and one a (wine) cupbearer, one killed and one lived, and so on.

In His first coming Jesus came as the son of Joseph, the Suffering Servant who was exalted from a place of condemnation to a place of exaltation in one day just like Joseph. In His second coming He will come as Messiah the son of David, the one who had set up the capital of God in Jerusalem in God's name. He will reign from Jerusalem when He returns.

The Kingdom-Now people are into Replacement Theology, thinking they are the new Israel and they will set up the new Kingdom for Jesus to take over when He returns. They are generally Post-Millennial; they think that the Millennium has come and passed and Jesus is already reigning, Satan being already bound. Well, if Satan is bound, who is doing his work?! It can be shown from pre-Nicean writings that it was widely taught and believed in the early church that the apostles believed there had to be a millennial reign of Christ on earth.

From a Jewish perspective, if there will be no Millennium, Jesus was not the Messiah. In order to be the Messiah, He had to fulfill *all* the Messianic prophecies, both those relating to the son of Joseph, a Suffering Servant in Isaiah, and especially those relating to the son of David. But in fact Jesus did not fulfill all the Messianic prophecies. In His first coming He fulfilled only the son of Joseph prophecies; the Suffering Servant prophecies. When He returns He will fulfill the son of David prophecies as a great King. That is why from a Jewish perspective there has to be a Millennium when the Davidic Messiah reigns on earth for Jesus to have been the Messiah. He will rule with justice and with an iron scepter.

Just as at His first coming God needed the Roman Empire and its roads to carry the good news of Jesus to all the world, so at His second coming Jesus will need a worldwide communication system in place so that He can rule all the world. And it can be clearly seen emerging.

Looking further at these patristic writings, it is unpalatable the way people call them "fathers." In Ephesians 2:20 the apostles and prophets are the foundations of the church with Jesus as the cornerstone. *They* were the fathers, *they* wrote the Scriptures. These other people who came along later very often distorted the original teachings of the Bible. It is therefore difficult to understand why people insist on calling them "fathers." They may have fathered churches, but the churches that they fathered are Eastern Orthodoxy, Roman Catholicism, etc. They were not the fathers of Christianity. The Apostles and the prophets were the fathers and, biblically speaking, no one else.

Increasing Error and the "Greecing" of the Church

Justin Martyr (c. 100 - 165) wrote two very effective apologies and the second one went a long way towards provoking a persecution. He also debated with a Jew named Trypho, and a record of that debate survives to this day. It is the first recorded debate between a major Christian scholar and a Jewish scholar.

Two ways of thinking were being applied to Scripture, the Hebrew way and the Greek way. The Hebrew way asserts, "Trust God and then you will understand." The Greek way supposes, "First understand, then you will trust God." God uses **BOTH** of these ways of thinking.

The Bible never teaches a blind faith. The Book of Isaiah opens with God saying, "*Come now, let us reason together, says the LORD.*" And in John 5 Jesus appealed to rules of evidence to show why people should believe in Him. Paul argued by "*proving from the Scriptures that Jesus was the Messiah*" (Acts 28:23), as did Apollos (Acts 18:28) and Peter (Acts 2:36). Jesus probably taught Peter (Lk. 24:44).

God will use the Greek way of thinking to get people to become believers. But after they become believers He expects them to follow the Hebrew way of thinking. Believers walk by faith, not by sight. Paul talked about "*Jews who seek a sign, whereas Greeks seek wisdom*" (1 Co. 1:22), and this is what he was getting at. God will use the Greek way of thinking to bring someone to the point of faith, but after they have come to believe that Jesus is the Lord He expects them to stop behaving like Greeks and begin behaving like Hebrews—Messianic Hebrews. Act in faith and then comes understanding.

A Different Gospel

It is one thing to recontextualize the Gospel, but it is another thing to reinterpret it or redefine it.

When the Wycliffe translators went to a certain tribe in equatorial Africa, a people who never saw snow, they translated Isaiah 1:18, which reads, "Your sins shall be white as snow" as "Your sins shall be white as coconut." That is perfectly acceptable. They are not redefining the Gospel; they are only recontextualizing it in terms that those people can grasp. But when something is redefined, it is a problem. And many of these early church fathers started redefining Scripture in Greek terms, in the kind of terms used by Aristotle and Plato.

Chapter 1 of John's Gospel is presented in very Hebrew terms. Every Greek would have been able to agree with John's Gospel until he got to the point where he said, *"The Word became flesh"* (Jn. 1:14), because he had this Platonic Greek world view that the spirit is good and the flesh is bad. Genesis said that the flesh was very good; it is just that it is fallen. Once these Greek and Platonic ideas came into the church, Christianity became redefined. It was taken out of its Jewish context and put into a Greek context, which became another gospel.

This got particularly perverted with the emergence of Roman Catholicism and Eastern Orthodoxy. Augustine said that the only good thing about getting married is having children that will be celibate! He thought all sex was evil and wrong. People later picked up the idea that all sex was sin. The idea anyone had to be celibate, and that it was holier to be a monk or a nun, is nowhere to be found in Scripture. It was all because of the Greek philosophical idea that the physical world was bad.

Some people said that Jesus could not possibly have been God in human flesh. They insist that He was totally God and therefore Spirit. Thus, if He walked on the beach He would not leave any footprints; He only looked human. Many of these fathers started taking on these Greek ideas, not simply explaining the Gospel to Greeks but redefining it in Greek terms. They could not believe it as it stood, so they invented explanations as liberals still do.

Some of the church fathers tried to defend the church against these heretical influences. Others later actually propagated them. Looking back, it is easy to see that Christianity was getting further and further away from its Jewish roots just as Rabbinic Judaism was also getting further and further away from its Mosaic roots.

Five Philosophies That Became Roman Catholicism and Eastern Orthodoxy

To sum up, there were five major opposing religious philosophies coming against the church, as follows:

First there were the Greco-Roman religions based on astrology. Today there is a huge resurgence in astrology. A visitor to the ruins of the synagogue at Kibbutz Alpha in Northern Israel would be shown a mosaic on the floor with astrological inscriptions. And at the Domitian Abbey in Jerusalem the visitor sees three concentric circles on the floor in a mosaic. The innermost circle depicts the twelve sons of Jacob, the patriarchs of Israel. The next circle shows, corresponding to them, the twelve apostles. And the outer circle depicts the zodiac. To us Zeus, Jupiter, Mercury, Cupid are but mythical characters, but Paul, writing in Greek, referred to them as demons (Greek,

64

demonoi) as he was quoting the Septuagint translation of Moses who referred to other gods as "*Shedim*," meaning "devils." Today Greek classics are read simply as literature, but to the early church it was considered demonic because it involved idolatry.

The early Christians were up against a big problem. Homosexuality and bisexuality were not only culturally endemic to much of the Greek and Roman world, but there was a definite religious flavor both to cult prostitution and to homosexuality and bisexuality. The early Christians were in conflict with this. There can be no doubt that there is a coming conflict between Bible-believing Christians and the homosexual world that is going to end up in the same way. Rampant persecution of Christians by gangs of homosexuals—that is what happened in the early church, reflecting the story of Sodom (Gen. 19).

Second there was the mystery religion of Babylon. Auricular confession, sacraments, the round communion wafer or "host" representing the sun-god and so on—these things originated in Babylon and found their way to Pergamum through the Greek and Roman world, and from there into Freemasonry, Roman Catholicism, etc.

Third was Stoicism. The Emperor Marcus Aurelius was a Stoic. It was the opposite of Epicurean. It emphasized things like mortification. "Do not touch, do not handle," do not do this, do not do that. Paul wrote against this when he said,

> "These are matters which have, to be sure, the appearance of wisdom in self-made religion and self-abasement and severe treatment of the body, but are of no value against fleshly indulgence." (Col. 2:23)

The manifestations of Stoicism can be seen today in Roman Catholicism where, because they add the idea that one must partly atone for one's own sin, there is an emphasis on self-abasement of the very kind Paul warned against as "*of religious appearance but having no spiritual value*" (1 Ti. 4:8)—for instance, the way Catholics and others fall face down and prostrate themselves in a show of apparent humility and submission to their mother church.

This used to be exploited by Roman Catholicism during the early Renaissance when they needed to find ways of raising money to build their cathedrals and basilicas. This was the idea of indulgences (payment for sins), or money paid to get one's mother out of Purgatory and such by, for example, paying the priest to pray for her. One finds in Rome the *Scala Sancta*—the sacred stairs, where weak, elderly ladies go up and down saying the rosary. In Guadalupe, Mexico, you see the same thing. In Brother Andre's cathedral in Montreal they have his heart in a jar, and they go up the stairs saying their rosaries. This kind of mortification was not a crucifying of the flesh in a biblical sense, it was the idea of self-atonement, that one somehow paid for their own sins or accumulated enough grace by doing certain things. These ideas did not have much appeal to the common people. They attracted only certain intellectuals and aristocrats in reaction to the Epicureans who were devoted to sensual pleasure.

Fourth there was Rabbinic Judaism. This is not the faith of the original Jewish Christians who were the Nazarenes and doctrinally sound. There were two later heretical sects, one called the Elkasites who were basically Gnostic, and the other called the Ebionites. In Israel today there are Ebionites, Jews who believe that Jesus is the Messiah but deny His divinity.

The fifth was Emperor worship—the kissing of his rings, his feet and so on.

Those five things, Greco-Roman religion, Babylonian mystery religion, Stoicism, Judaism and Emperor worship, all of which faced the church at Smyrna and the second- and third-century Christians, combined to form what has come to be recognized as Roman Catholicism and Eastern Orthodoxy.

Holocaust in Yugoslavia

In the West the focus is on Roman Catholicism as there is little interaction with Eastern Orthodoxy. But when in the Middle East the emphasis shifted to the Syrian Orthodox Church, the Greek Orthodox Church, etc., there was a split from Rome in a schism during the Middle Ages. The dividing line was in what became modern Yugoslavia, where the Greek-speaking East met the Latin-speaking West. It was also where the Muslim world confronted the Christian world for centuries. The things happening today in that area of the world have roots that go all the way back to those days. In time the Serbs went with the Orthodox tradition and were Greek-speaking, while the Croats went with the Latin tradition.

In the 1930's and 1940's there was a terrible holocaust similar to what was perpetrated against the Jews but it was carried out by Roman Catholic Croatians with some Muslim help against the Orthodox Serbs. This was not simply done with the participation of the Roman Catholic Church, but at the behest of the Roman Catholic hierarchy. And they killed over 700,000 Serbs. The only way that an Eastern Orthodox person could save his life was to be baptized into the Roman Catholic Church. This was carried out with the de facto endorsement of the Vatican. What is seen today is simply a continuation of the conflict that has been going on for such a long time in that part of the world.

Identity of the Renaissance Popes

During the Renaissance, the popes sought to identify themselves with certain of the pagan emperors who persecuted the church. In the papal chapels in the Vatican are seen the coats of arms of certain popes. These were adopted from the pagan emperors. During this period the rival banking families of Italy such as the Bourgeois and Medici families vied by a combination of intrigue, subterfuge, simony, and military threat to engineer the appointment of one of their clan to the position of pontiff. In the same manner as the pagan emperors had been head of Rome's religious Pantheon uniting religion, economy, and state with the title "*Pontificus Maximus*," so they wanted to identify with these emperors to show a relationship between imperial Rome and papal Rome. Papal Rome has now almost certainly killed many more Christians than pagan Rome. But the inscriptions can be witnessed in the Renaissance on the papal coats of arms in their palaces and chapels, and on their tombs.

The Principal Persecutors

The first Emperor to persecute the church significantly (Claudius was relatively moderate) was Nero who, according to Eusebius, killed Peter and Paul. Eusebius (c. 260 - c. 340), Bishop of Caesarea in Palestine, wrote the first comprehensive history of the church, *The Church from Christ to Constantine*.

Nero had a strange relationship with his mother. It very closely approximated what is seen in the Old Testament with Queen Athaliah and her son (2 Ki.). The son put the mother up to strange things, and the son turned against the mother. There is a deep typology in this. Nero began by being benevolent towards Christians and even, seemingly, towards the Jews. But he was falsely benevolent in order to gain their confidence, later revealing his true colors. This was the trap the popes laid for the Huguenots as previously discussed.

It is important to understand how the early church associated emperor worship with the Antichrist. The Antichrist will be like Nero. Initially he will show benevolence ("*confirm a covenant*" - Dan. 9:27) in order to seduce people into thinking what a wonderful chap he is. The verses in Revelation where it talks about th horn—a counterfeit of Christ who was, who is not, and who is to come—were taken by the early Christians to apply to Nero who would somehow be reincarnated (Rev. 17:10). The first person whose name was found to number 666 from the numerals representing the letters of his name was Nero. And when Rome burned under Nero the early Christians, identifying Rome with Babylon, said, "This is what Isaiah and Jeremiah were talking about: 'Fallen, fallen is Babylon'" (Is. 47, Jer. 51). It was later, of course, written into the book of Revelation.

Nero and all the other emperors went first against the Christians, and subsequently against the Jews. Not long after Nero's persecution of Christians a general named Titus went to Israel, put down a Jewish rebellion and destroyed the Temple in AD 70. That campaign ensued almost directly after Nero. The Jews had enjoyed a period of unprecedented prosperity while the church was being persecuted. Somehow that will be repeated at the end. The emperor of the world to come will somehow give himself the appearance of benevolence, even deceiving Christians to a point, certainly deceiving the Jews who will seem to have their messianic prosperity, but then he will show his true colors. That is what happened with Titus.

The same thing happened in the second century. There was tremendous persecution of the church, then there was the Bar Kochba rebellion and a genocidal holocaust perpetrated against the Jews. Up to the 1920s, the greatest bloodbath in Jewish history was what happened under Bar Kochba's Rebellion. The Jews of Israel were virtually obliterated and driven into the Diaspora for nearly two millennia.

It is critical to understand the theological relationship between anti-Semitism and the persecution of the Body of Christ. It is like heads and tails, the two sides of the same coin. One can distinguish between them, but one can never separate them. God said in Genesis 3:15, *I will put enmity between you and the woman, and between your seed and her seed.* The woman Eve represented Israel and also, by extension, the Body of Christ.

Remember who the Communists persecuted the most? Jews and born-again Christians. And who did the Roman Catholic Church persecute the most? Jews and born-again Christians. Today, who do the Muslims hate the most? Jews and born-again Christians. The reasons for this are not simply coincidental, or even historical or sociological, the reasons are really theological and spiritual. It all goes back to Genesis 3—the enmity between Satan and God's chosen people.

Persecution for Ten Days

Jesus told the church at Smyrna,

> "*Do not fear what you are about to suffer. Behold, the devil is about to cast some of you into prison, so that you will be tested, and you will have tribulation for ten days. Be faithful until death, and I will give you the crown of life.*" (Rev. 2:10)

Smyrna

In order to understand this it helps to borrow a theological term from the Roman Catholics, *Sensus Plenio*. The term "day" does not mean literal days, it means ten periods (as in the dark and light periods of Genesis, where the evening and the morning were the first day). So the reference is to the ten major periods of persecution under the reign of ten devil-possessed emperors during this time, as follows:

- Domitian in 81 – 96;
- Trajan, 98 – 117;
- Hadrian, 117 - 138;
- Antonius Pius, 138 – 161;
- Marcus Aurelius, 161- 180;
- Commodus, 177 – 192;
- Septimus Severitus, whose name gave us the word "severity," 192–211;
- Decius, 251 – 251, a terrible man who mercifully did not last long;
- And finally the two worst, Valerian and then Diocletian, who died in about 285.

Compromise

The persecutors who did the most damage to the Christians were the emperors such as Decius who enticed them to compromise, essentially in three major ways:

- First, there were the *liberecate*. These people purchased a document saying they had worshipped the emperor when they had not done so.
- Then there were the *thurificate*. They were religious about it. They would not sacrifice to the emperor properly, but they would burn incense.
- And finally there were the *sacrifacate*. They would actually, openly, sacrifice to the emperor.

The Emperor Diocletian was influenced by someone called Porphyrie who wanted to use the school system to propagate the religious ideas of the Roman Empire. This brought Christians into sharp conflict with the education system.

Once again the same kind of trend is happening today. Many Christian parents will not put their children in a state school; they are homeschooling them or putting them in private Evangelical schools despite the financial cost. Why? In Britain for instance, at a Church of England school, a very godly Christian headmaster disclosed the contents of the manual for Religious Education in Shropshire. On the front cover was a rabbi reading Torah, a Roman Catholic priest saying mass, a Muslim imam facing Mecca, a Hindu, a Buddhist monk, etc. the very first lesson it contains is a lesson on pilgrimages and it said (and remember this is an instruction manual for teachers) "These should be highlighted and pressed upon the children because they are colorful and meaningful." The whole philosophy behind it is New Age and an attempt at social engineering to try to bring harmony to a multi-ethnic society by conveying the idea that there is a common legitimacy to all faiths. The aim is to influence children at as young and impressionable an age as possible through songs, festivals, stories, picture books and so on. This was just the lesson on pilgrimages. The Catholics go to Lourdes, the Jews have the pilgrim feasts, Muslims have the Hajj to Mecca, Hindus have Rama and Sitra. This is what is required by law to be taught to young children in British state schools, and even Church of England schools are now utilizing this curriculum. But if this is examined carefully it can be seen that they have been enticed into finding a way to compromise their Evangelical Christianity. In other words, as it was in the beginning, it is the same today. *"There is nothing new under the sun."*

During a dispute with the Baptist Union of Great Britain, when they went into the inter-church process that included ecumenical unity with Rome, some said, "Listen, I am a Baptist and I am simply standing up for the traditional Baptist understanding of the Scriptures concerning Roman Catholicism and other non-Evangelical churches."

They replied, "What Baptist tradition?"

To which some replied, "John Bunyan, William Carey, Charles Spurgeon."

The President of the Baptist Union then said, "O well, they all disagreed with each other, didn't they?"

But it was pointed out to him, "Well not concerning the Church of Rome they didn't; do you want to hear some quotes from Spurgeon?"

But he did not. He changed the subject. He just compromised with Rome.

In the Church of England the same kind of thing happened. Liberal Anglo-Catholic bishops have said it is not required to believe in the resurrection or the virgin birth to be a Christian. George Carey wrote a book, *The Meeting of Waters*, calling for ecumenical reunion with Rome. Even "Evangelical" or "Bible-believing" bishops do not want to rock the boat; they do not want to speak out. Thurificate, burn incense to the false gods, participate in their false rituals occasionally for the sake of unity, it is the same thing in another form. *"There is nothing new under the sun."*

Now most people in the Baptist Union, or the Evangelicals in the Church of England or the Assemblies of God, would protest at these heresies and affirm what mainstream Evangelicals believe, what the Bible says. But almost without realizing it they get into thurificate. They began compromising in order to avoid being persecuted. This led to division in the early church and it can only cause the same thing today.

The reason the early Christians seem to have been total pacifists was not so much that they were pacifists as a matter of doctrine, but being in the Roman legions entailed worshipping the emperor and invoking the blessings of pagan gods, which the Christians could not do. However, as the empire began to decline, Rome started looking for scapegoats to blame. Christians, and later Jews, became the scapegoats. So Rome began asserting the need for a central religion to hold the empire together.

Christians wrote "apologies" to defend the faith before the Roman world and the emperors. In AD 125 Quadratus wrote an apology to the Emperor Hadrian, famous for the wall in Northern Britain. He emphasized the healing miracles and the monotheism of the early church. There are people called "cessationists" who believe the false doctrine that the gifts of the Holy Spirit ceased with the death of the original Apostles. However, there exist clear second-century historical records that these gifts continued beyond the time of the Apostles.

The point is this: only true believers were willing to be massacred and to see their families massacred rather than deny that Jesus is Lord. God used persecution and suffering to make the church zealous and to purify it from heresy and from false belief.

Persecution Today

It was Tertullian who said that the blood of the martyrs is the seed of the church. The more the church was persecuted, the more it grew.

When first migrating to Israel in the 1970s and pursuing high-profile evangelism to be conducted in Israel openly and similarly to how *Jews for Jesus* do it in America, people said this approach was wrong. But what happened is that the congregation in Jerusalem was fire-bombed. Tiberius and the Baptist House were fire-bombed. In the early 1980s, when the religious parties made a coalition with the Likud. The rabbis began feeling their roots politically as never before, and there was tremendous pressure and persecution against the local Body of Christ. That persecution did much to unite the church and to get it moving evangelistically. At present there are tremendous Israeli evangelists out on the streets with tracts, lifting up Yeshua, and spreading the Gospel more actively than has ever been done since the early centuries of the church in that area of the world. The church became very inward-looking with the Apostles, but after the martyrdom of Stephen persecution broke out and it became missions-oriented and outward looking.

The Dilemma of Laodicea

False doctrines continually infiltrated into the church, and as they infiltrated, persecution always filtered out the false believers. Persecution is not good; it is bad and it comes from the devil, but God very often has a purpose in it and it can end up doing the church more good than it does harm. Indeed,

> "We know that in all things God works for the good of those who love him, who have been called according to his purpose." (Rom. 8:28)

It has become the personal view of many that the church in the West has become so materialistic, so lukewarm, so much in the character of the church of Laodicea and so deluded by the false doctrines of so many false teachers, that perhaps the only hope for the church in the West is a persecution. No one should pray for persecution. It should never be desired personally or wished on anybody. Nonetheless things in the West have gone so far for so long, and so much false doctrine and compromise has come into the Body of Christ, that unless there is a persecution the church is not going to be corrected. People want to *"have their ears tickled"* as Paul warned Timothy (2 Ti. 4:3), and that is what they get: a tickling of their ears, but not sound doctrine.

The biggest deception came during and after these persecutions: it is called "Gnosticism." It was against this Gnosticism that Irenaeus wrote *Against all Heresies*.

The modern New Age Movement is rooted in neo-Gnosticism and Hinduistic thought and is again infiltrating mainstream Christianity, including much of supposed Evangelism via such deceptions as the Ecumenical and Inter-Faith Movements and the Emergent Church. This was initially facilitated in large part by a charismatic movement that, due to a popular lack of discernment, witnessed the counterfeiting of authentic biblically charismatic gifts, replaced authentic spirituality with a combination of emotionalism and mysticism, and supplanted biblical doctrine with experience-based theology.

Courtesy of figures such as Chuck Colson however, this deception has made popular inroads into most bastions of traditional Western Evangelicism. The counterfeit revivals of the Kansas City false prophets, the Toronto Experience, Brownsville Assemblies of God in Pensacola, Florida, and the Lakeland fiasco of Todd Bentley have seen Hinduistic practices such as Kundalini Yoga masquerade as Christian charismata. The repetitive singing of choruses with unbiblical lyrics as supposed worship has in effect been a mantra predisposing Christians to manipulation and deception where they become inundated by false doctrine through singing repeated clichés that are often simply not scriptural. This has been seen most often in the Vineyard Movement of the late John Wimber. Once respected Evangelical scholars, such as J. I. Packer, have lent credence to the ecumenical and interfaith leanings of Chuck Colson and former Evangelical, Peter Kreeft. Former Dallas Seminary professor Jack Deere has likewise written an apologetic for the Latter Rain deceptions of the Kansas City false prophets (a collection of sexual predators such as Bob Jones and homosexuals and drunkards such as Paul Cain). Deere's defense of these false doctrines and false prophecies made by the Kansas City false prophets and Mike Bickel was based purely on a Gnostic spiritualization of the Book of Joel out of all reasonable historical and exegetical context.

Mormonism is likewise predicated on the Gnostic revelations of its founders, yet we have witnessed once trusted Evangelical scholars such as Craig Blomberg of Western Seminary in Denver, academics such as Craig Hazen of Talbot Seminary, and apologists such as Ravi Zacharias, seeking a compromised rapprochement with Mormonism. This downward trend however, has reached new depths of demonic depravity in the phenomenon of the Emergent Church with its guru Brian McLaren and its proponents Dan Kimball and Rick Warren who forwarded the book promoting it.

We are experiencing for the third time the invasion of Western Christendom by Eastern religion and Gnosticism. The first time was in the ear or Origen, Basilides, and Valentinus in Alexandria in the Post-Nicean Patristic era when the Gnostic hermeneutics of Alexandria rivaled the hermeneutics of Antioch.

The second time was when the Crusades brought the influences of Buddhism, Hinduism, and Islam into Europe with everything from counting prayers on beads, to the burning of incense and candles before icons, to auto-flagellation copied from Shia Muslims commemorating the death of Ali at the Battle of Karbala.

The third time Eastern religion and Gnosticism have permeated Western Christianity is at the present time. The Emergent Church literally seeks to return to the Dark Ages, viewing not the New Testament, but the mystical Monasticism of the fifth through eighth centuries, as the ideal model for Christian spirituality. And to this end the Emergent Church movement has embraced everything from labyrinths, ritual prayer walks, contemplative prayer, Lectio Divina, meditative visualization techniques often involving icons, incense, candles, repetitive chanting, etc. The adaptation of visualization methodology in contemplative prayer originated with the brainwashing techniques of the Jesuit founder Ignatius Loyola, whose followers were responsible for the genocide and torture of thousands upon thousands of born-again Christians.

Loyola taught if the church (meaning the pope) said, "it is daylight when it is dark we must believe it is daylight." This perverse version of spirituality demanded the suspension of all critical faculties and abandonment of objective standards of truth, as well as the supersession of ecclesiastical and papal authority over Scripture. Acquiescence to the Toronto, Pensacola, and Lakeland deceptions likewise demands an abandonment of spiritual discernment, reason, and the capacity to reason biblically. It is no coincidence that the patriarch of the modern New Age Movement in the Western world was also a Jesuit, the late Teilhard de Chardin. What *is* astounding however, is that professing Evangelicals such as Joyce Huggett and Richard Foster, the author of *The Celebration of Discipline*, have incorporated such demonic formulas into their self-designed templates of Christian discipleship and prayer.

All of these pseudo-Christian trends however, have a common characteristic: *all* derive from Gnosticism and/or involve a doctrinal compromise with it. Those resisting these demonic trends will face ostracism and, ultimately, persecution by those being swallowed up in its advancing tide just the same as transpired in the early centuries of the church. The apostate church will turn on the faithful one, and will split Evangelicism.

A more shocking example of Eastern religion is contained in the book *The Fourth Dimension* by David Yonggi Cho, the Korean Christian mystic. Cho states that the subconscious imagination is one's spirit, when in fact it is one's soul that is a function of the mind. In his doctrine Cho advocates visualization of one's desires in one's imagination and speaking it into being with a Word-Faith formula. His claim is that Hindus and Buddhists have known this for centuries, but now Jesus Christ has shown it to him. Cho teaches pure oriental shamanism, yet calls it "Christianity." We do not know if Mr. Cho is a Christian or not, but he is certainly in terms of his beliefs a Buddhist and a Hindu.

The issue of Gnosticism will be revisited in the study of the church at Pergamum, but essentially God used persecution during the era of the church of Smyrna. He let it happen to keep the church refined and pruned and it did the church more good than harm. The blood of the martyrs was the seed of the church.

There is no doubt that just as this was the truth in the early church, it is going to be the truth before Jesus comes back.

Chapter 3

Pergamum: "Divorced," "Spiritual Adultery"
4th Century to Early Middle Ages

| 1st | 2nd | 3rd | 4th | 5th | 6th | 7th | 8th | 9th | 10th | 11th | 12th | 13th | 14th | 15th | 16th | 17th | 18th | 19th | 20th |

Apostolic Church

Pre-Nicean Church

Rise of the Institutional Church

The Dark Ages

The Reformation

Great Awakening

Apostate Church

"And to the angel of the church in Pergamum write:

"'The One who has the sharp two-edged sword says this:

"'"I know where you dwell, where Satan's throne is; and you hold fast My name, and did not deny My faith even in the days of Antipas, My witness, My faithful one, who was killed among you, where Satan dwells. But I have a few things against you, because you have there some who hold the teaching of Balaam, who kept teaching Balak to put a stumbling block before the sons of Israel, to eat things sacrificed to idols and to commit acts of immorality. So you also have some who in the same way hold the teaching *of the Nicolaitans. Therefore repent; or else I am coming to you quickly, and I will make war against them with the sword of My mouth. He who has an ear, let him hear what the Spirit says to the churches. To him who overcomes, to him I will give some of the hidden manna, and I will give him a white stone, and a new name written on the stone which no one knows but he who receives it.""" (Rev. 2:12-17)*

The City of Pergamum

Pergamum, today called "Bergma," was a seat of learning with a library of over 200,000 books, hand-written of course. The word "parchment" is derived from its name. The population is estimated to have been 120,000 and it was the seat of the Roman proconsul.

Pergamum was rife with occult centers. There were temples dedicated to the emperor, to Zeus, Athena, Dionysus, Demeter, Hera and Asclepius the "savior god" represented by a snake. However, unlike the bronze snake which God told Moses to set up, the Christians associated the serpent symbol of Asclepius with Satan.

The altar to Zeus was very prominent, standing 90 feet square and 20 feet high on a ledge jutting out from a hillside 800 feet above the city. It looked like a giant chair, one reason why it was *"where Satan's throne is"* (Rev. 2:13). The twelve large cap stones are today on view in Berlin while the ruins of the foundation remain in Bergma. It was also the first seat of Emperor worship—a temple for the worship of Augustus Caesar, being authorized in 29 BC. Smoke would rise from countless sacrifices every day, a sight no one could miss. Thus the Christians were being drawn into sacrifices to idols by eating sacrificial meat, sexual immorality, the teachings of Balaam (the soothsayer of Numbers 22) and the practices of the Nicolaitans from all of which, Jesus said, they must repent.

Pergamum was a place where Zoroastrian philosophy and theosophy originating in Persia found a beachhead to the West. On the mount overlooking the city, adjacent the altar of Zeus, was the Temple of Mithras from Egypt and the South. From the North and West came Athena worship. The city also had a temple of Dionysus, an androgynous son of Zeus in Greek mythology whose worship involved an out-of-control ecstasy which was seen as a spiritually-induced madness in part generated by music designed to sensually manipulate the worshipers.

Today much of the phenomena we see in deceptions such as the Toronto Experience, the failed revival in Pensacola, Florida, and the Lakeland fiasco are very much in the character of Dionysus worship more than in the character of Christ. The fruit of the Spirit is always "self-control" (*egkrateia*); when one is out of control, God is not in control. Hyper-charismatic lunacy of the modern age (not to be confused with a scriptural understanding of still-operating Holy Spirit gifts) has its first incipient expression in Corinth, but its pivotal expression in Pergamum.

As Zeus (whom the Romans called "Jupiter") was a corruption of the Greek term *Theos* (meaning "God"), so his son Dionysus was a corruption of Christ, as was Hercules who had Zeus as his father but a human mother and came as a superman to bring a kind of salvation to the common people. Dionysus was variously said to be the son of different Greek female pagan cult deities. Thus it is easy to see why the motifs of Dionysus became incipient in the paganizing of the church after the era of Constantine.

The worship of Athena in Pergamum was second only to her worship in Athens. Athens and Pergamum were the Lourdes and Fatima of their day as centers of female cult veneration. The concept of perpetual virginity and virgin nuns as brides of Christ were inspired by these influences from Pergamum that had their origins in the Semiramus and Tammuz worship arriving in Asia Minor from Babylon in the East, but which were, via Pergamum, incorporated into the Pantheon of Imperial Rome with emperor as pontiff. Once in Rome, the vestal virgins became the blueprint for female monasticism known as convent nunneries.

In short, Pergamum, like Alexandria, was the gateway by which the mystery religions originating in ancient Babylon found their way into the Greco-Roman world. It is the geographical point where the paganism of North, East, West, and South converged more than at any other single location.

What Really Came from Pergamum
That Is Once Again With Us Today

Not least of all however, was the temple of Asclepius Soter, the "Savior Healer" of the Hellenistic world. On this site in the lower city below the ridge line of the temples of Zeus, Mithras, and Athena above, was found the adjacent hospital in the temple complex whose most important figure was Galen of Pergamum. It was Galen of Pergamum whose philosophy of healing, based on Asclepius worship, resulted in a clinical approach seeing a relationship between human temperaments and four primary bodily fluids. The modern "shape" personality profiling is not a new phenomenon, but a variation of an old one of pagan origin, diagnosing someone psychiatrically and psychologically as well as spiritually by their temperament orientation as being either melancholic, sanguine, choleric, or phlegmatic. Modern innovations of this ancient superstition are central to the philosophy of discipleship held by Rick Warren and his Purpose-Driven agenda, and are used by some churches as a means to supposedly identify the spiritual gifts of regenerate Christians.

Biblical psychology views man as *imagio Dei*, being made in the image and likeness of the triune God. Therefore we have a body, a soul (mind), and a spirit corresponding to the incarnated Jesus as God in the flesh in the mind of the Father and the Holy Spirit. In the scriptural understanding of the psychological make-up of man, the spirit is distinct from the soul while in Eastern religions and psychology the spiritual or metaphysical aspect of man is a function of the mind or soul. Hebrews 4:12 instructs Christians to separate the two, while in psychology, shamanism, Sufi Islam, Buddhism, Hinduism, and in the positive thinking psychology-based theology of the late Norman Vincent Peale (copied by Robert Schuller, Yonggi Cho, and a host of others) the soul and spirit are essentially treated as one entity.

Additionally, God breathed into Adam and he became a living soul. Thus, what people are psychologically, intellectually and emotionally is a homogeneous blend of what they are spiritually with what they are organically. In other words, mental illness for instance never originates in the mind. Deleterious behavior or abnormality is caused either by something being wrong physiologically (e.g., hyperthyroidism, allergic delirium, or a reaction to a drug) or else it is the product of something wrong spiritually, or conceivably some combination of the two. A few biblically Evangelical clinicians such as Dr. Kurt Koch and Jay Adams seem to have understood this scripturally. Most proponents of Christian psychology however, have not.

Biblical psychology recognizes the tripartite nature of man and assesses human behavior accordingly as we see in the Book of Proverbs. Most so-called Christian psychology is not Christian but is mere psychology that uses Christian jargon. Psychology itself (apart from psychiatric medicine, bio-psychology, and neuro-psychology which deal with the relationship between metabolism and behavior) is pseudo-science. It is also pseudo-theology manifesting itself as the de facto religion of Humanism. It is not organic and therefore non-quantitative. Thus it is not actual science any more than it is actual theology (unless in one's mind man is deified).

The con job we call "psychology" originated in large part in Pergamum. The con job we call spirituality and behaviorism which too much of the modern church pretends is Christian also has its ontogeny in Pergamum.

Future Historical Prophetic Antitype

While the Pergamum church of the late first century is the type, the antitype it prefigures is the period from the Nicean Patristic Era through the Dark Ages. Historically this was the period where biblical Christianity saw its last remaining vestiges of apostolic doctrine preserved in reasonable tact. It was early during this era when Priscillian became the first known Christian pastor in Iberia to be martyred for his faith not by the Pagan world but by the church for upholding scriptural orthodoxy against the tide of heterodoxy and apostasy that was gaining rapid momentum. It was also in this period that Europe was overrun by Viking invasions.

An early form of Monasticism began with the Desert Fathers who were semi-mystics who attempted to escape the growing worldliness of the post-Nicean church by adopting a hermit lifestyle in the deserts of the Middle East. It was during this time that East met West and Buddhist monks who came as far west as Alexandria began to deposit Eastern religious influences within Christian monasticism. An alternative monasticism emerged among the Celts where peninsulas and islands in Ireland, Scotland, England, and Wales provided the respite from the world that the desert gave to the monks of the Middle East.

Certain traditions of Byzantine spirituality made their way into the British Isles as a by-product of Viking incursion which spanned from Russia to the Atlantic. With this, Irish monks of the Celtic church led by figures such as Columbkille, St. Ives, and St. Boniface, sought to preserve biblical manuscripts in scriptoriums, libraries, and monastic communities while the Vikings burned everything in print. It is of little doubt that the Celtic church played a key role in the preservation of Christian civilization during the Viking period which otherwise put the lid on Western Christendom completing the grotesque oppression that would become the Dark Ages. Unlike the hermit monks of the East or the later monks of Benedictine and Trappist monasteries, the Celtic monks were outgoing preachers and diligent scholars whose skills in accurately copying biblical codices and manuscripts rivaled that of the ancient Hebrew scribes.

It was in this age beginning with Constantine that the church began to first absorb superstition and idolatrous influences from the Greco-Roman world that once persecuted it. Constantine's conversion has been debated for centuries. He in fact claimed similar visions to the one he is said to have had of the cross in the sky at Malvern Bridge and was never baptized until the end of his life. In essence, Constantine converted to Christianity but allowed pagan coinage and practices to both abound and integrate into

Christendom. In order to deter further collapse of the Roman Empire he relocated his capital to Istanbul and saw Christianity as a socially uniting force between the Latin West and Greek East of his domain. As Augustine Platonized the church philosophically and Constantine bequeathed imperial titles and properties to the Bishop in Rome, what had been Christianity once again was transformed into Christendom, and the seminal of origins of what would become Roman Catholicism and Eastern Orthodoxy had been planted. The hybrid paganizing of the church had commenced.

Early Charismaniacs

Tertullian wrote in a legal format defending Christianity to the Roman government. Some consider that he may have been a lawyer. Tertullian was orderly, well thought-out and biblical in his approach to doctrine, constructing well-orchestrated explanations of Christian beliefs in defense of the church. But later Tertullian went totally off the rails. How could somebody of his caliber stray so dramatically? That may puzzle modern believers until they have themselves witnessed Christians, people they always previously thought were thoroughly biblical, totally ordered and well thought-out in their theology, go totally off the rails in the same direction.

It was Tertullian who rejected any compatibility of biblical theology with pagan philosophies. Yet later this same figure embraced a primordial kind of "charismania" called Montanism, whose experiential doctrines were as much rooted in oriental Gnosticism as they were in Scripture. It began as a group of people following others who called themselves prophets. Their epicenter was a city in the province of Phrygia called Pepuza. People went on pilgrimages to Pepuza from all over the Christian world to get an impartation evidenced by ecstatic experiences as others would do seventeen centuries later on junkets to Toronto and Pensacola. Their name came from Montanus (c. 300) but some of the leading figures were women, so-called prophetesses who made wild predictions in the name of the Lord which generally failed to happen. What they regarded as "Christian spirituality" was in effect pseudo-Christian mysticism, and what they regarded as "prophecy" was more akin to clairvoyance and Shamanism.

To grasp how these women operated, just observe their latter-day equivalents such as Cindy Jacobs, who erroneously prophesied that Zimbabwe would blossom in the 1990s just before the diametric opposite took place. Carol Arnott, Stacey Campbell, Suzanne Hinn, Patricia King, Cindy Jacobs, and other would-be prophetesses who mislead undiscerning Christians today have their prototypes in the false prophetesses of Montanism.

Pergamum

The capacity of women to mislead the church is always an indictment of Christian males for their failure to assume responsibility and for relinquishing their divinely assigned role of headship to erroneous women is today seen in the combination of true and seriously flawed scriptural teaching of money preacheress Joyce Meyer, but is far from being a new phenomenon. Be it the scandal of Aimee Semple McPherson or of Kathryn Kuhlman running off with the husband of another woman and remaining in ministry after her "repentance," the divorce and remarriage cycle of Paula White, the spectacle of Juanita Bynum fighting with her husband in a car park after doing a Christian marriage seminar, or the "dancing elephant" dreams of Jessa Hasbrook (who adulterously took off with Todd Bentley after he abandoned his wife and children) are latter-day examples of the very kind of madness that transpired in Phrygia with the prophetesses of Montanism. It is not a new style of debacle, and it parallels how the late Tammy Faye Bakker and Jan Crouch recapitulate the saga of Ahab and Queen Jezebel in the eyes of many observers.

The Montanists began with honorable motives, and they were very concerned about something most believers are concerned about: the role of the gifts of the Holy Spirit, power, and dynamism in the ministry. Tertullian was sympathetic to such aims but became enthralled with the excited frenzy that it had degenerated into. Later Irenaeus would defend the belief and practice of charismatic gifts but denounced the Montanist error into which Tertullian had plunged. That a champion of the faith fell vulnerable to this kind of spiritual seduction should have served as a warning to later generations. Too often however, this has not been the case, and many Christian leaders who should know better confuse biblical charismata with experiential charismania.

The gifts of the Spirit and supernatural manifestations were in the church of the Apostles, so where are they now? As a result of the Montanists and the false prophets, the gifts of the Spirit are discredited or have ceased in the eyes of many Christians.

So much of that is true today. There are modern-day people of Baptist and Brethren backgrounds who would be open to the gifts of the Spirit if there were not so many hyper-charismatic maniacs ("charismaniacs" as opposed to "charismatics") who hold extreme doctrines based on extreme ideas that are not scriptural. Their error is compounded by further embracing Kingdom Now theology, believing that the kingdom is coming into being *now, before* Jesus returns, under *their* authority and leadership. This doctrine has surfaced many times in history under many different banners but they all have the same essential beliefs. As will be seen when studying the church at Sardis, in the 16th century, the Anabaptists fell into this deception in Munster through following the Zwickau Prophets. It was much the same recently with the Kansas City Vineyard Prophets who made predictions that did not happen. This is exactly the same thing that happened to Tertullian. He got caught up in Kingdom Now theology and hyper-charismatic extremism.

No one initially expects that any of the good teachers of their own generation would be deceived by this Triumphalism and publicly identify themselves with these false prophets and false teachers. But that is what happened in the early church, and it is happening today. *"There is nothing new under the sun."*

Gnosticism

This leads logically into the age of the church of Pergamum. Something crept into the church from the Greek world which originated in the Babylonian world before: Gnosticism. There were many different strains of Gnosticism. Philo, who believed in an unorthodox form of Judaism, was almost a contemporary of the Apostles. He was based in Alexandria in Egypt which at that time was more Greek than African or Arab. Ideas began coming into the church. There is the "deductive" approach, which is doctrine, and the "inductive" approach, which is illumination. Typology is fine and biblical. It can be said that Isaac, Joseph and Moses are types of Jesus, but no doctrine can ever be based on it. Doctrine can only be arrived at deductively, taking *out* of Scripture what it actually says by exegesis. But if someone goes further and claims some mystical insight into the symbols or typology they would be "Gnostic." The Greek word *"gnosis"* essentially means "mystic knowledge."

Gnosticism is neither "inductive" nor "deductive" but "mystical." A Gnostic claims to have additional knowledge above and beyond what Scripture says. It is a very easy trap to fall into, which is why so many people fall into it. Basically pride leads people into it, and pride "cometh before a fall." (Prov. 16:18) Induction is acceptable for illumination, to explain or *illustrate* doctrine, but never as the *basis* of it.

Because the Septuagint, authored in Alexandria, put the Hebrew Scriptures into Greek, and because the Intertestamental Apocrypha was in Greek (just as the New Testament would be largely Greek), Philo mixed Gnostic Greek hermeneutics with pure Jewish methods. It was at Alexandria that the schism in early Christian hermeneutics originated. The Alexandrian school would always be colored by Philo, later influencing Clement of Alexandria and Origen. Conversely the Antiochan school was closer to the midrashic method of hermeneutics evident in the New Testament and the Dead Sea Scrolls.

Be that as it may, the church was becoming more and more Gentile and less and less Jewish. For instance, the Greek idea that the spirit is "good" and the flesh is "bad" became accepted. The flesh is certainly inherently fallen but, as God created it, it is certainly not "bad." God saw that all He had made was very good (Gen. 1:31).

A main propagator of this was Manchean. It was also the view held by the Roman writer Cicero. They also had their own ideas about cosmology and Zoroastrianism which came from the East and from Babylon. Gnosticism comes in many forms but they all come from the East. In Hinduism the Gnostic is the guru or the Brahman priest, the highest order of the caste society. He goes to Krishna and Vishnu; congregants go to their god only through him. In Zoroastrianism, the ancient religion of Persia, practitioners go through the Zoroastrian priest to their god.

These ideas infiltrated not only Christianity but also Judaism. Thanks to Philo it was already incipient in Judaism before it infiltrated the church. Hassidic Judaism is based on Gnosticism. Hassidic Jews teach that God is the *Ein Soph*, that He has no essence, only attributes. This is a Gnostic concept which in the Middle Ages was incorporated into Judaism via *Caballa* (Jewish mysticism whose chief work is the *Zohar*). The *Rebbe* (their name for the rabbi) has the *gnosis*, the mystic knowledge. He is the descendent of someone called Baal Shem To, the founder of the Hassidic movement in Europe a few centuries ago. And through some kind of male line of descent his spirit becomes reincarnated in the Hindu sense within the Rebbe.

So there arose two ways to God: through the Torah or through the *T'sadic*, that is, the Rebbe. *T'sadic* means "the Righteous One," the very term used by Stephen for Jesus. But they call the Rebbe the Righteous One! His word becomes the word of God to the point of arranging marriages, deciding where followers should live, where they should go, work, or study. If he says it, that is the word of God. He goes to God through Torah, he claims, but followers can go to God only through him. It is totally controlling, so of course one's relationship with the Rebbe completely replaces one's relationship with God the Father, Jesus and the Holy Spirit. Instead, the Rebbe becomes the counselor.

Roman Catholicism took on these Gnostic ideas. The pope falsely claims to be the heir of Peter and thereby further claims to have inherited some special mystic knowledge to enable him alone to interpret the Bible correctly. Thus, instead of reading what the Bible actually says, they decided it meant whatever the pope said it meant because only he had the *gnosis*, and only he could interpret it. It is so easy to believe that the trained and senior professional "priest" knows better than everyone else, but each individual must trust in God and must test every man rather than accept such claims at face value.

Therefore when the pope speaks *Ex Cathedra* (from his throne in St. Peters in Rome) he is considered to be infallible in matters of faith and morals because he is the heir of Peter and he has the *gnosis*, the mystic knowledge. This became official Roman Catholic doctrine in 1870.

This is how they can reinterpret so radically a plain statement by Mary, "*My soul exalts the Lord and my spirit has rejoiced in God my Savior*" (Lk. 1:46-47). In plain words, Mary says she needs to be saved. "Ah," they say, "but you don't understand it. Only the pope can understand it; he has the gnosis. Mary did not have any sin; she does not need to be saved."

This clearly goes against the plain biblical meaning.

Sufi Islam is the charismatic form of Islam and a reaction to the Stoicism of Sharia and Din, the legalistic expressions of Islam and of Islamic Fundamentalism. The Shias go to Allah their god through the imam, such as Khomeini in Iran. Sufis go through the Suf, who goes to Allah through the Koran. They go to their god only through him. This Gnosticism is found in all of the false religions.

Alexandria was almost the interface where East met West. Buddhist monks came from India to Alexandria and there they met Jews and Christians. East came West long before Marco Polo went East.

Later on liberal scholars in the 19th and 20th Centuries were influenced by German Rationalism. Chief among these was Rudolf Bultmann, a man who said that salvation equals knowledge. He claimed to have a *gnosis*, a mystic knowledge, a way for him to interpret the Bible critically and in a way that Jesus intended which everyone else did not understand. When Jesus talked about salvation, "salvation" to Bultmann just meant attaining a higher level of understanding and wisdom. The church had it wrong, he said, because they did not have his *gnosis*. This "Higher Criticism" is, in principle, Gnosticism.

When Gnosticism comes into the church, people usually claim they have understood things that the Apostles understood but have long since been lost. Today it is quite frightening when looking at the proponents of Restorationism and some of the house churches. It is the same mentality.

Instead of "Who is your confessor, who is your pope, your rebbe, your Brahmin, your guru" they ask, "Who is your apostle?" Very similarly, the leaders of Restorationism teach things that are flagrantly contrary to the Word of God.

While reading a book by Kevin Connor, a Restorationist and would-be theologian in Australia, it was observed that he was taking things totally out of any reasonable context. (This is not an issue about these people personally [they may have faith in Christ Jesus], but rather the discernment of what they have published, and testing it against Scripture.) One said that the Book of Revelation is not about the Last Days, that the phrase "the Last Days" only meant the days surrounding AD 70, and they therefore conclude that it has no future meaning or even any further meaning. This totally distorts the plain meaning of the context. Such errors originate from Gnostic ideas. They think they know best!

The classic example is the Manifest Sons of God, the "Joel's Army" doctrine. Joel 2 plainly says that this army of locusts Joel describes is an evil army which God used to judge Israel, but which God will later destroy. Restorationism says it is the Manifest Sons of God, that it is the church triumphant. Who wants to be part of an army that God will destroy? And how did they get that idea? *Gnosis*. Someone had the mystic knowledge. They thought *they* knew best.

There are other ways of arriving at those doctrines. They used Preterism and Historicism. They say that Biblical prophecies were fulfilled totally in the early church and have no future meaning. Another idea was Replacement Theology, an idea that God had no further purpose for either Israel or the Jews. This became, of course, anti-Semitic in character.

A recent example is a tape from America issued publicly by Rick Godwin. (This is not an attack on him personally, but rather testing what he said.) Rick Godwin said that Israel had nothing to do with God or the plans or purposes of God. He said the church is Israel and if Christians run around saying that God has any purpose for Israel or the Jews it will cause the Muslim Arabs to hate the church. Therefore no one should say these things because the Muslims will not like the church.

That is what he said on his tape. And he points people to David Chilton in America, one of his mentors, who teaches and basically boasts of having a book in his computer for when the Muslims drive Israel into the sea. These are the same conclusions that the Gnostics reached in the early church. Israel was spiritualized as meaning "the church." They used the same kind of false hermeneutics.

Another conclusion they arrived at was that there would be no eternal punishment in hell. One of the main figures who took on Gnostic ideas in the early church in Alexandria was Origen (185 - 253). Origen said that Satan would be saved, that this idea of eternal hell did not exist and that there is no eternal damnation. Yet Revelation 20:10 states categorically,

> "And the devil who deceived them was thrown into the lake of fire and brimstone, where the beast and the false prophet are also; and they will be tormented day and night **forever and ever.**"

Today people who teach that there is no eternal damnation arrive at their conclusions the same way. It is shocking to note some of the people who have taken on these ideas. What more could God have done? He sent prophet after prophet, but they were mostly killed. So finally He sent His only Son to die in our place, for we deserve to die and He did not. They say a God of love could not send anyone to hell. God is slow to anger, but that means He does get angry. It just takes him a while. Jesus said, "*Fear Him who is able to destroy both soul and body in hell*" (Mt. 10:28). But what do these false teachers propagate? Truly, "*There is nothing new under the sun.*"

The Greek term *anion tou aniones* ("forever and ever" or literally, "from age to ages") translates the Hebrew idiom *olama olamim* ("world to worlds," "age to ages"). This term is used to describe the eternal glory of God, the perpetual high priesthood of Jesus, and the endless longevity of our salvation. It is also used for "the smoke of their torment going up forever and ever" (Rev. 14:14). If hell is not eternal and conscious, but rather a place of annihilation, neither is there any exegetical basis to conclude that heaven is eternal and conscious. Yet, in disregard of this exegetical truth, figures such as England's John Stott and Roger Forster, as well as most Emergent Church leaders, dismiss the reality of eternal hell clearly spoken of in Scripture. One certainly cannot prove from Scripture that hell is not eternal and conscious; the thrust of Scripture supports the opposite contention.

Such notions are, again, not new, but date to the time of Origen in the post-Nicean Patristic period. Today some of the deniers of eternal hell even hold to an ultimate reconciliation with the salvation of Satan himself. But there were multiple other deceivers who surfaced once the Apostles were gone. Those whose deceptions were sequestered by true apostolic authority began to take root. Before long, matters became so convoluted that biblical orthodoxy became simply another strain of Christianity surrounded by multiple other strains holding fundamentally deviant doctrines proclaimed by false teachers, false prophets, and false apostles. Various expressions of Gnosticism in particular wreaked havoc on the Body of Christ.

Pergamum

In the second century Irenaeus of Lyon, who originated in Asia Minor, was a disciple of Polycarp, who in turn had been a disciple of the apostle John. Irenaeus earnestly defended mainstream biblical orthodoxy against the Gnostics and other heretics and left a treatise facilitating the identification of such deceptions for future generations. In a sense we might say that Irenaeus was the first Dr. Walter Martin, the 20th-century apologist who equipped the church to evangelize pseudo-Christian cults and refute their deviant doctrines.

Arius (c. 250 - 336) taught that Jesus was not of the same substance as the Father but was a created being. This is now known as the Arian heresy. Today we call them Jehovah's Witnesses; it is the same Christology.

Athanasius was the main opponent of the Arians. The Athanasian creed says of Jesus, "being of one substance (Latin, *consubstantiabilis*) with the Father." Athanasius was persecuted for his belief in one God and three persons and he also played a role in bringing monasticism into the church.

Monasticism did not begin as a bad thing. The church became carnal, very much associated with the world and worldliness, and there were Christians who wanted to live in communities apart from the world. That was all, and that was how it began, and they wanted to seek God contemplatively. Over time, influences from the East, particularly Buddhism which had monks as in Thailand today who have to beg for their food, began to come into Christendom. But it did not begin that way. There was a very positive monastic movement that came to the British Isles, particularly Ireland, and it played a very positive evangelistic role in Europe after the Viking invasions. These were the Celts to whom this discussion will return later.

The Judaizers in the early church were the legalists who added to the Gospel. There were also Sabbatarian and dietary legalists such as we read about in Galatians. Today we have Seventh-day Adventists; it is the same theology.

Marcion, a Gnostic of the second century, taught there was no creator God. This prefigured evolution. Under a Gnostic influence he drew a radical difference between the Gods of the two Testaments. Deuteronomy states nine times, "Love the LORD" and as for wrath, Revelation is full of the wrath of the Lamb! Jesus and the Father are certainly "one" (Jn. 10:30).

Jerome (342 - 420) translated the Bible into Latin to give people the Vulgate, Latin being the common or "vulgar" tongue. However, he not only translated both Testaments but he took the Old Testament from the Hebrew instead of from the Septuagint, the Greek version translated in 270 BC. He pointed out from Romans that the Old Testament canon was given to the Jews. This was much to his credit.

John Chrysostom (345 - 407) was an eloquent speaker if not much of a theological thinker. He became known as the man with the golden mouth. He was one of the people most responsible for introducing a strong anti-Semitic mentality into the church. He was trying to oppose the introduction of Judaization, but he set a precedent which proved very, very unfortunate in a number of ways.

At a much later point in history Thomas Aquinas (1225 - 1274) claimed that the Bible was allegorical, whereas to a Jew it is literal unless the context demands otherwise. Such a dichotomy in scriptural interpretation between the Antiochean and Alexandrian Schools of thought in the early church would later divide Judaism, with chassidic Jews taking a mystical allegorical interpretation of Torah on the basis of Caballah, and non chassidic orthodox Jews who accept Caballah in principle but downplay it in practice. Thus Greek ideas gradually replaced Jewish ideas. This was all done under the heading of "Scholasticism" but these "scholars" had some strange ideas. For example, a pope said the 70 years when the pope was forced to live in Avignon under military threat was the Babylonian captivity! (We shall look more closely at Aquinas in the chapter section dealing with the church of Thyatira.)

If someone adds, for instance, a role for Jesus' mother Mary as "co-redemtrix," it most certainly takes away from the role of Jesus whose sacrifice on the cross (and His alone) paid the price for sin. If they add doing time in Purgatory, they take away from 1 John 1:7: *"the blood of Jesus His Son cleanses us from all sin." All.* So why would someone need to go to Purgatory even for one second? If they are required to pay for "indulgences" (their sins) or do penance for them themselves, then again the blood of Jesus did not actually cover them. If one must attend the "mass" or meetings regularly to earn salvation, then faith in the blood of Jesus is not sufficient by itself. If one must listen to visions of Mary, then they are in conflict with her last recorded words, *"Whatever He says to you, do it"* (Jn. 2:5). Even His Father said, *"Listen to Him"* (Jesus) (Mt. 17:5). Christianity is *"from faith to faith"* (Rom. 1:17). Do not add or take away.

When the Bishop of Rome claims the title *Pontificus Maximus*, and then it is learned that this is the same title the Roman Emperors used, and before them the Emperors of Babylon with their mystery religions, it is both frightening and enlightening.

In Switzerland Pope John Paul II said that Switzerland cannot remain an island anymore. In some way Rome or a Roman system will rule the world again. Daniel saw four visions which would rule until the end. The fourth empire of iron, representing Rome, never dies; it continues in one form or another to the very end. Daniel 7:23 refers to "*a fourth kingdom*" that "*will devour the whole earth and tread it down and crush it.*" Revelation 17:9 speaks about the woman and the seven hills, which plainly represent Rome. The European Union was founded on the Treaty of Rome and Rome was founded on seven hills.

God commanded the Jews in Deuteronomy 7:2, "Make no treaty." What is the point of a treaty with someone who is not true to their word? Did the Treaty of Versailles prevent the Second World War? *God* knows what is best!

Rome was the capital of the world's false religious system in the days of the early church. Within the Pantheon in Rome all the idols of all the countries of the Roman Empire were worshipped together, all set around the eternal fire representing the sun and the sun-god Apollo. When the Emperor Constantine became a "Christian" in 321 a cross was placed in the Pantheon. Constantine did not get rid of all the idols; he just added a cross to his collection. So it can be seen where all the Roman Catholic symbols came from. If they are not present in the New Testament they most certainly came from these false religions.

The Deity of Jesus

All present-day believers are victims of the councils of Nicea in 325 and Chalcedon in 451. The purpose of studying history is not for what it was, but for what its effect has produced on the present-day generation.

At the Council at Chalcedon the delegate bishops defended the deity of Jesus against heretics with a low Christology who were attacking it. They began by saying that Jesus did not walk on the water because He was a *man* powered by the Holy Spirit, therefore He walked on the water because He was *God*. And they said Jesus did not feed the five thousand by the power of the Holy Spirit but that He did it because He was God. In other words, in order to defend His deity against heretics, they understated His humanity and overstated His divinity, if that is possible.

The Bible teaches something called "*kenosis.*"

"... *Christ Jesus, who, although He existed in the form of God, did not regard equality with God a thing to be grasped, but emptied Himself, taking the form of a bond-servant, and being made in the likeness of men. Being found in appearance as a man, He humbled Himself by becoming obedient to the point of death, even death on a cross. (Phil. 2:5b-8)*

Jesus was God, He was in very nature God, but He did not count that as something to be grasped. But He took the form of a servant—the people's servant. And what a price He paid for them, willingly.

A way to explain it is to look at *The Prince and the Pauper*, a fictional book by Mark Twain about King Edward VI. The little Prince found someone who looked like him and could have been his identical twin. They swapped roles so that the Prince could view the outside world from the perspective of a pauper. Meanwhile his father, King Henry VIII, died. And while the new king was out playing, the pauper boy was almost crowned king accidentally. The point is that the Prince was the Prince but he had placed himself in a position where he could not use his power.

Jesus was in very nature God; somehow He was God. Although He was distinct from the Father He was one with Him. So Jesus *could* have fed the five thousand, He *could* have walked on the water, He *could* have turned the stone to bread **IF** He was the Son of God. Bear in mind how Satan tempted Him in the desert and that He could have come down from the cross or raised Himself from the dead. But for others' sakes He laid aside His majesty. The Gospels teach that He fed the five thousand miraculously by the power of the Holy Spirit. He walked on the water miraculously by the power of the Holy Spirit. And He raised the dead little girl miraculously by the power of the Holy Spirit. But Chalcedon concluded that, no, He did it because He was God. They were not overstating His deity but they were understating His humanity. As pure God He would not have needed the Holy Spirit.

"Therefore, since the children share in flesh and blood, He Himself likewise also partook of the same, that through death He might render powerless him who had the power of death, that is, the devil," (Heb. 2:14)

This laid the base for cessationism, the idea that the Holy Spirit ceased to act. Instead of having a Trinitarian understanding of the Godhead, they replaced it by asserting "Jesus only."

Tertullian was the first person to use the word "trinity." He held up a twig with three branches, later imitated by brother Patrick in Ireland with the shamrock. Meanwhile, instead of having a Trinitarian Christology (a view of God based on the Father, the Son and the Holy Spirit), they wound up with a binitarian Christology, emphasizing the divine Sonship of Jesus but negating a balanced emphasis including the Holy Spirit. The role and ministry of the Holy Spirit was put to one side. They were only concerned with the Father and the Son. The Holy Spirit did not figure very prominently into their view and He began to be suppressed.

The Reformers followed Chalcedon. They did not see much place for the study of the Holy Spirit. Calvin wrote about the Holy Spirit but his idea was that the gifts of the Spirit had ceased. The Roman Catholic Church was claiming many bogus miracles with which the Protestants wanted no association. This turned them against miracles because they did not want to be identified with Rome.

On the Roman Catholic side, the effect of this was much worse. Because Jesus was God and His humanity was downplayed, they needed a mediator between God and man. Originally Jesus was God who became a man to be that mediator. "For there is...one mediator between God and men, the man Jesus Christ" (1 Ti. 2:5). But no, having absorbed the error of Chalcedon, they needed another mediator, so they appointed Mary as the Mediatrix in order to get to Jesus. The things seen today originally go back to this council.

The other council was Nicea in 325. During the age of Smyrna, persecution was God's vehicle to keep the church purified. False believers would always be weeded out; only the truly saved would be willing to die for their faith. People had a choice: they could either backslide or die.

Constantine

At this time the Roman Empire was starting to collapse and it all began to go wrong in the city of York in England, which for two years was the functional capitol of the Roman Empire. It was where Constantine was a general and where he became Emperor. He observed in Christians a willingness to die for something. He also saw their morality, and he began to see the practical expediency of having Christianity as the religion of the state.

The story is told of his victory at Malvern Bridge where he claimed to have seen a cross in the sky and heard a voice telling him, "In this, conquer." But he reported many visions to do with pagan gods often during his life. Most objective historians seem to agree that it was probably a political maneuver to make use of the increasing number of Christians. Whatever Constantine's motivation, his declaration making Christianity the official religion of the Roman Empire set the stage for spiritual error that would see the purity of the faith suffer.

> "Behold, days are coming," declares the LORD, "when I will make a new covenant with the house of Israel and with the house of Judah, not like the covenant which I made with their fathers in the day I took them by the hand to bring them out of the land of Egypt..."But this is the covenant which

The Dilemma of Laodicea

I will make with the house of Israel after those days," declares the LORD, *"I will put My law within them and on their heart I will write it; and I will be their God, and they shall be My people." (Jer. 31:31-33)*

This does not call for a response from the rulers of the state and its religion, but mandates an individual response to it.

Addressing the New Covenant that would be made through the blood Jesus, God said, "It will not be like the covenant I made with their fathers." It was never to be a state church. But politically motivated, Constantine made it a state church once again. The persecution stopped, so persecution was no longer the purifying element it had been. Note what happened to the state church; the very thing that Jesus died to get rid of, Constantine put back.

This opened the door to all kinds of problems. Into the Pantheon of Rome went all kinds of new gods. Who was the pagan god of gift giving? Well, that is Saint Nicholas. Who was the pagan god of love? Call that one Saint Valentine. Who was Minerva, or Astarte, or Ishtar, or Diana of Ephesus? Was she called the Queen of Heaven? Ah yes, that is in Jeremiah 44 four times. Call her Mary. Never mind that she was a false pagan goddess! Tammuz is mentioned in Ezekiel 8:14. Tammuz, the Babylonian god worshipped with his mother holding him as a baby as a precursor to the Madonna and Child. Hislop, in *The Two Babylons*, explains how Tammuz is the reincarnated spirit child of Nimrod. This seems to be the origin of all Madonna-and-Child icons.

The traditions associated with emperor worship became absorbed into the medieval papacy when Constantine moved his capitol eastward from Rome to Constantinople, again for political reasons. The Empire was fragmenting and he thought that by moving eastward he could achieve more cohesion. So he bequeathed the imperial inheritance in Rome to the bishop in Rome. The bishops in Rome in turn began claiming primacy and lineage from Peter.

One of the first to do so was Gregory I (aka, Pope Gregory the Great) in 598. But Fulton J. Sheen from New York, one of the predominant Roman Catholic theological writers of the 20th century, admitted there is no proof of papal succession to Peter, and even no reference to the issue until the fifth century. Eusebius wrote about succession to the Apostles, but not papal succession. There were many patriarchs, many "popes," before Gregory. In contrast, as recorded in Acts 15, at the Council of Jerusalem it was James who presided, not Peter. There was a time when Paul rebuked Peter in the presence of all (Gal. 2:11), among other problems that call into question the idea of Peter as the first pope. There is no evidence of the infallibility of

Peter; rather the reverse. But the kissing of the ring, carrying on a chair, enthronement as God–all these came from the veneration and worship of the emperors.

Cyprian and Sacramentalism

Cyprian of Carthage, who became bishop in 249, brought about a negative change at this time. Although Cyprian was later actually martyred for his faith, he misunderstood two basic things: the unity of the institutional church and Sacramentalism. There was a lot of debate about whether or not those who had compromised the name of Jesus by the annual oath to Caesar and emperor worship could be restored to fellowship.

The Novatians took a strict view of this, not automatically accepting back into fellowship those who recanted their faith, but the institutional church took a broader view. The native North African Christians were called Berbers. The Berber people today are Muslims. They were forced to embrace Islam at the point of a sword or die. But in the early centuries of the church they were very good Christians who were Indo-Europeans anthropologically and gave many martyrs. They had some very strict views. They were willing to die for Jesus, and they could not see how anybody could know Jesus and not be willing to die for Him. They would even count it a privilege. That set the stage for something known as the Novation Schism.

Cyprian said one cannot have God as his Father unless he has the church as his mother, so he began looking to the idea of the institutional church. The Novationists began setting up independent rival churches, saying they were not against Cyprian but were independent of the institutional (mother) church which they did not believe was holding to the biblical standard. Whether they were right or wrong is another issue, but they were accused of being schismatic. Cyprian supported this idea of a central institution.

Cyprian was also a sacramentalist. He took on ideas that originated in Babylon and propagated them on a broad level into something called *Ex Opere Operato*. This claims that the sacramental things have in themselves power and efficacy to dispense grace. For example, one such application holds that a baby can be baptized even though the baby has no choice, and even though the person baptizing the baby may not believe in it himself. But if it is pronounced, "I baptize thee in the name of the Father, and of the Son, and of the Holy Spirit," the baby becomes a Catholic. (Or Orthodox; a split took place later.) Cyprian took on these ideas, including transubstantiation, the idea that bread and wine literally become the body and blood of Jesus. He and those who followed him ignored the fact that there is no suggestion of the bread and wine becoming literal flesh and blood at the Last Supper under the prayer of Jesus Himself. But Cyprian applied the words like a magic spell from Babylon. And never mind if the person believed and came to repentance.

When studying the Passover and the Lord's Supper from the original Jewish perspective, it can be seen that the concept of transubstantiation is alien to the Jewish understanding of the Passover. It is only when a Jewish concept is extracted—the Jewish Pesach, the Jewish Seder—and misapplied into a totally different context alien to its own, that anyone can arrive at this doctrine of transubstantiation. This says the bread and wine actually become Jesus incarnate. It is important to remember that Roman Catholicism actually worships the bread and wine as Jesus incarnate. It *worships* it. And then it performs an act of cannibalism when it eats it. It is utterly, utterly pagan, totally unbiblical, and certainly alien from the original Jewish context of the Scriptures.

This was Cyprian. He was a major influence on Augustine of Hippo (354 - 430) who is the pivotal character to be discussed in detail further on.

Ambrose

Ambrose (340 - 397), Bishop of Milan, was a pivotal influence on Augustine. Ambrose tried to use the church to control the state in a way somewhat similar to what Calvin's followers did in Geneva later, and, to a degree, the Puritans did in the UK. Whenever that happened it always caused all kinds of problems. Again, it was to be "*a new covenant, not like the one I made with their fathers.*"

It was never intended that there should be a church state or a state church. But Ambrose would actually force the emperors to submit to the authority of the church under threat of excommunication! The Roman Catholic Church did this for centuries. It would even force people to go to war under threat of excommunication. This affected England (the Norman Conquest of 1066 spread the power of Rome) and then Ireland.

The Roman Catholic Takeover of Ireland

People in Ireland have no idea how the English were first involved in their country. It was through a Norman king of England, Henry II. He was French; he was not even an Anglo-Saxon. Henry II (1154 – 1189) was threatened with excommunication by Pope Adrian IV if he would not invade Ireland, put an end to the Celtic church and force the Irish to become

Roman Catholic. The Irish people have no idea that the pope sent the English into their country under such a threat.

The popes have always used their power politically, and anyone would be very foolish to think that they would not do so today if they had the capacity. In fact, through the Jesuits and through *Opus Dei*, a Roman Catholic cult founded by a political fascist in Spain called Jose Marie Escrive—who was canonized a saint by Pope John Paul II in 2002—they are continually trying to extend their influence.

They certainly did this in the Second World War with international fascism of every sort: Franco in Spain, Peron in Argentina, Mussolini in Italy, Hitler in Germany who made a concordat with the Roman Catholic Bishops. In every case they have done this, and they still do it today through *Opus Dei*. It never changes.

What was the final result of the influence of Cyprian and Ambrose? Cyprian of Carthage was a sacramentalist who believed in the unified institution. And Ambrose believed that the church should control the state. Ambrose had the idea of spiritualizing the Old Testament. He took this from the Gnostic influences in Alexandria and spiritualized the Old Testament to a high degree, which made it acceptable to Platonists. Together, these two brought sacramentalism and these Gnostic, spiritualized influences into the church.

Augustine, Sexual Perverts and a Doctrine of Demons

Augustine of Hippo had been involved with Manichean who adopted the Greek idea that the flesh is evil. Hence the idea of repressed sexuality has been institutionalized in Roman Catholicism to this day. The attitude that all sex is wrong originated here. It is utter perversion of the Word of God, utter heresy.

This explains why so many priests are constantly caught up in scandals such as the pedophiles under Bishop Casey and the court case in Ireland. *The Richard Sipes Report* on sexual misconduct among Roman Catholic clergy stated that at any given time at least 40 per cent of the Roman Catholic clergy in the United States and Great Britain are sexually active in some way. These have taken an oath of celibacy before God, but they are long-term pedophiles, homosexuals, sadomasochists and so on.

There are four psychiatric institutions in England for treating pedophile Roman-Catholic priests. At one of them, Gracewell in Birmingham, the chief psychotherapist admitted that the Roman Catholic Church is a magnet for people with deep sexual problems. Some of them come into the church either to repress their sexuality because they see the priesthood as totally celibate, or because they see it as a way to get access to children. Ireland will not admit to the problem; they just send such people abroad to be treated. But it is a very widespread problem. There are major scandals of this nature in America.

In Great Britain the Roman Catholic Archbishop of Birmingham was found to have transferred a known pedophile priest to seven different parishes, and he molested children in every one.

In Wales, Bishop John Aloysius Ryan, with a history of immoral relationships with women, was found protecting pedophile priests.

Cardinal Roger Mahoney of Los Angeles, the Roman Catholic Bishop of Green Bay, was similarly caught protecting pedophile priests from the law. In Boston Cardinal Bernard Law was forced out of office after affirming his widespread practice of protecting sex pervert priests at the expense of not protecting the children whose lives they were destroying. Such scandals have been massive in Africa, Latin America and Europe, but the largest number of priests in the Western world found to practice pedophilia have been of Irish descent.

In the Diocese of Amarillo, Texas, the bishop was caught recruiting convicted pedophiles on parole from prison in a half-way house to be priests and to work with children.

In Australia, a child-abusing nun who procured little girls to have sex with priests was falsely claimed to be dead by the church when her crimes were exposed, only to be found hiding in a convent in Wellington, New Zealand.

The Vatican knew of these scandals and did nothing, not even accepting the resignation of Law when it was first offered. In his 2002 visit to Canada, John Paul II skirted from Montreal to Latin America, avoiding the United States in order to avoid answering questions about his own failure to tackle this travesty. He implemented only a too-little-too-late policy in order to appear to be dealing with it in a public relations ploy designed to stem the tide of revelations. Under his heir Pope Benedict xvi the scandals worsened when it was revealed that in his previous role as Joseph Radzinger he was complicit in not defrocking pedophile clergy.

It is well-documented that through its "rat-route" the Roman Catholic Church protected Nazi war criminals from justice, and indeed Pope John Paul II lauded Archbishop Stepinac, the Nazi war criminal from Yugoslavia.

John Paul II also refused to hand over Bishop Paul Marcinkus, president of the Vatican Bank, to the Italian police when he was wanted for questioning in connection with the Ambrosiano Bank scandal, known as the Calvi affair. Over 200 people were brutally murdered (including Calvi himself who was found hanging under Blackfriars Bridge in London) and this all resulted in the Vatican paying hundreds of millions of dollars in compensation to defrauded depositors. It is therefore little surprise that, under John Paul II, the papacy, which had protected Nazi war criminals and gangsters, would now protect criminal sex pervert priests who victimize children.

The Roman Catholic Church initially attempted to say that this was not purely a Roman Catholic problem, when in fact it is statistically *largely* a Roman Catholic and Anglo-Catholic phenomenon. There are far fewer instances of this kind of outrage in Protestantism, the Eastern Orthodox Church and Judaism.

The actual source of this clerical celibacy, condemned in the New Testament as "a doctrine of demons" (1 Ti. 4:1), was none other than Augustine, who introduced the Gnostic ideas of Mancheanism. They asserted that sex was a necessary evil. Because Augustine was never recognized as a church father by the Eastern Church, to this day the Eastern Orthodox Church has normal matrimony for its clergy which even the pope permits for the Eastern branches of the Roman Church. We will re-examine these issues in further detail when we consider the Church of Thyatira.

Augustine's Doctrine of the Visible and the Invisible Church

The real long-term damage that Augustine did to the church was his invention of a doctrine called the "visible" and the "invisible" church. The gist is that the church is made up of the truly converted and the nominal, and only God knows the difference. In some ways that is true. In denominational churches are found individuals who do have a personal relationship with Jesus, even though their doctrines may be questionable. Being born again is the criterion.

So what happened? Well, they put back the Old Covenant. Instead of circumcising babies, they began "baptizing" them. The rite of initiation is part of the system of the state church. So what was the end result? The same thing that occurred in Old Testament Israel.

What a witness the church is to the people of England! "Oh, I am an Anglican; I was baptized, I am a full member of the church; the baptismal card says so." The only time some of these people go to church is when they are "baptized" or married or buried. Or maybe Mothering Sunday, Christmas and Easter. And they think they are Christians. Their church has told them so. They are Christians culturally, socially and in some sense religiously, and they probably try to keep some of the Ten Commandments. But if they are not circumcised in heart they are back at step one.

It is important to understand what went wrong. To reform the church, to realign the church with what the Apostles taught, the unbiblical marriage between church and state had to be severed. Instead of doing that, Luther, Calvin, Zwingli, Henry VIII, John Knox—what did they do? They replaced a Roman Catholic state church with a Protestant state church.

The doctrine of the visible and invisible church also had to be thrown out. And what did the reformers do? Luther said, *Cuius regio, eius religio.* "Whatever your noble or ruler is, that is what your religion should be."

Hooker, who wrote the *Thirty-Nine Articles* for the Church of England, basically said that a citizen of the British Empire was a member of the Church of England, and a member of the Church of England was a citizen of the British Empire. Thus, just as Constantine did, they put the very thing back that Jesus sought to get rid of.

Therefore people thought they were in a relationship with God because they were in a national covenant rather than an individual one. John Calvin Christianized this with something called Reformed Theology or Covenant Theology. But the relationship between the Old and New Covenants is both evolutionary and revolutionary; it is both continuous and discontinuous. One cannot come down on one side or the other. It is true that the church is a *continuity* of Israel, but not the *replacement* for it.

Calvinism – the Gospel in a New Context – and Redefined in the Process

While Calvin and Arminius historically were products of a later age more suited to our review of the church of Sardis, it is prudent at this point to touch on Calvinism because of its theological and philosophical relationship to Augustine. By the 16th-century Rationalism had begun to emerge. So Calvin and others tried to recontextualize the Gospel in the light of what was then a rational world view. But as previously discussed, it had become a Greek world view. The Reformers were influenced by 16th-century humanists, people who studied the Greek and Latin classics and studied the Bible as literature. But they had very Greek ideas. Calvin had a very black-and-white view which was in line with a 16th-century world view and he tried to recontextualize the Gospel for his age. But in the end he actually ended up redefining it. This was the same thing that happened in the early church. He changed it.

Pergamum

Replacement Theology—the church is the new Israel? Covenant Theology? The opposite was, of course, Dispensationalism, introduced by people such as Schofield and Darby. They emphasized the discontinuity of separate eras, or "dispensations." The point is that there is truth in both, but when one tries to come down firmly on one side or the other, one is wasting one's time. Just hold them in tension with a Jewish mind-set!

In Geneva, Calvin—who knew that most of the people in his churches were not Christians—tried to convert them after they came into his churches. He baptized the babies, etc. It is not biblical.

Jeremiah promised that the Messiah would come and give a new covenant that would not be like the one made with their fathers. Jesus did it, Paul explained it, and then Constantine came and undid it. Augustine undid it. The medieval papacy undid it. And then, in the name of reforming the church and going back to the Bible, Luther comes, and puts *back* that Old Covenant! Calvin and Zwingli did the same. The church is remarried to the state by all these people. Jeremiah said it should not be like that.

It is not that these people did not do good things, but they got one thing, which is very fundamental, very wrong. And, within one generation of the Reformers, Protestantism was nominalized. Today Protestantism has degenerated more than Roman Catholicism. No Roman Catholic Bishop denies the resurrection or the virgin birth as do many of their Protestant counterparts today. But it all goes back to Constantine, Nicea, Augustine. Christianity became the religion of the state.

To reform the church it is necessary to get rid of the marriage of church and state, the Erastianism, and the idea of the visible and invisible church. It is also mandated to get rid of Replacement Theology. And there must be a return to interpreting the New Testament and the Hebrew Scriptures as a Jewish book instead of as a Greek book. They failed to do all of those things.

There were people called non-conformists who tried to do those things— the early Baptists, the Anabaptists and so on. But what happened to those people, which will be seen in the church at Sardis, is that the Reformers persecuted them.

Pelagius (died c. 420) was a heretical monk in England who denied original sin. Augustine first became known because he rightly refuted Pelagianism. But never underestimate the importance of the damage that was also done by Augustine. Today's Pelagians preach that the unconverted are all created "in the image of God" (Gen. 1:27). But this is how Adam was created before the fall. After the fall Adam had another son "*in his own likeness, in his own image*" (Gen. 5:3), and this is the image of the fallen Adam in which, alas, all are born. Currently it is the practice of Calvinists to somehow try to associate Arminianism and the ideas of John Wesley with Pelagianism.

Arminius

Jacob Arminius (died 1609) reacted against Calvinism, and in effect made God the author of sin. Arminianists believe that the death of Jesus as an atonement for sin is a sacrifice where God is willing to save all even though He foreknows those who will repent and accept Christ (2 Pe. 3:9; 1 Ti. 4:10). Arminianism does not deny original sin. Denying original sin denies man's fallen nature. The fact of the matter is that Arminianism is the via media between the two errors of Calvinism and the heresy of Pelagianism.

Predestination and the Sadducees

This entire issue about eternàl security and predestination does not begin with Calvin or Arminius or even with Pelagius or Augustine; it goes right back to the Old Testament. The Sadducees were fatalistic determinists. The Pharisees said that all is foreseen and foreordained, but the choice is personal. Jesus agreed with the Pharisees. He said, *"For the Son of man is to go just as it is written of Him; but woe to that man by whom the Son of Man is betrayed"* (Mk. 14:21). The Jewish mind was able to hold the two in tension; the Greek mind could not. That was the root.

Augustine took on the ideas of Alexandria courtesy of Ambrose. He adopted transubstantiation and began defining it in more specific terms. But he also used allegory. He would refer to Luke 14:23, *"Compel them to come in"* to the wedding feast. So he reasoned that the church could use violence to compel people to become Christians.

There was a split in the church in North Africa caused by the Donatists who said all their leaders were immoral, so they could not (biblically) follow them; they had to have their own church. Yet some of their own leaders were also immoral!

Augustine, under the influence of Cyprian, claimed to stand for unity in the church, and against the schism. He said, "The church is holy, no matter how unholy the men who run it, simply because it is Christ's church." Hence, when the Roman Catholic Church is confronted with the Spanish Inquisition, the papal wars, the corruption of the papacy, its role in the holocaust and so on, its leaders will not deny those things, but they will still say it is the "Holy" Roman Catholic Church because Jesus died to make it holy.

Augustine also argued for the sacramental ideas of *Ex Opere Operato*, that the sacrament is valid no matter who administers it, although it does not become efficacious until a person accepts the Roman Catholic faith.

The tragedy is that the Protestant Reformation, instead of going back to the New Testament, went back to Augustine. Both Catholicism and Protestantism draw from Chalcedon and both are built on Augustine. A return to the New Testament is what is mandated *before* Chalcedon and *before* Augustine.

Cyril, Nestorius and Priscillian

Afterward Cyril of Alexandria began persecuting other Christians who were followers of Nestorius—who denied *Theotikos*, the divine motherhood of Mary. Indeed, *Theotikos* is a pagan concept alien to biblical thought, and the term is not found in Scripture. Those who opposed this falsehood experienced persecution. Later, the Nestorians themselves went into severe doctrinal error.

Priscillian, in the West in Iberia, was one of the first major figures to be executed by the established church for standing up for the truth. The church moved further and further and further away from the truth and became more and more institutionalized and Erastrian, involved with politics, ever increasingly Hellenized and Platonized, and strayed further and further from its Jewish roots.

Subsequently a split began to occur between the Greek-speaking East and the Latin-speaking West which resulted during the Middle Ages in the split between Eastern Orthodoxy and Roman Catholicism.

The Faithful Few

Nonetheless, God has always had a faithful remnant. Even from earliest times there were people such as the early Nistorians who began well. There were the Paulicans who as missionaries went all the way to China. The Armenian Empire became Christian in 301 *before* the Roman Empire. There was a remnant that went all the way to the Far East, Thomas being one of the first.

Biblical Christianity, or something close to it, was preserved in the West mainly by the Celtic church. The Byzantine Empire in the East was judged by God through Islam as a reaction against the idolatry of the church. This is the source of the term "Pergamum." What does "Pergamum" mean? It means "divorced."

It needs to be understood why God uses the term "divorced." When Israel sinned, Israel sinned. But when Israel went after other gods, Israel was called a harlot and an adulteress. Idolatry equals spiritual adultery. Israel was to be Yahweh's bride and Yahweh was to be Israel's husband. *Ba'al* in Hebrew, for "God" and "Husband" are the same word.

The Dilemma of Laodicea

Hence, what it comes down to is that idolatry equals spiritual adultery. And adultery in the sense of turning away from God for false gods equals spiritual idolatry. As Hosea and the prophets lamented, "O daughter of Zion, you have played the harlot."

The same thing began to happen in the church, and just as God gave Israel a certificate of divorce in Jeremiah 3:8, so the same thing began to happen in the church when it introduced idolatry.

Pergamum and Jesus

"And to the angel of the church in Pergamum write: The One who has the sharp two-edged sword says this:" (Rev. 2:12)

To Pergamum the aspect that Jesus reminded them of was, *"The One who has the...two-edged sword."* It separates flesh from spirit, rightly dividing the Word of God (Heb. 4:12) and separating that which is biblical from that which is not.

"'I know where you dwell, where Satan's throne is; and you hold fast My name, and did not deny My faith even in the days of Antipas, My witness, My faithful one, who was killed among you, where Satan dwells." (Rev. 2:13)

"Where Satan dwells." It is very probable that this is alluding to the Temple of Zeus which was excavated and moved to East Berlin in the 1930s by German archaeologists. It resembles a huge throne. Understand that the mystery religion was a false religion that began in Babylon under Nimrod (Gen. 10). It found its way through Asia Minor, through the city of Pergamum particularly, into Athens and the Greek world and from there to the Roman world. But Pergamum was the channel for these Babylonian mystery religions. *"Where Satan dwells."* It was a church in the city where Satan dwelt. When the practices of transubstantiation and priestcraft are taking place, that is a place where Satan dwells and a place where Christ will employ the two-edged sword with no compromise.

"You hold fast my name." Remember, all they had to do to live peacefully under *Pax Romana* was to say once a year, "Caesar is Lord." (Similarly, Islam has a one-line creed.) But this denied the name of Jesus as one's Lord and God. Evidently Antipas did not deny the name of Jesus, and paid the price.

"'But I have a few things against you, because you have there some who hold the teaching of Balaam, who kept teaching Balak to put a stumbling block before the sons of Israel, to eat things sacrificed to idols and to commit acts of immorality. 'So you also have some who in the same way hold the teaching of the Nicolaitans." (Rev. 2:14-15)

Pergamum

Something which was not biblical, plainly, was eating food sacrificed to idols—transubstantiation. Balaam was a sorcerer, an idolater, and a professional curser. And the practices of the Nicolaitans were discussed previously.

Of all the debates surrounding the ordination of women, not one has come from the fact that the Bible says *every* Christian is a priest. If people stuck to the Bible to begin with, they would not have these debates and schisms over things which do not exist. The Nicolaitans were a clergy class having power over or above other people. Remember, this was a Gnostic influence.

> "'Therefore repent; or else I am coming to you quickly, and I will make war against them with the sword of My mouth. 'He who has an ear, let him hear what the Spirit says to the churches. To him who overcomes, to him I will give some of the hidden manna, and I will give him a white stone, and a new name written on the stone which no one knows but he who receives it.'" (Rev. 2:16-17)

Note that Jesus appeals to individuals, affirming the New Covenant, and He singles people out with the singular tense, "To *him* who overcomes."

At the end of this promise Jesus is drawing on things mainly from the book of Isaiah.

> "To them I will give in My house and within My walls a memorial, And a name better than that of sons and daughters; I will give them an everlasting name which will not be cut off." (Is. 56:5)

Jesus is saying that the promises given through Isaiah to Israel would now be fulfilled in Jesus.

> "The nations will see your righteousness, And all kings your glory; And you will be called by a new name Which the mouth of the LORD will designate." (Is. 62:2)

And in Exodus it teaches about the secret manna, or the hidden manna:

> Moses said to Aaron, "Take a jar and put an omerful of manna in it, and place it before the LORD to be kept throughout your generations." (Ex. 16:33)

Similarly, in Revelation 14:3 there was a secret song that only those who had been redeemed could learn.

These are the Old Testament promises that God is saying will be fulfilled for the overcomers.

The Idolatry of the Mass

"You...hold the teaching of Balaam, who kept teaching Balak to put a stumbling block before the sons of Israel, to eat things sacrificed to idols and to commit acts of immorality." (Rev. 2:14)

Christians were murdered in the tens of thousands for refusing to participate in this idolatry. Yet today there are major Evangelical leaders now saying it is acceptable to do it. To tell someone to continue practicing this immorality is no different than telling a homosexual who gets saved to stay a homosexual, or a drunkard who gets saved to keep drinking. Telling someone to remain in a church that practices transubstantiation and to continue practicing and participating in idolatry is no different. They must come out. They must stop believing those doctrines of Satan.

Christians who stand up against what goes wrong in Pergamum have to be prepared to go the way of Antipas. It happened in this country; it happened in the Reformation: people who stand up against these things must be prepared to pay the price of Antipas. But just look again how Jesus spoke of Antipas: "My witness, my faithful one." Would it not be wonderful to meet Jesus and be greeted with, "My witness, my faithful one"? It is worth dying for! However, the way Antipas died was very brutal. It was not very pleasant, the way they removed him. But then the flowers grew where they had burned him. This is found in *The Martyr's Mirror* or *Foxe's Book of Martyrs*.

That is the church in Pergamum.

Conclusion

The main points are these:

First, the two-edged sword. When those things that are flagrantly immoral begin coming into the Body of Christ there can be no compromise in dealing with them. No compromise. It is not taking a position against the people; the proper stance is always *for* the people. But in order to be *for* the people it is necessary to be *against* the deception that destroys the people.

Second, Protestantism and Catholicism both draw from Chalcedon. And they both draw, unfortunately, from Augustine. The key is to go back to the original teaching of the Apostles.

Third, remember that these same heresies witnessed in the Body of Christ today are simply a recapitulation of the heresies that existed in the early church. The ones that are outside the Body of Christ are not the most concerning. The ones that cause the most trembling are the ones that get inside the Body of Christ. They got into the early church and, unfortunately, they are certainly getting in today.

Pergamum

Nonetheless, no matter how bad the church, how dark the age, there has always been a faithful remnant. The prayer for any Christians at any time in any church is that, by the grace of the Lord, they would be in that faithful remnant.

Chapter 4
Thyatira: "Continuing Sacrifice"
11th Century Onward

1st	2nd	3rd	4th	5th	6th	7th	8th	9th	10th	11th	12th	13th	14th	15th	16th	17th	18th	19th	20th

Apostolic Church

Pre-Nicean Church

Rise of the Institutional Church

The Dark Ages

The Reformation

Great Awakening

Apostate Church

The City of Thyatira

Thyatira, 35 miles down the road from Pergamum, was a busy market town and commercial center for the wool trade and the dyeing industry. Lydia, the first convert in Europe, came from Thyatira (Acts 16:14) and was a seller of purple dye. This came from a little shellfish called the murex. A similar method was used for manufacturing the dyes for the ritual fabrics in the Jerusalem temple, where dyes were prepared from crushed crustaceans harvested from the seabed near Caesarea. From the throat of each murex just one drop of purple dye could be extracted. Pliny the Elder relates that this dye was so expensive that one pound cost a thousand denarii – that is, three years wages.

Lydia was probably a woman of considerable means and Thyatira a place of considerable prosperity, although not as salubrious as Laodicea. Like today, wherever people prosper they can afford to indulge in the evil drugs of the day, in their case learning Satan's deep secrets about the occult.

The Letter of Jesus to the Angel of the Church

"And to the angel of the church in Thyatira write:

The Son of God, who has eyes like a flame of fire, and His feet are like burnished bronze, says this:

'I know your deeds, and your love and faith and service and perseverance, and that your deeds of late are greater than at first. 'But I have this against you, that you tolerate the woman Jezebel, who calls herself a prophetess, and she teaches and leads My bond-servants astray so that they commit acts of immorality and eat things sacrificed to idols. I gave her time to repent, and she does not want to repent of her immorality. Behold, I will throw her on a bed of sickness, and those who commit adultery with her into great tribulation, unless they repent of her deeds. And I will kill her children with pestilence, and all the churches will know that I am He who searches the minds and hearts; and I will give to each one of you according to your deeds. But I say to you, the rest who are in Thyatira, who do not hold this teaching, who have not known the deep things of Satan, as they call them—I place no other burden on you. Nevertheless what you have, hold fast until I come.

'He who overcomes, and he who keeps My deeds until the end, to him I will give authority over the nations; and he shall rule them with a rod of iron, as the vessels of the potter are broken to pieces, as I also have received authority from My Father; and I will give him the morning star. He who has an ear, let him hear what the Spirit says to the churches.'" (Rev. 2:18-29)

Future Historical Prophetic Antitype

In the period after the Crusades, the seeds of the Renaissance were planted because the influences of the Islamic Golden Age, and more importantly the still-surviving Greco-Roman civilization of the Byzantium Empire, still existed in Constantinople, the Balkans, and the Levant. The Holy Roman Empire wound up with rival capitals in Ravenna and Istanbul.

Thyatira

What had been the Latin-speaking West had fragmented into a number of primordial romance languages being colloquially spoken, with Latin the reserve of monastic intellectuals, lawyers, court bureaucrats, royalty, and more educated vassals. The Greek-speaking East however, had remained more culturally cohesive throughout the Byzantine Age until it was nearly squeezed to death by the Crusades attacking from the West and North, and Mohammedans attacking from the East and South. The political split between East and West was directly proportionate and exasperated by a theological split that ended with the pope of Rome claiming primacy against the patriarch of Constantinople.

The Western church followed the Latin Vulgate while the Eastern church held to the original Greek New Testament and the Septuagint. The Western church was, in the final analysis, to be identified by the Platonism of Augustine, while the Eastern church did not accept Augustine as a church father, looking more to Chrysostom and other of the Antiochan fathers and figures such as Gregory of Naziunzus (who was also canonized by Rome). Although churches of both East and West were sacramentalist, the Eastern church emphasized theosis, where God became one with man rather than man becoming one with God. Also, the church in the West held to a hyper-sacramentalist view of salvation as opposed to the philosophical view of the East. While both were ritualistic and venerated icons, the West emphasized Eucharistic veneration and, progressively, a unique veneration of Mary as Co-Mediatrix called "hyper-dulia." The East however, stressed a metaphysical power of icons as windows into the supernatural world.

Finally, there were disputes of primacy with the church of the East claiming the original Greek New Testament Scriptures and the West claiming a bogus papal dynasty from Peter. This saw the church in the East holding to a more Episcopal ecclesiology based on a Magesterium of bishops and scholars, while in the West bequeathal of the pontifical and imperial attributes of the emperor to the pope resulted in what would eventually become a papal monarchy where the Magesterium is subordinated to someone claiming to be heir of Peter and Vicar of Christ. These theological, ecclesiological, and cultural differences fueled a schism that invariably became political, then degenerated further into military conflict. The Western Crusades killed not only Muslims, but Eastern Christians and Jews alike.

This legacy endures to the present time. Under the Ustashi Nazi Archbishop Stepinac in the early 1940s, 750,000 Eastern Orthodox Serbs plus the entire Yugoslavian Jewish community and a smaller number of Muslims were exterminated in the Holocaust with the knowledge of the

Vatican. Eastern Orthodox victims, however, were able to gain a reprieve and save their lives if they agreed to convert to Roman Catholicism. This murderous legacy was perpetuated in the papacy of Pope John Paul II who beatified Stepinac and canonized the fascist Jose Marie Escrive, the fascist pro-Nazi founder of the Roman Catholic "*Opus Dei*" movement in Franco's Spain. At this time the Vatican pressed Germany and other EU countries to grant diplomatic recognition to Roman Catholic Croatia in the continuing three-way battle between Roman Catholics, Eastern Orthodox, and Muslims dating back to the 11th century. These tensions were artificially contained during the Communist dictatorship of Marshall Tito but re-exploded like a tinderbox with the collapse of the Iron Curtain.

It is imperative that we recognize that the Vatican has a very long memory. It greatly views contemporary history, and sets its present political goals, in light of its centuries-old history of genocide and desire for religious and political hegemony that has never subsided. From the 11th century to the present, the situation has remained the same in the Balkans and the aims have not changed when viewed through the Vatican's eyes. The same remains equally true regarding modern Vatican diplomatic policy and papal ambitions in the Middle East, especially concerning Israel and Jerusalem.

As the Crusaders invaded, certain bishops of the Greek Orthodox tradition entered into a negotiated settlement with the papacy to save their lives and the lives of their congregants. In these arrangements these Eastern Orthodox Christians-turned Roman Catholic would be able to retain their identities as an Eastern Rite, still holding to the Byzantine tradition, liturgical use of the Greek language, and the vestments and rituals of the Eastern church, even allowing their clergy to marry. Hence in Roman Catholicism marriage is outlawed (this forbidding to marry is blasted as a doctrine of demons in the New Testament – 1 Ti. 4:3) for its clergy of the Latin Rite while it is permitted for the clergy of the Eastern Rite as the price for persuading these elements of the Eastern church such as Marionite Catholics to come back under the governance and jurisdiction of the pope. It is not inexplicable therefore that the widespread pedophilia among Roman Catholic clergy of the Western Rite is much less common than the Eastern Rite. Today we see the Vatican willing to dialog and negotiate similar compromises with Anglo-Catholicism and other Protestant sects in the same way, allowing them to retain the outward dressing of their own identities and to hold certain practices alien to mainstream Roman Catholicism as an inducement for them to likewise acquiesce to the demands of the pope that they kneel down and kiss his ring in a return to Rome.

Thyatira

Prior to the Crusades however, the Dark Ages were at their darkest. Only small biblically Evangelical sects such as John Wycliffe's Lollards in England and the Waldenseans of the Piedmont Valleys above Turin, Italy, endured under notorious persecution, yet faithfully sustained some semblance of biblical Christianity.

Most of the clergy in the mainstream church were mendicant, meaning they were completely uneducated and often illiterate; like so many modern hyper-Pentecostals and hyper-charismatics, their beliefs were largely constituted by a thin list of clichés. The only knowledge the serfs and peasant masses had of Christianity was gleaned from things like passion plays and reenactments of the Nativity at Christmas festivals. Custody of the sacred canons was confined to the repository of monasteries where the texts would always be read through the prism of neo-classic Greco-Roman philosophy by the minority of clergy who could even read.

Sociologically the peasant classes, serfs, and in some cases servants, were doomed to a meager subsistence, plagued by disease and want in the beckoning servitude of the nobility and bishops. Christian service to God was viewed in strict Augustinian terms: "The only good thing about marriage is having children who would be celibate." The common people were mere breeding stock, often of less value than cattle, existing merely to populate convents and monasteries as a necessary evil. Viking invasion, Feudalism, and Roman Catholicism reduced Western Civilization to centuries of misery where the general population was stripped of dignity, upward mobility, and above all *the* saving faith taught in the Scriptures. All learning and education, even to the level that it did exist, was in the domain of a corrupt, idolatrous church where superstition and morally bankrupt Greek philosophy were part and parcel of the Roman Catholic distortion of Christianity.

It is little wonder that Jesus employed such superlatives in addressing that age in the character of Thyatira as the Jezebel motif of seduction and immorality, idolatry and eating food sacrificed to idols (pointing to the Eucharist), and other such practices that Christ Himself labeled as "the deep things of Satan." This is the lowest point Christian civilization has reached up until this point. Its treachery, idolatry, and heresy will only be eclipsed by the apostate church of the coming Antichrist, of which the pope is a type.

As the Apostles taught, there are many false prophets and many antichrists, (1 Jn. 2:18), and the spirit of Antichrist has always operated both in the world and in unscriptural churches. All of these, as always, point to the ultimate Antichrist, the two beasts of Revelation – one political, and one religious known as the "False Prophet." The relationship between the medieval popes and the emperors of the Holy Roman Empire that moved to murder and damper any expression of scriptural Christianity for centuries must be understood as historically typological foreshadowing the coming, ultimate Antichrist and False Prophet.

Territorial Spirits

During "the age of Thyatira" the god Apollo, the sun-god of Babylon, was the patron of the guilds. Citizenship in Thyatira was centered around the trade guilds—men belonging to their appropriate guild. This pagan practice of patron gods was incorporated into Byzantine Christianity and also into Roman Catholicism in the form of canonized patron saints. Just as at Thyatira they trusted in patron gods, the Catholic and Orthodox believers put their trust in patron saints instead of in the Lord.

By the early Middle Ages these pagan superstitions had been Christianized (or Christianity had become paganized). These things are actually manifestations of what Paul called "principalities" in his Epistle to the Ephesians which today is unfortunately mistranslated by the charismatic colloquialism "Territorial Spirits."

These local demonic powers are actually satanic beings associated with a particular location as seen in Daniel 10 with the "Prince of Persia" (the demonic power behind Shia Islam in modern Iran) and the demons in Gerasene in Mark 5, where these demons pleaded not to be sent out of the region. Moses and Paul both defined idols as "demons" (*shedim* in Hebrew and *demonoi* in Greek).

Binding and Loosing

In the Bible people were simply called to repent of this idolatry as they were of any other sin and the Gospel was the weapon used against it. Today, under the false and unbiblical ideas propagated by such people as John Dawson, Youth with a Mission, C. Peter Wagner, the late John Wimber, George Otis Jr. and Roger Forster, the scriptural strategy of evangelism to confront these local demonic powers is foolishly replaced by a distortion of the actual meaning of binding and loosing.

Biblically, binding and loosing was a phrase Jesus used in reference to the Apostles. It concerns their apostolic authority to define doctrine and to deal with unrepentant sin in the church; it has nothing to do with binding Satan. The foolhardy strategy of popular charismania to supposedly bind these spirits is not biblical and does not work. It was certainly not the strategy of Paul in Athens when the idols vexed him in Acts 17. This error is compounded by the obvious error of ecumenism, where these same charismaniac leaders will accept the validity of the parallel Roman Catholic myth of "canonization" of saints. This is unbiblical. Just as all believers are priests, so all believers are saints; they are being sanctified. But only Jesus, not the pope, will decide who is acceptable to His Father. So "canonization" simply propagates the proliferation of these demonic powers.

The classic example is the pseudo-Christianization of Diana of Ephesus whose attributes are perpetuated by the veneration of Mary the mother of Jesus, when in fact the real Mary of the Gospels has nothing in common with Diana who represents Ishtar, the Queen of Heaven mentioned in Jeremiah 44.

Hence, Thyatira becomes representative of that age we call the Dark Ages from the 8th to the 16th centuries. Roman Catholicism became an institutionalized hybrid of pagan religions with roots in ancient Babylon, whose occult practices became the predominant expression of the visible church.

Food Sacrificed to Idols, etc.

The ancient city was laid out in districts according to the guilds as their bazaar still is to this day, and no one could avoid living in a district devoted to a particular guild. The power of the guilds would have made it very difficult for any Christian to earn a living without belonging to the guild. But membership involved attendance at guild banquets, essentially feasts in the temple, where food was sacrificed to idols and Apollo was worshipped. After too much wine, sexual debauchery often followed. Jezebel evidently taught that this was permissible (Rev. 2:20, 1 Co. 6:12 and the whole of chapter 8 address this theme). Paul explains that although food sacrificed to idols cannot harm, if eaten with a weaker brother it could cause him to fall into sin. If that were the case, Paul said, he would never eat meat again. In other words his aim was not to avoid the food, but to avoid leading a brother to sin.

What is of particular interest, however, is that the Phoenician priesthood of Jezebel, and their Baal worship that infiltrated Israel during the reign of Ahab, had a priestly celibacy where homosexuality and pedophilia were common results. The idea of sex as dirty, introduced into the church by Augustine, paved the way for clerical celibacy in the Western church.

Hypocritically, the Roman Catholic Church allows matrimony for the priests of its Eastern Rites which re-acquiesced to papal authority to avoid persecution during the Crusades, but disallows it for the priests of the Latin

Rite. Why it is alright for some and not for others, however, is not the first question. Neither is it why they have enforced clerical celibacy when Paul wrote, *"Do we not have a right to take along a believing wife, even as the rest of the apostles and the brothers of the Lord and Cephas (Peter)?"* (1 Co. 9:5).

The real question is why do the church leaders ordain "priests" to begin with when the Bible teaches that *all* believers are priests?! The priestly class was a Levitical institution of Old Testament Israel fulfilled in Christ. According to the Old Testament, Jews should have priests, not rabbis; and according to the New Testament, Christians should all be priests under the same High Priest—the Lord Jesus!

Jesus taught, *"... the rulers of the Gentiles lord it over them, and their great men exercise authority over them. Not so with you"* (Mt. 20:25-26). Also, Jesus plainly castigated the use of the religious title "rabbi," (meaning "teacher," derived from the Hebrew word for "great") and the religious title "father." Both terms usurp the place of God, according to Jesus, as there is only one Teacher and one true Father, both of whom are in heaven (Mt. 23:8-11). Jesus prayed to the Holy Father in John 17:11, and no one should dare to usurp that title. Neither biological fathers nor fathers in the faith are referred to as titles of ecclesiastical office.

The first misuse of the religious title "father" for ecclesiastical purposes was in reference to the so-called "Church Fathers" of the first centuries. Some of the pre-Nicean "fathers," particularly Irenaeus and Justin Martyr, indeed tried to preserve the apostolic tradition against heresy, and some of the later ones at least made practical literary contributions (such were Jerome with his Vulgate (Latin Bible) and Eusebius with his *History of the Church from Christ to Constantine*). But the effect of most of these "fathers" was negative, tearing the church away from its Judaic and biblical origins and redefining Christian dogma in the light of secular Greek philosophy. Such Christian literature tends to take the reader away from the God-breathed Scriptures and into the opinions of the writer.

Although Augustine rightly withstood the Pelagianism that denied original sin, it is Augustine who rewrote Christianity as a Platonic religion. Thomas Aquinas (1225 - 1274), in his *Summa Theologica*, later rewrote it as an Aristotelian religion; similarly Maimonides (1135 - 1204) redefined Judaism in Aristotelian terms much influenced by Greek philosophy in a total departure from biblical Judaism. The seminal influence for what transpired in rabbinic Judaism and Christianity stemmed from the world of Islam when Averroes and Avicenna, two Arab religious philosophers, began to "Aristotelianize" Islam.

Thyatira

Christians today sometimes die due to a distortion of the Bible's teaching on healing. People erroneously prophesy or claim healings by faith, neglect medical treatment and die prematurely. This is in no way to say that God cannot and does not heal miraculously, but the hyper-faith corruption of certain biblical texts results in self-inflicted death. Today, just as in the days of Irenaeus who sought his martyr's crown, "*My people perish for lack of knowledge*" (Hos. 4:6). "*For I can testify about them that they have a zeal for God, but their zeal is not based on knowledge.*" (Rom. 10:2)

The Papacy

Pope Gregory I (540 - 604) is often considered to have established the papacy. Known as Gregory the Great, he was the son of a Roman senator. The papacy developed continuously but it was defined in its present form in 1870 when the popes, who had already ascribed to themselves the title of "Holy Father" in rejection of the plain teaching of Jesus in Matthew 23, and had taken the title Jesus gave the Father in John 17:11, now ascribed to themselves the divine attribute of infallibility when speaking *Ex-Cathedra* from his throne in St. Peter's in Rome. This was a pronouncement by Pius IX. He supported the pro-slavery confederacy during the American Civil War and issued a Papal Encyclical (*Quanta Curia*) denouncing democracy. He implicitly reaffirmed the church's right to use violence in the aftermath of the tyrannical Papal State.

The road to the papacy was paved by Augustine and those who influenced him, particularly Ambrose of Milan and Cyprian of Carthage, fulfilling the Apostle Paul's prophecy in Acts 20:29-30 that after the Apostles...

"*Wolves will come in among you...and from among your own selves men will arise, speaking perverse things, to draw away the disciples after them.*"

The Word of God explains in Ephesians 2:20...

"*having been built on the foundation of the apostles and prophets, Christ Jesus Himself being the chief cornerstone.*"

When the popes came along, the rightful doctrinal paternity of the church was cemented over and a false doctrinal paternity was laid in its place. This was the sad legacy of the church fathers. A Judaic New Testament faith was redefined as a Hellenistic one and Tertullian's greatest fear of Babylon replacing Jerusalem was the consequence. Soon the Roman Catholic priests mimicked the Babylonian priests and became celibate with what the New Testament calls "*doctrines of demons*" (1 Ti. 4:1-3).

The Greek term *antichristos* is an ambiguous term meaning "in place of" as well as "against." Thus the Latin title the pope ascribed to himself, *Vicarius Christos*, the "Vicar of Christ," in Greek is literally translated "Antichrist." His other Latin title, the "Pontiff," is the title of the pagan emperor of Rome, *Pontificus Maximus*, the supreme bridge-builder between faiths as head of the Pantheon, the hall of idols in Rome.

Thus today can be seen an example of an Antichrist receiving ritual acts of emperor worship such as genuflecting and ring-kissing, and at the same time trying to unite all faiths just as the pagan emperor, the *Pontificus Maximus*, head of the religions, had always done in the Roman Empire. And at the same time he teaches that men must not marry, which the Bible said would happen and was a thing taught by demons. Jesus referred to celibacy in Matthew 19:12 when He said,

"There are also eunuchs who made themselves eunuchs for the sake of the kingdom of God. He who is able to accept this, let him accept it."

So if one desires to renounce marriage, fine, and if they do not, fine. But if they teach that men must not marry, that is something that Paul said men would teach and it comes from demons. In every case the wrong spirit seeks to take control, and in such a way that man cannot continue to serve the Lord Jesus.

When what is natural is suppressed, what is unnatural and perverse will replace it. Yet the popes would have everyone believe that the widespread pedophilia among the clergy, and the orchestrated campaigns by their hierarchy to cover it up and protect these perverts at the expense of innocent children whose lives they have destroyed, is unrelated to the doctrine of celibacy. Contrary to this bogus assertion however, it is largely a phenomenon of Roman Catholicism.

The avalanche of degenerative change which began with the church fathers gained astounding momentum during the age of Thyatira to the point that mainstream Christendom became full-fledged idolatry and immorality riding on the back of political and financial corruption.

Continuing Sacrifice – The Church of the Middle Ages

Do not forget that these seven churches literally existed at the end of the first century. They correspond to various ages in history and they teach about the seven kinds of church that can exist generally, but they also specifically represent the seven kinds of church that will exist in the Last Days before the beginning of Revelation proper in chapter 4. Hence the curses and the blessings and the promises for this church that applied to people at Thyatira also applied to people during the Middle Ages when the seductions that existed embryonically in Thyatira had become full-blown and universal. They also apply to people in that kind of church in the Last Days.

For instance, there was great tribulation in the Middle Ages. The epidemics known today—AIDS, cancer, you name it—all the known diseases put together, have not killed nearly as many people in the Western world as the Bubonic Plague. Most people who have not read history do not begin to understand the impact of the Black Death. Historically and sociologically it was an unprecedented phenomenon. History has never seen anything like the Bubonic Plague, before or since. There was not a single family in Europe that did not experience multiple deaths. No one knows the exact percentage, but just as about one-third of the world's Jews died in the holocaust, one-third of Western Europe's population died in the Bubonic Plague, which they called the Black Death. The great tribulation of this time in history prefigures the Great Tribulation that will come about at the end of the world.

Ramifications of Continuing Sacrifice

There had been no systematic or philosophically comprehensive explanation of transubstantiation that was agreed on until Thomas Aquinas defined the doctrine of transubstantiation in terms of the debunked physics and chemistry of Aristotle. Aristotelian philosophy exploded in the Islamic world, which was having its Golden Age when Roman Catholicism plunged Europe into the Dark Ages until the Renaissance. Moses Maimonides, known in Judaism as the "Rambam," was a rabbi who authored two major works: *Mishneh Torah* and *A Guide for the Perplexed* in which he rewrote and redefined Judaism as an Aristotelian religion, among other things rejecting the miraculous and attributing supernatural phenomena of the Old Testament to the sphere of the scientific explicable. With the approach of the Renaissance after the Crusades came the influences of the Islamic and Byzantium worlds back to Europe. The old Platonic factions of Roman Catholicism dating back to Augustine were challenged by new Aristotelian factions that not infrequently resulted in hostile rivalries among competing religious orders.

This period would see the rise of Joachim of Fiori who would teach a new doctrine of the Holy Spirit that would have its later parody in John Wimber and the Vineyard Movement centuries later. Joachim taught there were three ages in the divine economy, the age of the father being the Old Testament, the age of the Son being the New Testament, and now a new charismatic age of the Holy Spirit that would establish a new religious order. Few if any modern adherents to Kingdom Now Theology blending

Reconstructionism with charismatic extremism, or members of Mike Bickel's International House of Prayer, would have any notion that they are mimicking the accolades of Joachim of Fiori.

However, this tumultuous period would also witness the rise of harbingers not only of the Reformation, but of a popular rediscovery of biblical Evangelicalism that had for centuries been the domain of persecuted Evangelical sects dating back to the Novationists of the post-Nicean period, followed by the Waldenseans, the Lollard followers of John Wycliffe, and the Bohemian Brethren followers of Jan Huss. Among the earliest of these however, was the Italian champion of the Gospel, Savaranola of Florence, who, prior to his martyrdom by the papacy, decried the idolatry and the moral and financial corruption of the established church, and pointed crowds back towards a biblical faith.

There were a number of mainly sad figures who lived and wrote at this time, including Ablehard, William Ockham, Anselm, and a host of others whose works have largely faded into historical obscurity if not oblivion, but who helped frame the religious thinking of the time. Each was engrossed in the endless game of trying to understand and explain the prevailing versions of Christianity in light of the evolving philosophies and shifting world views of the era in which they lived, which was largely static but even in the Dark Ages was often punctuated by storms of change.

This has been an intricate and often pathetic endeavor undertaken by successive generations of philosophers and theologians throughout the history of the church. While the unchanging philosophy of God is the divine philosophy found in the twelve chapters of the book of Ecclesiastes, what St. Paul in his Epistle to the Colossians ridicules as the vain philosophies of the world, mutate ad infinitum, futilely leaving a trail of ultimately hopeless figures consumed by the endeavor of making sense of truths that are eternal to a world view that is transient. As we shall see when we reach our discussions of Laodicea, the necessity of representing the immutable truths of Scripture to those whose outlooks are defined by the world views of the era in which they happen to live and by the *zeitgeist* (or spirit of whatever age they happen to live in) has too often ended in an obsessed effort to make scriptural truth fit the world view instead of making the world view accommodate scriptural truth. (We shall examine this later when we contrast recontextualization with redefinition.) It was the period between the post-Nicean church and the decades leading up to the Renaissance that this spectacle left Christian theology in the doldrums of endemic malaise.

Thyatira

In the darkest of periods during the Crusades, Bernard of Clairvaux left a marred legacy when he posed a theological argument for the Children's Crusades. As radical Islam today uses children as suicide bombers promising them the eternal blessings of martyrdom, it was the Catholicism of Bernhard who fulfilled this barbaric function during the Crusades. While Catholic Europe was in the dismal clutches of Medieval darkness, Islam triumphed in literature, science, and architecture, and had an economy so advanced one could sign a check in Baghdad and cash it in Morocco. The Islam of that day was Westernized, not fundamentalist, and was intellectually controlled from Cairo and not by the Saudi Wahabists as today. It was politically and strategically led by Turks more often than Arabs. At that time it was the Muslim who was relatively civilized and tolerant; it was the European Catholic who was the intolerant savage who sent his child on suicide missions.

This began to change with the Renaissance that would later see as its result the rise of the Humanist scholarship that would pave the way for the Reformation. But it began with an avalanche of Aristotelian philosophy into Europe. Just as Maimonides rewrote Judaism as an Aristotelian religion, so too Thomas Aquinas would reinterpret European Catholicism as an Aristotelian philosophy with his *Suma Theologia*.

The doctrine of the Roman Catholic mass teaches that Jesus continues to die again sacrificially by sacramental means. Rejection of this doctrine more than any other accounted for the martyrdom of the most Bible-believing Christians from the Renaissance to the 17th century. The continually reiterated refrain of New Testament soteriology (the study of the doctrine of salvation) was that the atonement of Christ on the cross was once and for all sufficient for all time with the multiple Old Testament sacrifices being only shadows of the substance found in Christ. His death was to be once and for all, and all sufficient (1 Pe. 3:18; Heb. 7:27; Heb. 9:12; Heb. 10:12-14). The doctrine of the mass constitutes a fundamental rejection of the sufficiency of the once-and-for-all death of Jesus, and reverts to the Old Testament practice of a separate priesthood and continuing sacrifices in direct abrogation of the unambiguous teaching of the Epistle to the Hebrews. Moreover it distorts the context of John 6 where Jesus followed His discourse on eating His flesh and drinking His blood with the admonition that the flesh profits nothing (Jn. 6:63). The Last Supper in which the Lord's Supper was instituted was a Jewish Paschal meal which is a memorial ritual in which Jesus said, "Do this in remembrance of Me," and not a reenactment of His death understood in context.

The Dilemma of Laodicea

The practice of holding up communion elements before the graven image of a risen Christ once again hanging dead on a crucifix and pronouncing it Christ incarnate in which He dies again with the elements to be literally worshiped and eaten defies all biblical and reasonable rationale. The cannibalistic consumption of blood is directly forbidden by the New Testament in Acts 15. Yet such a vampire religion and the worship of bread and wine as Christ incarnate is focal to Roman Catholicism in which supernatural powers to transform organic matter into a physically present Jesus Christ are ascribed to a priest. Apart from the priesthood of all believers the Apostles recognized no New Testament priesthood, but such a clergy class stank of the Nicolaitanism in no uncertain terms condemned by Christ Himself.

Jesus warned repeatedly in the Olivet Discourse against those who claimed any physical return by Him apart from His return to the Mt. of Olives just as He left. He warned His disciples not to go anywhere where it was claimed He was physically present (Mt. 24:26-27; Lk. 17:23-24). Yet in each Roman Catholic mass (and also in high church Anglo-Catholicism and certain churches of Eastern Orthodoxy) it is claimed that Jesus returns physically in a form to be worshiped, killed again, and ceremonially eaten. This is indeed food sacrificed to idols and is the thrust of the spirit of Jezebel seducing Christians into idolatry and ritual cannibalism (Rev. 2:20).

The problem medieval Catholicism faced was explaining transubstantiation philosophically and scientifically in an Aristotelian era. In fact there are probably no two things less logically compatible than Christianity and Aristotle's philosophy, but making them appear compatible was the task assumed by Thomas Aquinas. It is strange to us that today even certain supposedly Evangelical theologians such as Norman Geisler (educated at the Roman Catholic Loyola University) imagine the speculations of Aquinas (known as "Thomist") can find harmony not only with Christianity generally, but somehow in his mind be congruous with conservative Evangelicism.

To furnish a justification for transubstantiation, Aquinas drew on the pseudo-scientific philosophy of "accidents" based on Aristotle's ignorance of particle physics and molecular chemistry. Before the Enlightenment, astronomy and astrology had been one and the same. Medicine and pharmacology and folk medicine had been the same. The same was true of alchemy where there was not much practical distinction between chemistry and magic. Chemical changes of electron transfers from orbitals between atoms was not known of; hence a chemical reaction could not be understood in the modern sense. Chemical changes were therefore explained as "accidents" where a substance could be one thing but appear to be another. An alchemist would combine chemical elements and form a compound, but the compound and the chemical was misunderstood as simply being a change of appearance, not of substance.

This of course is a laughable misunderstanding of chemistry and physics, and the world view deriving from it is equally ludicrous. Yet this is how Aquinas explained transubstantiation where the bread and wine would be the mere appearance, but the substance would actually be the protoplasm of Jesus Christ after the priest uttered his magic phrase: "Hoc est corpus meum" (from where we get the colloquialism "hocus pocus"). Absurdity of absurdities however, the Roman Catholic doctrine of *Semper Eadem* ("always the same") will not allow them to change a *De Fide* doctrine. Thus while scientifically debunked as preposterous, the Roman Catholic Church must still hold to the belief.

Today most Catholics say it is Christ incarnate by faith. The doctrine itself, however, maintains that it *is* His actual protoplasm scientifically defined by Aristotle's archaic misunderstanding of physical science.

The Relevant Aspect of Jesus

The relevant aspects of Jesus as He appeared in Revelation 1 that He mentions to Thyatira have to do with judgment. He is the Son of God who has been appointed to judge (Acts 17:31); He has eyes that see everything; He has the flame of fire and the feet of burnished bronze. Those things have to do with judgment in biblical typology. Such can be drawn on the construction of the tabernacle for this—the purifying with fire and so on. He is looking for what is wrong, and His eyes of blazing fire are looking, judgmentally, on this church.

Jesus also commends what is right, getting straight to the heart of the problem, which is the woman Jezebel. She appears in Revelation; the wicked woman, and all the wicked women in the Bible typify the woman Jezebel in some way—the sexually-immoral Moabite women in Numbers 25, Potiphar's wife, Delilah, Queen Athaliah, the woman Jezebel herself, Herodias, the seductress in Proverbs 5 and 7—*all* of these wicked women typify in some way the spirit of false religion which can be called "Jezebel." She is a seductress, a harlot, someone who is out to seduce God's servants to commit acts of immorality, specifically to eat food sacrificed to idols.

Please notice that Jesus raised no objection to Jezebel on account of her gender, nor to her being a teacher; He found fault only with what she taught. The early third-century school led by Origen had woman and men in attendance in equal status. Two women of this school, Herais and Potomiana, suffered martyrdom for their faith. Jesus is not opposed to women. Look at the list of women Paul affirmed in Romans 16. Jesus simply never tolerated false teaching. As well as showing up the false teaching of the Pharisees and teachers of the Law in the Gospels while He was on earth, Jesus in this instance rebuked the church at Thyatira for tolerating false teaching. Jesus wants the people of the church collectively to challenge false teaching, not to tolerate it.

Observe that the things that are wrong in Thyatira are built progressively upon the things that were wrong in Pergamum. One of the things wrong with Pergamum was that they tolerated those who held to the teaching of the Nicolaitans, lording it over the laity. A priestly class became established, setting themselves up over the people. Not a class of servants, but the opposite, almost a class of religious aristocracy similar to the Pharisees at the time of Jesus. They were a Christianized version of the same people. Remember, Jesus hated the practices of the Nicolaitans and commended the church of Ephesus for hating them, too. No one knows for sure of all of the practices of the Nicolaitans, but we do know what the construction of the Greek word means and that Jesus hated their practices. Unlike Ephesus, Pergamum tolerated them. This is the result.

Origin of the Immaculate Conception

It is critically important to understand that from the beginning people were trying to get into the church and do things that were not of God. The evil seductress was always there trying to seduce God's people as she had always been right through the Old Testament. In the pre-Nicean church before AD 325, there were people who followed the teaching of the Apostles fairly accurately, such as Justin Martyr and Irenaeus, and they also prevented Jezebel from getting too far for too long. But that began to change for the worse about the time when Constantine made Christianity the religion of the state.

However, look what Paul said in 2 Thessalonians 2:7...

"For the mystery of lawlessness is already at work; only he who now restrains will do so until he is taken out of the way."

It was already there about thirty years **before** John wrote Revelation. The spirit of seduction was already around at the time of the Apostles. But it becomes amplified and mushrooms in the Last Days.

Studying Pergamum reveals what happened when Constantine made Christianity the religion of the state. As emperor he was head of the

122

Pantheon of Rome, and his title was *Pontificus Maximus*, the Pontiff. That title was taken on by the medieval papacy and now the pope is the Pontiff, the head of the Pantheon, where he changes the names of the Greco-Roman folk gods and festivals and gives them Christian-sounding labels. The most significant thing in all this is what the popes say happened to Mary, the mother of Jesus. Remember the riot in Ephesus?

> *When they heard this and were filled with rage, they began crying out, saying, "Great is Artemis of the Ephesians! (Acts 19:28)*

When Paul contested the worship of Diana it led to uproar.

Today in South America and the Philippines the same thing happens. There are tremendous Evangelical revivals in these poorer Catholic countries and nothing stirs up the Catholic priesthood more than the agitation they experience when they think Mary is being offended. But understand, of course, that it is not Mary who is offended when worship turns to Jesus; it is Minerva, Diana, Artemis. These can be seen in the Vatican Museum and it is striking. One can observe the Madonnas and statues of "Mary" from different periods of history. There are five museums in the Vatican and the continuity is visible from Artemis worship to female cult deities to fertility goddesses, etc. It matches exactly. This came about from something called *In Parte Chalcedon*, the Council of Chalcedon. There were people who were defending the deity of Jesus. They had a high Christology and they were defending it against heretics who denied the deity of Jesus. Some people had accepted Him as a prophet from Nazareth who healed the sick and raised the dead, but nothing more, and denied that He is the Son of God just as Mohammed did in his *Sura Miriam* several hundred years later.

The results of Chalcedon are present to this very day. They affirmed Jesus as fully God and co-substantial with the Father, for He now shares His Father's throne (Rev. 3:21). But they subsequently lost Him as the only Mediator, inventing the idea that Mary is a Mediatrix to enable one's approach her Son, who is God. Next, they regarded Mary as the "Mother of God" and "Queen of Heaven." Thus, she must not be sleeping in the dust, but must be alive and well in heaven. All this is invention, adding to Scripture, which God tells us again and again not to do.

However, for Mary to be co-redeemer, in their thinking she had to be conceived without sin. So they invented the doctrine of the Immaculate Conception. Previously the ancient Babylonian concept of *Theotikos* ("Mother of God") was discussed, a term not found in the Bible but having its origins with Semiramis and Nimrod and manifesting itself at various points in biblical history in different forms such as Tammuz, whose worship the Lord hated (Ez. 8:14). Tammuz was portrayed as being held by his Madonna mother as a helpless babe, while the focus was placed on his mother. This is the exact nature of the spirit of Jezebel. Just as Queen Jezebel used the position of her husband, King Ahab, for her own glory, so an apostate church in the character of a wicked woman uses her husband as a vehicle to glorify herself and obtain power. A faithful bride, however, seeks the honor of her husband, who in turn honors her.

Roman Catholics should know that their two most important theologians, Augustine of Hippo (354 - 430) and Thomas Aquinas (1225 - 1274), both *denied* the Immaculate Conception. Most Catholics do not know that, but their two greatest theological thinkers both denied it. So did most popes. It did not become an official doctrine until relatively recently, declared by Pius IX in 1870.

Mary was the greatest woman who ever lived. The Scripture says that the angel Gabriel, *Gabri-El*–the "Mighty One of God," told her that she was "*Blessed among women*" (Lk. 1:28). There is no question that she was the greatest. She may also be "The chosen lady" of the second letter of John (2 Jn. 1:1). But Mary said, "*My spirit has rejoiced in God my Savior*" (Lk. 1:47). Mary certainly said she needed a Savior. The Church of Rome had to say, "No she did not." Who should be believed, Mary or a pope? Let us believe Mary!

Many Roman Catholics believe that Jesus said, "When you honor My mother you are honoring Me." That is not in the Bible, but many people are led to believe that it is. It goes back to this period. And because Mary became a mother-figure and they adore her, one must be very sensitive when talking to Roman Catholics about her. The most effective way is to look at Mary herself. She said she needed a Savior. Who am I going to believe? Or ask why Mary brought a sin offering when Jesus was born. Or quote Mary's last recorded words, "*Whatever He says to you, do it*" (Jn. 2:5). Deal with it that way.

So the Nicolaitans paved the way. Then Constantine made the Roman Empire "Christian," and the Bishop of Rome took over the title of *Pontificus Maximus* and became the head the gods of the Pantheon. Next the dead began to be called saints. The god of gift-giving became Saint Nicholas; the pagan god of love became Saint Valentine, etc. But then there was Gnosticism: it is not what the *Bible* says is important, it is what the *person* says who has the *gnosis*, the mystical and experiential revelation or knowledge. This is Gnosticism. It is in all false cults in some way.

Thyatira

Within Roman Catholicism Gnosticism is central in its pure sense. Most people who are Gnostics claim that their leader, the person with the *gnosis*, has it because of some kind of descent. With Roman Catholicism, it is a claim that the pope is an heir or successor to Peter. This form of Gnosticism in the Roman Catholic Church, the way they interpret the Bible, is called *Sensus Plenior* in Latin, the "fullest sense." And only the person who has the *gnosis*, the pope, as the successor to Peter can properly interpret the Bible. That is to say, in order to understand the Bible correctly, one has to be under the pope; otherwise, they say, one is under deception. They have a constitution called *Lumen Gentium*—"The Light of the People." In this constitution it specifies that only the church can interpret the Bible, and only through something called the *Magesterium*. This is the hierarchy of the church under the headship of the pope, but he has the final word. Hence, even though their greatest theologians denied the Immaculate Conception, once the pope says it is a truth, and he has the *gnosis* so no one can argue with him, there is no higher authority.

So the Gnosticism that came into Pergamum, and the Nicolaitanism that also came into Pergamum, set the stage for what happened at Thyatira.

Pagan Practices

Even before Satan began to paganize Christendom he tried to Judaize it, to deceive them into going back under the Law and to apply legalistic Old Testament tenets to the Christian community where those tenets are not reiterated in the New Testament, starting with circumcision. The Council of Jerusalem in AD 51 (Acts 15:29) did not require Gentile Christians to meet any such requirements of the Law. They decided, "*That you abstain from things sacrificed to idols and from blood and from things strangled and from fornication.*"

Much could be said about the pagan origins of many Roman Catholic beliefs. To quote from Cardinal John Henry Newman, the greatest Roman Catholic theological thinker Great Britain has ever produced (they want to have him canonized as a saint) in his treatise called *The Development of the Christian Religion*, Cardinal Newman said this: "At least seventy percent of the rights, rituals, customs and traditions of Roman Catholicism are of pagan origin."

In Jerusalem resides the Evangelical Institute of Holy Land Studies and another place called the Pontifical Institute of Holy Land Studies. Here one can talk to the Jesuit scholars and confront them with the evidence and they will not deny it. A good book to read is Alexander Hislop's classic *The Two Babylons* first published in 1858. He uses archaeology and anthropology to demonstrate the exact pagan origins of these things. (It would be great if someone would produce a more modern version of it; it is tedious to read but well worth reading.)

So instead of a priesthood of all believers, which is what the New Testament teaches (1 Pe. 2:9, fulfilling Ex.19:6), they go back to a special priesthood like the Levites in the Old Testament. Roman Catholics believe their priests have special powers that other people do not have: to forgive sins and to transubstantiate bread and wine into the actual flesh and blood of Jesus. They put back the Levitical priesthood. It is Judaization.

The true church should be a dynamic tabernacle, each member a temple of the Holy Spirit. But it can be seen how Roman Catholicism reintroduces the altar and on it the tabernacle, a box, where God lives. That is what they believe! So it is like the Holy of Holies, the *Qodesh Qodesh'im* in Hebrew or, as Catholics would call it, the *Sanctum Sanctorum*. The Tabernacle is back; He is in one place and He is fixed.

While giving out tracts to Roman Catholics in Battersea Park when they had a celebration for Mary, the late Cardinal Hume came in a limousine to give the benediction with the "monstrance." In other words, as far as they were concerned, Jesus Christ had just arrived in a Mercedes limo! One would think He would at least have had a police escort. After all, He is God! This is what it comes to.

So, instead of having a dynamic tabernacle there is a static one just like in Judaism. It puts Judaism back. Except that it goes beyond that.

In Hebrew they say *lach toch brit*, "to cut a covenant."

> "Behold, days are coming," declares the LORD, "when I will make a new covenant with the house of Israel and with the house of Judah, not like the covenant which I made with their fathers in the day I took them by the hand to bring them out of the land of Egypt, My covenant which they broke, although I was a husband to them," declares the LORD (Jer. 31:31-32)

It will be different. There was going to be a new covenant and God was going to write it on people's hearts individually; it was not going to be a national covenant. Paul explains this in Romans: they are not all Israel who say they are Israel (Rom. 9:6). That is what Jesus says, "They say they are Jews who are not Jews" (Rev. 3:9).

The New Covenant

"*I will make a new covenant*" And Jesus has done so. The Old Covenant idea that people who are in a state church are in a covenant relationship with God does not apply anymore! And in any case it applied *only* to Israel! This state church was on its way out the window just as Jeremiah prophesied.

However, the very things that Jesus died to get rid of, they started putting back. It will be seen how the Reformation failed to restore biblical Christianity because in order to restore biblical Christianity one had to break the unbiblical marriage between church and state which the Reformers did not do. They just replaced a Catholic marriage with a Protestant marriage of church and state.

Is it clear what happened? Satan made it a state church. And instead of people being baptized upon confession of faith in Jesus like the 3,000 who repented and were baptized on the day of Pentecost in Acts 2:38 or the Ethiopian in Acts 8:37, they started baptizing unbelieving babies who could not understand. It was the same as circumcision; it brought back a national covenant and a national state religion. They always hoped that these Gnostic rules would result in salvation, but the New Covenant is based on faith, not rules.

And the results can be seen today in this kind of thinking. It is called "Erastianism," when religion becomes an institution of the state. Today in Britain members of Parliament who are Muslims, Hindus, unsaved Jews or Atheists appoint Bishops for the Church of England. A New Age monarch could become the head of the church. This is what went wrong in the Old Testament, and this is what God said He was going to get rid of through Jeremiah, through John the Baptist, through Paul (and through the writer to the Hebrews), and this is what Satan manages to put back. It is beginning to happen.

So what happened to Thyatira is based on what happened previously. Particularly Nicolaitanism, Gnosticism and, above all, Judaism. God's idea was that Jesus would die once for the sins of the whole world; He would be the perfect Passover Lamb once for all, replacing all the normal Passover lambs that were only a symbol of Jesus.

Jesus, High Priest and King

For it is attested of Him,
"YOU *(Jesus)* ARE A PRIEST FOREVER ACCORDING TO THE ORDER OF MELCHIZEDEK." *(Heb. 7:17)*

Jesus is the real High Priest now, in the order of Melchizedek, not of Aaron.

Jesus is also a King, the Son of David. And Jesus is unique. Kings had to be descendants of David and priests had to be descendants of Aaron. The Jewish authorities knew that only the Messiah could be **both** a king and a priest which the prophet Moses wrote about in Deuteronomy 18.

But Jesus was not a descendent of Aaron, He was not even a Levite – He was from the tribe of Judah! So how could He be a priest at all? How helpful the writer of the Epistle to the Hebrews has been by showing us that He is a priest in the *"order of Melchizedek."*

When Jesus was hanging on the cross He was the High Priest making atonement for sins on the altar. But then Pilate put up the sign, "THIS IS JESUS, THE KING OF THE JEWS" (Mk. 15:26). Only Christ/Messiah could be both king and priest. Everyone agreed that He was a prophet, but he was also *The* Prophet, the one Moses wrote about in the Law.

Now consider this: in Christ Jesus *all* believers are priests and *all* believers are kings. In Him, and only in Him, all believers have both a regal and a priestly stature.

> *"[Jesus] who does not need daily, like those high priests, to offer up sacrifices, first for His own sins and then for the sins of the people, because this He did once for all when He offered up Himself." (Heb. 7:27)*

Jesus died once and for all; is it, finished. The Law is fulfilled by Jesus. He becomes our righteousness and the sacrificial system is finished.

> *"So Christ also, having been offered once to bear the sins of many, will appear a second time for salvation without reference to sin, to those who eagerly await Him. (Heb. 9:28)*

A sacrifice offered once.

> *"For by one offering He has perfected for all time those who are sanctified." (Heb. 10:14)*

Once! It has been done! There is no longer a "priest" making sacrifices every day, again and again, except for each believer's sacrifice of praise, each believer's worship.

Therefore it can be seen what happens when the church gets Judaized. The "mass" is invented. The priests come in offering what they call "the sacrifice of the mass" in which they claim Jesus dies again. It is a re-presentation of the actual sacrifice of Calvary. It is vague and mystical, but they say the bread and wine becomes transubstantiated, that it turns into Jesus and it should be worshipped. Roman Catholic documents actually teach that it is to be *worshipped*. And then what amounts to an act of cannibalism is carried out: they eat Him. That is what happens; it is utterly cannibalistic. That is the pagan aspect. In reality the disciples never ate His flesh or drank His blood, because His words were obviously symbolic, no question.

The mass is probably the most central doctrine of Roman Catholicism and it fundamentally denies the Gospel as the New Testament teaches it. It is a fundamental denial of the completed work of Jesus on the cross. Remember John Henry Newman, and their own literature. Jesus is our High Priest and our King.

Further Decline

As we have already explained, Augustine of Hippo (c. 343 - 430) tried to make Christianity Platonic. Platonism, essentially, means to treat plain things as representing abstract ideas. It tends to treat almost everything allegorically.

There was a reaction against the Platonization of the church in a movement called Medieval Scholasticism whose main figure was Thomas Aquinas. This led to the Jansenist Schism within the Roman Catholic Church. Long before the Reformation there were factions and schisms within the church theologically. The Reformation merely took theological schism and brought it to its natural conclusions institutionally in the form of a forced split, much the same as the Eastern Orthodox church took a combination of cultural, political and theological differences to an institutional split between Rome and Constantinople. The papacy has only ever ultimately cared about institutional schism. Theological schism has plagued the Roman church from the time of the Novationist Schism onwards.

The first attempted institutional split was the Donatist Schism of the fourth century, opposed by Augustine. Before long the incipient Roman Catholic Church began murdering people within its own ranks to try to maintain an institutional unity after doctrinal unity disappeared. And as for spiritual unity, well, what spirit was there to bring unity? Spiritual unity did not exist.

Among the victims who tried in earnest to maintain a biblical Christianity, Priscillian, a bishop in Iberia, was murdered at an early point. Girolamo Savonarola (1452 - 1498) was murdered in Italy during the Renaissance in an age when Cardinal Rau of Florence denounced the New Testament writings of Paul as disgusting, and urged that the Greek and Latin classics be read for religious purposes instead.

Challenging the Pope Meant Death

From the Novatians to the Waldenseans to the Lollards of John Wycliffe in England to the Bohemian Brethren of Huss, those who tried to split from Rome institutionally on doctrinal grounds were always exterminated by the papacy and its surrogates. This continued until the social and political changes that precipitated the Reformation allowed the Reformers to survive what others had always been slaughtered for.

The Dilemma of Laodicea

On the hollow basis of institutional unity, Rome would have everyone believe that it is one church with one dogma, which in real terms is not and never has been the actual case. Before the Reformation the Dominicans fought their rivals the Franciscans. If Platonic Roman Catholicism tended to allegorize the literal, the Aristotelian religious orders of Roman Catholicism tended to literalize the symbolic. In order to justify the cannibalism of the mass and to explain transubstantiation in a final form (previously there had been three versions of it), Aquinas absurdly used Aristotle's philosophy of "accidents." Before the superstitious aspects of alchemy was debunked, Aristotle's belief was that matter can have an appearance which is its mere "accidents" but at a particle level it can physically be an entirely different substance.

In the modern age when the nature of compounds is understood in terms of molecular formulas based on the valence of atoms, it is now common knowledge that the visible properties of something are not mere "accidents." They are the result of what they are on a chemical level. What something looks, tastes and smells like is a result of what it is physically, not because of its appearance.

Today the Roman Catholic Church, in the face of all this, now tries to defend its absolute lunacy on the basis of "faith," that it is something spiritually different from what it appears to be because it has been "consecrated" by a special "priest" with special "powers." But the official doctrine, as formally set out by Aquinas, specifies it is not spiritual but literal and physical. A quantitative analysis would confirm that their Eucharist is not protoplasm but grain and fermented grape juice. Yet because the Eucharist is a *De Fide* doctrine, a doctrine of the faith, *Semper Eadem* applies, and science must be rejected. It is therefore easy to see why the Roman church so persecuted the early scientists.

Augustine wrote *The City of God*, claiming that although Rome was finally destroyed, the kingdom of God lasts forever. He wrote his *Confessions* in which he laid the groundwork for trouble in the Middle Ages. Augustine's hermeneutics, his way of interpreting the Bible, was totally Greek.

For example, consider the Good Samaritan. Augustine said going down from Jerusalem to Jericho could be the plight of fallen man. The inn was the church. The Levite and the High Priest, the Cohen, cannot help someone who has been mugged, showing that the Law cannot save and so they cannot help this person who was the victim of a crime. Then a Good Samaritan came along representing a Christian or Christianity and he could help him, and he brought him into the church. Could be, but then he said that the coins meant something, that the innkeeper was St. Paul and he went on and on and on. This was Greek hermeneutics which began with Philo and others in Alexandria and people who later copied them, particularly Origen (c. 185 - 253). So this whole philosophical process is introduced.

For over a thousand years Roman Catholicism reigned. Anyone who desires to know what a Roman Catholic world would be like merely has to look at what a Roman Catholic world *was* like for over a thousand years. And if they want to know what a Roman Catholic Church would do in the world if it had its way in the world, if it could do anything it wanted in the world, all one has to do is look at what it *did.* The Byzantine and even the Islamic Empires had their golden ages while, under Roman Catholicism, Europe went into the Dark Ages.

Eastern Influence

In the Roman Catholic constitution, *Lumen Gentium*, as we have already pointed out, there is something called *Semper Eadem*, Latin for "always the same." Its origins are actually in the philosophy of the medieval Islamic world. Later when the Crusaders began bringing from the East the Islamic and Byzantine influences into Europe, Greco-Roman culture was rediscovered. The result was what is now called the Renaissance. Moorish arches and Gothic architecture with flying buttresses came from the Muslim world. At that time the Muslims were far ahead in architecture, literature, medicine, mathematics, science, philosophy. European Jews were considered primitive. It was the Sephardic Jews in Spain and North Africa who were the learned ones. Today it is almost the opposite. But back in Islam's golden age the popes wanted to control the spice trade with the East because the economy of the West depended on the spices from the East much as the West depends so heavily on oil from the Middle East today.

Western visitors to present-day Morocco are often shocked if they have never been to the Muslim world before. Upon arrival they will observe little Arab girls wearing white gowns, looking exactly like little Catholic girls dressed for their first communion, counting prayers on beads. Alexander Hislop's book *The Two Babylons* explains the true origins of these things, and visitors to Morocco can see for themselves how these things were copied from Hindus and Muslims.

This is where they got such traditions. They will tell you the Rosary came from St. Dominic. St. Dominic was someone who said all women had to be suspected of being witches because they have a curved rib, having been made by God from the rib of Adam. Therefore, as a rib is curved, so all women are crooked. As a result, they would do terrible gynecological tortures on women to find out if they were witches. This was St. Dominic who gave them the Rosary; he was the first to carry out inquisitions on a wide scale.

So it was that these Eastern influences began to come into Roman Catholicism, including *Idj T'had*. In Islam there is Sharia and Din, religious law and religious codification of the Quran and things derived from it. Once something is determined to be legally binding in Islam, in Sharia and Din, the principle of *Idj T'had* takes over; it cannot be changed. This came into Roman Catholicism, and they say *Semper Eadem*, "always the same." Once a doctrine has been officially proclaimed in the Roman Catholic Church through the process known as *Ex Cathedra*, meaning "from the chair of Peter," it cannot be changed.

There are people today saying that the Roman Catholic Church changed with the Second Vatican Council. But the Second Vatican Council documents all affirm the Council of Trent (1545) in the time of the Counter Reformation. They cannot change these central doctrines. They can change the mass from Latin into English, French or the vernacular. They can change the outer packaging, but the doctrine must remain unchanged.

A few eyebrows were raised in a Bible College when they asked a student what he thought of the Church of Rome after the Second Vatican Council, and he told them bluntly, "It is like an old tart with a new dress. But when you lift it up you find the same knickers she has worn for the last two thousand years."

They cannot change! *Semper Eadem*. It has to be that way. The Principal of the Bible College mentioned above described it like this: imagine a car loaded with more and more accessories until it becomes so heavy that it cannot move or be driven. Yet continue to install more and more accessories, and they cannot take anything off, so the whole thing looks ridiculous, does not drive well, and does not go anywhere. But they cannot remove anything because of *Semper Eadem*.

Jeremiah 51 tells us this: Babylon cannot be healed. *Semper Eadem* fulfils that prophecy. All of these false religions come from Babylon, from Nimrod in Genesis 10, this has been previously considered. They found their way through Pergamum in Asia Minor into Greco-Roman civilization and from there into Eastern Orthodoxy, Roman Catholicism, Freemasonry, etc.

Consider this: one in every six Protestant males in Northern Ireland is a member of a Masonic Lodge or an Orange Lodge which is filled with Masonic influence. Why are the Protestants so upset about the Catholics when they themselves are even worse? Read the testimonies of some converted Masons, particularly some in the higher degrees of Freemasonry, and find out what it is. It is not just the Catholic Church that has been infiltrated by Jezebel's teaching about the so-called dark secrets of Satan. Even they would not go as far as the Masons, if you really know what masonry is.

Adding But Not Taking Away

So they add this, and add this, and add this, and they cannot take anything away.

It is the same with Judaism. In the Talmud, Rabbi Hillel said there would be no Messiah, for the Messiah came in the reign of King Hezekiah. Then his grandson Rabbi Yosef said, "God forgive my grandfather, Rabbi Hillel." There are blatant contradictions in the Talmud so another Rabbi has to come along with another theory to try to reconcile the contradictory opinions and it gets crazy. Loving the Talmud would be like loving the Yellow Pages! People try to make the Talmud seem like an organized body of opinion when it is not. It is really a disorganized body of controversy.

The Roman Catholic Church has people called the "fathers" and, strikingly, many Protestants hold to whatever these "fathers" taught. That was another failure of the Reformation as will be seen. The Reformers did not always go back to the Word of God; they went back to Augustine and to the "fathers" who began getting it wrong to begin with.

Contra-Scriptural Views of Sexuality

When the Bible specifies that there will be those teaching doctrines of demons and forbidding marriage (celibacy, 1 Ti. 4:3), it places the increase in this kind of demonic activity into the context of "the Last Days" when its significance will increase. This is seen happening today with pedophilia among Roman Catholic priests and nuns, and the criminal conspiracies of their Cardinals and Bishops to obstruct justice in order to preserve the status quo and their child-raping clergy.

With the release of the twin Ryan and Murphy Reports in the Republic of Ireland in late 2009, the disclosures horrified the Irish public with countless thousands of children having been proven to be victims of pedophilia perpetrated by Roman Catholic priests and nuns. In addition to prolific sexual abuse, an endemic history of emotional and physical abuse was uncovered in some cases that appeared to include defenseless children being used as sex toys for sado-masochistic lesbian and homosexual practices of the clergy. Due to the political and judicial influence of the Roman Catholic Church in Ireland however, it was agreed to preclude and exclude the possibility of even identifying the perpetrators, and none of the sex criminals were arrested or prosecuted as a direct result of the report.

In one case in Ireland a priest who had ritually raped ten little girls dressed as little brides for their first communion using the Eucharist altar as a bed to violate them was shielded by the Irish police when prosecutorial evidence in the custody of a senior Irish *Garda* police investigator disappeared. The Irish press reported that he was contacted, and help was enlisted in some fashion through his involvement in an organization called "The Knights of Columbus." This same police official shortly afterward was honored by Pope John Paul II with a medal and commendation for his service to the Roman church, not mentioning of course the pedophilia he was charged with investigating. Both reports in Ireland indicated collusion between the church and the police in sequestering evidence and pursuing the arrest and prosecution of dangerous pedophile sex criminals who were allowed by the church to continue their depravity and victimization of helpless little children. Virtually every bishop, archbishop, and cardinal in Ireland had been implicated in the protection of these child molesters. The same was largely true in Canada, Australia, New Zealand, and Great Britain, but was routinely worse in Roman Catholic countries such as Ireland, Austria, and Brazil.

In Austria the largest Roman Catholic seminary for training priests in Europe was closed under pressure from the Austrian government after the seminary was found to contain 40,000 hours of recorded child pornography, the largest cache of kiddy-porn in history. The volume of this material was staggering and outpaced the previous record of 8,000 hours of child pornography placed on the Internet by a Catholic priest from St. Joseph's church in New Castle, England. It was also reported in the Austrian and international press that the cardinal of Vienna had probable knowledge of what was taking place in the seminary. In effect, in studying for the priesthood, seminarians learned how to molest children. Much of the film footage was of older priests performing homosexual acts with younger ones.

In the United States former Governor William Keating of Kansas (himself a Catholic), who chaired the Roman Catholic Church's own investigation commission, complained of continual obfuscation by church authorities. He publicly announced that, based on his previous experience as an FBI agent and prosecutor, elements of the Roman Catholic Church were more secretive than the Mafia. Indeed, it is known in the law enforcement community and by district attorneys that both the Italian and Russian Mafias will not traffic in child pornography as it violates even their supposed code of ethics. The Roman Catholic clergy engages on a wide scale in something that even organized crime would consider too sick and evil to become involved in. Even professional gangsters would not do to little children what Roman Catholic clergy have done!

The second Irish report however, was *more* damning because it disclosed from its investigations an uncovered Roman Catholic teaching called *The Doctrine of Mental Reservation* where church hierarchy could mislead authorities in order to protect sex criminal priests and nuns without it being considered a lie or a sin. The Irish public was left not only indignant but stunned that their bishops, archbishops, and cardinals in effect said it is not a sin to lie in order to protect pedophiles at the cost of not protecting the victimized children, providing the child molester is a priest or a nun.

This demonstrates that the source of this outrage is not simply the misdeeds of a few. In fact, 177 out of 179 Roman Catholic diocese and archdiocese and their bishops in the United States have been proven responsible in court for the same kind of practice. The Catholic Church responded to Keating's pronouncement by Cardinal Mahoney of Los Angeles demanding the resignation of Keating. Shortly afterward the archdiocese of Los Angeles paid $660 million in damages plus legal fees as the price of what some legal editorialists called keeping Mahoney out of prison. His colleague, Cardinal Law of Boston, left the country amidst such scandals, and was promoted to archpriest of a Vatican cathedral in Rome by Pope John Paul II, for whom it was Law who said the funeral mass.

These facts are undeniable and well-documented. The Roman Catholic Church and its lawyers can only amplify moot points in the reported details. Any reasonable Catholic examining these facts would be left astounded if not flabbergasted.

The *Criminale Solicitaciones* directive, telling bishops to at all costs keep sex scandals uncovered even when they involve the violation of children and sex with animals, was uncovered in both Australia and the USA. It was first issued by Pope John XXIII, proving that the Vatican was cognizant of this cancer for at least some fifty years. It was then reissued by Cardinal Joseph Radzinger who is now Pope Benedict XVI at the behest of his predecessor John Paul II (Karol Wojtyla). When a litigation was launched against Benedict XVI by Daniel Shea and other American attorneys for the victims, the George W. Bush administration and Condoleezza Rice pressed the Justice Department to ask the court to dismiss the litigation because the pope is the chief of state of a nation given full diplomatic recognition by Ronald Reagan and cannot be prosecuted. The Vatican tried to persuade the public to believe that the document had to do with confessional secrecy as if bishops needed to be reminded of their obligation to keep things confessed in their sacrament of penance absolutely confidential. In actual fact however, clergy privilege is protected by law the same as attorney-client privilege and physician-patient privilege, as well as under constitutional provision for freedom of religion. Legally no defense of confessional secrecy could have been required. The Vatican instead petitioned the White House and the U.S. State Department for a political defense that simply saw the President, Secretary of State, and Attorney General asking the court to not allow the case to go forward, not for reasons based on the merits of the case, but for reasons of politics and diplomacy.

The *Criminale Solicitaciones* instruction and the *Doctrine of Mental Reservation* prove categorically that the source of this satanic corruption manifesting itself in the most appalling sex crimes imaginable is rooted in Roman Catholic false doctrine; again, St. Paul's "doctrine of demons" forbidding marriage (1 Ti. 4:3). It was not simply a matter of a *few* bad apples, but a rotten *barrel* right up to the highest echelons of the papacy and Roman Catholic hierarchy.

It was the Roman Catholic Church that organized the notorious *Rat Lines* facilitating the escape of numerous Nazi war criminals to Latin America, protecting them in convents and monasteries. Many of these Nazis murdered children, especially Gypsies and Jews. Now the same institution that protected the Nazi killers of children is protecting the rapists of children. The core reason points back to the corrupt doctrines first introduced in the fourth century, and that evolved through the Middle Ages.

The nascent origin of this subversion of the scriptural truth regarding marriage and sexuality is once again found in Augustine of Hippo, the ramifications of whose unfortunate influence lingers to the present day in many areas including the modern Roman Catholic pedophilia scandals. Augustine said the only good thing about marriage is having children who will be celibate. The false idea he was conveying was that the sin of Adam and Eve was sex. To this day Roman Catholicism has a very, very, *very* sinister hang-up about even marital sexuality. This discussion is not about *sinful* sexuality, but *marital* sexuality.

The monastic movements even taught flagellation rituals. The Crusaders saw the commemoration of the Battle of Kabala by Shia Moslems who would mutilate themselves and flagellate themselves and flagellate each other to commemorate the martyrdom of Mohammed's grandson Ali at the Battle of Kabala in AD 680 in Iraq. So this was brought back by them, along with the little girls in white gowns with the beads, and it became integrated into the body of doctrine. The nuns and monks began to flog each other and flagellate themselves as a form of penance. Given that normal sex was outlawed because marriage was outlawed, perverted sex was the inevitable consequence. Hence religious flagellation accounts for the prevalence of sadomasochism in Roman Catholic culture, as is evidenced in the original writings of Marquis de Sade who propagated this aberration of human sexuality.

In modern times in a magazine interview, the pop singer Madonna once accounted for the sadomasochistic images in her pop videos by attributing them to her strict Roman Catholic upbringing. It is crazy to beat one's self to make atonement for sin when the Bible says, "*By His stripes we are healed*" (Is. 53). Jesus was flogged for our sins.

The Introduction of Indulgences and Prayers for the Dead

And so they got further and further away from a righteousness that is by faith, and into a "righteousness by works." One of the most cruel of these "works" was the doctrine of Indulgences. During the Renaissance they needed a way to get money to build all the buildings, basilicas, cathedrals, etc., that they wanted. "Oh, your poor mother, she is in Purgatory and surely you want to get her out?" There was a priest named Tetzel who said you could sexually violate even Mary the Mother of Christ and be forgiven if you came up with the right price to purchase an indulgence.

Tetzel was a Dominican, the order that perpetrated the Inquisitions and were a rival order to, among others, the Augustinians, of which Luther was a member. Hence Luther's challenge to the sale of indulgences in his *95 Theses* at Wittenberg. It was Tetzel who preached,

"*When a coin into the box rings,*
A soul from Purgatory springs."

That is how they built the great cathedrals of the Renaissance. They preyed on people's fear of this totally unbiblical doctrine. Forgetting both Stephen's apology (Acts 7:48) that "*the Most High does not dwell in houses built by human hands*," and Peter's declaration that God's house on earth is made up of the believers themselves (1 Pe. 2:5), not only did they try to build a house by human hands but they exploited the laity who were the true house in order to do so! Nicolaitans! No wonder Jesus hated the practices of the Nicolaitans. He knew what would happen if the church tolerated them!

There is a reference in the Apocrypha, not the Bible, concerning the need to pray for the souls who have died and are waiting for their redemption. But when properly examined in its Jewish context it is people looking forward to when Messiah comes, so they are praying for the Messiah to come and bring the redemption.

The Celts

Since the time of the Apostles there have always been some Bible-believing Christians in spite of the proliferation of false Christianity. Rome persecuted them all, but one of the last places to resist Roman Catholicism was the British Isles. And the last place in the British Isles to resist was Ireland, specifically the North.

In the early Middle Ages the church became more worldly and the movement of Monasticism began in North Africa. It was basically people trying to escape the corruption and the materialism of the established church, so they began forming private communities. These were not monks as monks became—that began with Benedict—but they were just communities of people: men, women and children. Then they began taking on pagan influences. For instance, the convent comes from the tradition of the Vestal Virgins of pagan Rome. Nonetheless, a lot of Monasticism began with good intentions. But the place where it blossomed most was with the Celtic church in the British Isles.

When reading the *Confessions of Patrick* it is clear he knew nothing of Mary, or superstitions, or confessions, or Purgatory. The Vikings invaded continental Europe, totally obliterating Christianity throughout Western and Central Europe. Only Southern Italy was spared these invasions. Irish monks, following Patrick's successors, began sending missionaries to Iona in Scotland. Ninian went there, and also to Cornwall in England. St. Ives, St. Mawgan and the like were named after these people who were true believers, who began re-evangelizing England. They even re-evangelized continental Europe—Boniface going to the Germans—all the way down to Lake Constance (the Bodensee), where Huss would later be murdered after Rome broke its word promising him safe passage but then saying, "Holy Mother the church is not obliged to keep her promises to such people." The Celtic church was a tremendously faithful church. They had their own translation of the New Testament called the *Book of Cells*, and that was their belief. When all the manuscripts of the Bible were burned by the Vikings in the West and by the Muslims in the East, Irish monks copied the greatest body of manuscripts and codices extant today, and they come from that period. It was the Irish who preserved our Bibles. They have a wonderful missionary tradition.

Papal Destruction of Celtic Christianity

In AD 597 Augustine (not Augustine of Hippo but another Augustine) was sent to England by the pope to catholicize the Celtic church and bring it into submission to the papacy. He largely succeeded in England but the Welsh refused to submit to Roman authority. The story is told that prior to meeting Augustine the Celts in Wales asked their oldest elder, "How will we know when we meet him if he is a true man of God?" The old man replied, "If when you enter his presence, if he is a true man of God, he will rise to his feet to greet you." Well, they entered his presence, and Augustine remained seated.

It is interesting that Leviticus 19:32 says, "*Rise up before the gray headed* (the hoary head, AV) *and honor the aged.*" Perhaps the old Celt knew this. It used to be considered good manners to stand up when a visitor or an older person came into the room. When Stephen was stoned in Acts 7 he looked up and saw Jesus standing. Jesus is always the perfect example. Certainly Augustine is not.

In AD 664, after much political connivance, the English Celtic church, at a place called Whitby in Yorkshire, acquiesced to the authority of the papacy.

The Irish continued to hold on to the *Book of Cells* until Pope Adrian IV threatened to excommunicate Henry II, a Norman, if he did not invade Ireland and put an end to the Celtic church. Try telling an Irish Catholic that the way the English got involved with their country was because the pope sent them to put an end to biblical Christianity! They do not know their history but that is how it began.

Other Papal Envoys

Around 480 Benedict, based at Monte Casino, developed a rule for monastic orders. He was influenced by Basil the Great of the Capodicean fathers. Again, his intentions may have been good because the monks were, at this point, trying to react against corruption in the hierarchy.

Then came Gregory I, known as Gregory the Great. Some people said he had a lot of good points, but he was the last and most important of the founders of Roman Catholicism who were called the "doctors" of the church. Remember, Ambrose, Jerome, Augustine and Gregory are the four main founders of Roman Catholicism, not counting Constantine.

Gregory developed the doctrines of Purgatory and the mass. He was the grandson of Felix III who had also been a leader of the church in Rome. He began to proclaim himself as the ecumenical patriarch, the Bishop of Bishops, but having primacy over all other bishops. This was first claimed by Gregory. But it can be traced back to the concept of monoepiscopy, which began with Ignatius of Antioch (c. 35 - c. 110), probably the third Bishop of Antioch. Gregory was a turning point; he really led the way into the Dark Ages.

Anselm, around 1063, was known for faith-seeking understanding, and he wrote something called *Cur Deus Homo*. This gives full rise to the theme of the Greek/Hebrew way of thinking. The Greek way of thinking says, "Give me understanding, then I will believe." The Hebrew way of thinking says, "I will believe, then I will understand, then God will show me." God uses both of these. In Isaiah 1:18 he says, "*Come, let us reason together.*" God wants to reason with man concerning man's sin. God will use the Greek way of thinking to bring an unsaved person into an encounter with Himself. But after people get saved God expects them to shift from the Greek way of thinking to the Hebrew, and trust Him by faith. Then they will understand. There is a place for both. God uses the Greek way to get people saved but, once they are saved, He expects them to think the Hebrew way.

Abellard (c. 1079), following on the ideas of Anselm, said it is **not** by faith.

St. Bernard de Clairvaux (1090 - 1153) was their greatest theologian of the 12th century. But try telling a Roman Catholic that St. Bernard denied transubstantiation! St. Bernard said that it was not what Jesus was talking about when He said, "Unless you eat of the flesh of the Son of Man."

Peter Lombard (c. 1147) wrote the *Four Books of Sentences* and he began to define the seven sacraments. Sacramentalism took a firm root before Augustine with Cyprian in the third century, but it was formally canonized with Peter Lombard in 1147.

In 1250 there was the Fourth Lateran Council under Pope Innocent III, and what was innocent about him no one knows. He affirmed auricular confessions and transubstantiation.

This recalls what Jesus was talking about to Thyatira: food sacrificed to idols. There is an Aramaic prayer in the Sephardic Passover *Haggida*. It is the prayer Jesus would have said at the Last Supper because it is Aramaic. And it uses the language of an allegory:

> "*This is like the bread our fathers ate in the wilderness.*"

When it is understood what Jesus was doing in the Last Supper, and it is understood what Jesus was saying in John 6 ("I am the bread of heaven," "Unless you eat my flesh..."), it is impossible to come up with the doctrine of transubstantiation. When it is understood as "the evening meal" (Jn. 13:3),

140

it is impossible to arrive at the doctrine of transubstantiation. It is a memorial, it is a commemoration: *"Do this in remembrance of Me."* That is exactly what the Passover is about, remembering. Additionally there is the exact Aramaic prayer Jesus would have recited. Transubstantiation is totally crazy. Even their St. Bernard denied it. Nonetheless, Pope Innocent III thought differently and he claimed the *"sensus pleniore"* gnosis.

The Waldenseans and Others Who Stood Firm

At this time a very dynamic group of believers began evangelizing. They were called the Waldenseans. Simple people, forced to live at Piedmont in the higher Alps in Northern Italy, they watched their children die of exposure and hunger because as soon as they came down, the papal armies would exterminate them. These people were noble, Gospel-believing, Gospel-preaching people sending missionaries all over the place. There was never a time even in these dark times when God did not have faithful witnesses (like Antipas at Thyatira) and a true church. The Protestants like to believe that they rediscovered the Gospel when in fact there were people who had never lost it.

After this some people began to realize how bad things were. At an early point Francis of Assisi challenged the church. Many believe he was a true believer. He had some crazy doctrines, putting ashes in his food, etc. He said he was married to Lady Poverty, the bride of Christ, in a reaction against the materialism of the church.

One pope said, looking at the papal treasury, "We can no longer say, 'silver and gold have I none.'" A Roman Catholic saint then said to him, "Neither can we say, rise up and walk!"

Reacting against this, Francis of Assisi was one of the first major figures to try to change the Roman Catholic Church from within and failed. By going back to the love of Jesus and a simple Christ-centered faith, caring for the poor, living simply, he affected people in his own lifetime. The Franciscans were at an early stage in their later ugly history, initially more noble, and they were persecuted by the other Catholic religious orders. The fighting that went on between the religious orders is a whole area they do not want you to know about. One pope put another pope on trial and rival popes placed anathemas (curses and excommunication) on each other. Nonetheless, Francis of Assisi tried.

When the Renaissance began, back came the old conflict between the Aristotelians and the Platonists. At this point the main Platonist was Bonaventure, but the main Aristotelian was Aquinas. Currently the same thing is happening in the Muslim world today. We have elsewhere addressed the fact that Judaism went into a crisis and someone called Rambam, whose actual name was Moses Maimonides, went from Spain to North Africa and wrote what he called, *The Guide for the Perplexed*. He totally rewrote Judaism in Aristotelian terms. Thomas Aquinas wrote a Christianized version of it called *Suma Theologia*. The entire world view changed because of this avalanche of Aristotelianism that came from the Muslim world centered in Alexandria. Every time world views change there are major changes in philosophy. But if Rambam comes along and does it for Judaism, somebody has to come along and to it for Roman Catholicism.

Transmutation and Transubstantiation

The doctrine of transubstantiation, the eating of food sacrificed to idols that Jesus it talking about to Thyatira, is already going on, but how can it be explained to people with an Aristotelian world view? Aristotle had this idea of accidents and substance, hypostasis and accidents, wherein it is postulated that accidents (appearance) and substance can be different. As we have established, scientifically it is all nonsense, but at that time it was not because they did not know that transmutation of the elements is impossible; elements cannot mutate.

Consider a hypothetical Bert Jones. But the accidents of Bert Jones—is he married or single, does he have children, how much does he weigh, how much hair does he have, how many teeth—the accidents, the details, surrounding him are mutable, they can change. But Bert Jones is Bert Jones. It is a crazy thing, but Thomas Aquinas came along and said that in transubstantiation the accidents do not change, it is Bert Jones that changes. The bread and wine become Jesus even though it still looks like bread and wine. It is a totally Aristotelian idea, absolutely crazy, with no basis in science whatsoever. As the Enlightenment came and science progressed, people knew it was ridiculous, but *Semper Eadem*, they can't change it; *Idj T'had*, they cannot change it. Once it becomes part of the canon, it cannot be changed. The Roman Catholic Church cannot change it. Babylon cannot be healed (Jer. 51). Jeremiah said they would be sacrificing cakes to the Queen of Heaven and that is what they do.

In 1265 Duns Scotus came up with the idea of the Immaculate Conception, that Mary had no sin, but it was not proclaimed an official doctrine until the 19th century.

William of Ockham (c. 1324) taught "blind faith." However, he did question the authority of the pope to supersede Scripture, and that opened a door.

I Know Your Faith – The Message of Jesus to This Church

Returning to what Jesus is getting at in Revelation, He began by saying all these good things despite these abominations.

"I know your deeds, your love and faith and service and perseverance, and that your deeds of late are greater than at first."

It began with people like Francis of Assisi. It went on to people like the Catholic mystics. Later there were people such as Madame Guyon and Vincent de Paul who really cared for the poor. Tremendous people. Another was John Tyler who cared for the sick during the Black Plague. He said that the Black Plague and the decimation of Europe's population was a judgment because of sin. Thomas a Kempis wrote *The Imitation of Christ*. In England there was John Wycliffe and the Lollards. They tried to get back to the Word of God, but the bishops burned their English Bibles and the Lollards with them until enough Parliamentarians were converted to put a stop to it. These were true believers from the Roman Catholic Church who tried to change it from within.

During the height of the Renaissance when Savonarola tried to react against what he knew was idolatry, he began reading the Bible, for which they killed him. But he saw the corruption against which he stood. That same corruption still exists, and all but gone are the Savonarolas who are willing to stand on the Word of God and oppose it. He knew what idolatry was from reading the Bible, but they killed him. He was a monk in the style of Thyatira. Jesus knew his deeds, his love, his faith.

A most truthful book and film that describes Roman Catholicism is *The Name of the Rose*, authored by Umbert Ecco. It really shows what the whole church was like and it gets into the effects of Aristotle, the Platonists, the corruption and hypocrisy in the monasteries and the hierarchy. This book and film is essential for anyone wanting to truly grasp the flavor of the treachery, hypocrisy and debauchery of Roman Catholicism and what it is like in its own element. (I offer a caveat about one graphic sex scene between a novice monk and a peasant girl.)

Principal Heresies of Rome

Read a few doctrines of Roman Catholicism from their Catechism bearing their *nihil obstat* and *imprimatur*, confirming it as official Roman Catholic dogma.

Quoting from the Catechism of the Council of Trent: "It is lawful to have images in the church and to give honor and worship unto them. Images are put in the churches that they must be worshipped. Therefore those who do not worship these images are not true to the teachings of the church."

143

Remember, the Hebrew word "to worship, to genuflect, to bow down, to give obeisance," is all the same word, *histahavot*. Whenever someone kneels before a graven image they are committing an act of idolatry. Read the book of Esther or the book of Daniel.

Can Mary, the priests or the saints be anyone's mediators? Turning to the Roman Catholic *Bible* the answer is "no," Jesus is the only Mediator with the Father. But turning to the Roman Catholic Church the answer is "yes," they are our mediators. And so it goes on and on. It is a total replacement for the original ideas of the New Testament.

Here is a list of the principal heresies:

- Third century – Sacerdotal mass performed by "priests" was instituted by Cyprian.
- 300 – prayers for the dead
- 300 – The sign of the cross
- 320 – Wax candles
- 375 – The veneration of angels, dead saints and images
- 394 – The mass becomes a daily ritual
- 431 – The exaltation of Mary; the term Theotikos – "Mother of God," was first applied at the Council of Ephesus
- 500 – Priests wearing distinct clothing to separate them from the common people
- 526 – Extreme Unction
- 593 – The doctrine of Purgatory
- 600 – Latin required to be used in worship as official liturgy
- 600 – Prayers offered to Mary, dead saints and angels
- 610 – The first man officially declared to be pope, Boniface III
- 709 – Kissing the pope's feet, a custom coming from emperor worship
- 750 – Temporal powers of popes conferred by Pepin, king of the Franks (Jesus said his kingdom was not of this world and He refused political power)
- 786 – Veneration of the cross, images and relics was authorized
- 850 – The use of holy water (water mixed with salt and chrism and blessed by a priest)
- 890 – The veneration of St Joseph
- 927 – The College of Cardinals
- 965 – The baptism of bells instituted by John XIII
- 995 – The canonization of dead saints by Pope John XV
- 998 – Fasting on Fridays and for Lent

Thyatira

- 11th century – The mass made a sacrifice, attendance made obligatory
- 1079 – The celibacy of priests declared, a doctrine of demons according to Paul
- 1090 – The Rosary, of pagan origin, adopted by Peter the Hermit
- 1184 – The Inquisition and the use of violence and torture instituted by the Council of Verona
- 1150 – The sale of indulgences
- 12th century – The seven sacraments defined by Peter Lombard
- 1215 – Transubstantiation defined by Innocent III
- 1215 – Auricular confession, the sacrament of penance for sins, confessed to a priest instead of to God, instituted by Innocent III
- 1220 – Adoration of the wafer, saying it is God, decreed by Pope Honorius III
- 1229 – At the Council of Valencia the Bible was forbidden to laymen and the Bible was placed on the Index of Forbidden Books
- 1251 – The Scapular (a pair of small cloth squares joined by shoulder tapes and worn under the clothing on the breast and back as a sacrament) invented by Simon Stock of England, probably from Walthamstow
- 1414 – The cup was forbidden to the laity at Communion by the Council of Constance
- 1439 – Purgatory proclaimed as dogma by the Council of Florence
- 1545 – Tradition of the church was declared equal authority with the Bible by the Council of Trent (Jesus condemned teaching the traditions of men as doctrine as a hell-damning offense against God and man)
- 1546 – The apocryphal books added to the Bible at Council of Trent
- 1560 – The Creed of Pope Pius IV took the place of the earlier Creed
- 1854 – The Immaculate Conception of Mary was proclaimed by Pope Pius IX
- 1864 – The Syllabus of Errors was proclaimed by Pope Pius IX and ratified by the Vatican Council which condemned freedom of religion, freedom of conscience, freedom of speech, the press, scientific discoveries and authority of rulers not approved by the pope
- 1870 – Infallibility of the pope in matters of faith and morals
- 1950 – The Assumption of Mary was proclaimed by Pope Pius XII
- 1965 – Mary proclaimed the mother of the church by Pope Paul VI

Bloodshed and Genocide Continued and Rewarded by the Papacy

In 1492 Columbus discovered America. Genocide was used to steal the gold of the Incas and the Indians and bring it to Europe. The pope proclaimed that the year 1992 commemorated the 500th anniversary of the arrival of the Gospel in South America. He tried to canonize the Inquisitors such as Juniper Serra who tortured those Indians. But interestingly this same pope, John Paul II, visited a synagogue in Italy and, after 500 years, he admitted that the Spanish Inquisition was a mistake. What else is torturing and murdering half a million people? Just a "mistake"?! They even used to have "Jew Inspectors" and much more. The same pope, at that 500th anniversary of the Inquisition, tried to canonize Isabella, the very monarch who carried out these terrible deeds with the connivance of the church!

Once more, in *Opus Dei*, John Paul II canonized Jose Marie Escrive, a pro-Hitler political fascist.

Signor Monsignor Tissot, Roman Catholic Archbishop and a personal friend of Hitler, who was president of Nazi-occupied Slovakia, was the first man to transport Jewish children to Auschwitz, an estimated 100,000 of them. When he was hung for his war crimes they said, "Don't you know that you have killed tens of thousands of innocent people?" He replied, "Not people, Jews." He was never defrocked. He was a friend of the pope, a friend of Hitler, appointed to a Nazi political position, and he deported at least 100,000 children to the ovens.

Once again, as documented, John Paul II also paid homage to Archbishop Stepinac, the supporter of the Ustashi (the Croatian Nazi party) who murdered 750,000 Serbs, sparing only those who converted to Roman Catholicism. At the height of conflict in Yugoslavia, John Paul II used the German Catholic Church to pressure the German government to give diplomatic recognition to Croatia, inflaming tensions further.

The Roman Catholic clergy blessed Nazi emblems. The Pontifical Legate, Marcioni, received the Nazi salute, "Heil Hitler" from a group of Hitler Youth. This was the personal representative of Pope Pius XII.

Hitler came to power initially through a coalition with the Zentrum, the Catholic party of Bavaria headed by Hans von Papen, Privy Chamberlain to Pope Pius XI who, before becoming pope, had been Papal Nuncio to Germany. During the First World War Von Papen was a terrorist who committed the largest terrorist attack in the United Stated prior to September 11, 2001. He used Irish Catholic stevedores to plant pipe bombs on ships carrying war supplies to Britain and France, and carried out the infamous Black Tom attack in New York harbor creating the most devastating terrorist explosion that has ever occurred until modern times. Von Papen, the Bin Laden of his day, then slipped out of the USA and assumed his political position within the Roman Catholic Church that forged the alliance which bore Hitler to power. He was later sentenced as a war criminal at the Nuremburg trials. This terrorist's sentence was later commuted to eight years after the intervention of his mentor, Pius XII.

Today's problems in Yugoslavia go back to this time. There was a Holocaust committed by the Roman Catholic Church against the Orthodox Serbs and now can be seen its repercussions. The Serbs were suppressed by Tito, and now the suppression is taken out of the way. The pope's representative received the salute "Heil Hitler!" and killed little children. There are pictures of the Franciscan Brother Philipovitch in his Ustashi Nazi uniform as chief of the Jasinovak Concentration Camp.

Cardinal Michael Schmauss was a Jesuit who Pope John XXIII elevated to Cardinal and called "The Theologian of Munich." It was well known that he was the author of a Treatise called *Empire and State* in which he said it was the obligation of German-speaking Catholics to support Adolf Hitler because the Third Reich unites German people with Catholic Christianity.

When did John XXIII change his tune? After the Eichmann trials when it was discovered that it was the Vatican that got all these Nazi war criminals to South America.

Peron in Argentina, Jemayel in Lebanon, Franco in Spain, Hitler in Germany, Mussolini in Italy, every one of these fascist regimes was backed totally by the hierarchy of the Roman Catholic Church, every one of them. The German bishops made a treaty with Adolf Hitler in the late 1930s that gave him the blessings of Pope Pius XII.

Thus there was Fuhrer Hitler and Vice Fuhrer von Papen, Deputy Fuhrer to the Third Reich and Privy Chamberlain to Pope Pius XII, sentenced at Nuremburg and now, having already canonized Escrive, there are those in the Vatican wanting to beatify Stepinac and Pius XII!

"Were they ashamed because of the abomination they have done?
They were not even ashamed at all;
They did not even know how to blush.
Therefore they shall fall among those who fall;
At the time that I punish them,
They shall be cast down," says the LORD. *(Jer. 6:15)*
"There is nothing new under the sun!"

The Dilemma of Laodicea

In Franco's Spain the official press of the Roman Catholic Church eulogized Hitler as a great champion of the Catholic people.

Cardinal Innziger of Vienna said, "It is the obligation of Roman Catholics to support Adolf Hitler. Adolf Hitler is the envoy of God. Heil Hitler!"

These were not ordinary priests, they were the hierarchy. There were a lot of individual Catholics who did not support Hitler. But it was the hierarchy of the church. The hierarchy! Today, what are they doing? They have canonized the founder of Opus Dei, Jose Marie Escrive, a Nazi. What are they doing by trying to canonize Isabella who carried out the Inquisitions?

Prior to America's entry into the Second World War, while Britain was being bombed, and while Jews and Gypsies were being rounded up to be gassed and Europe was overrun, a Jesuit priest, the infamous Father Coughlin, preached his radio sermons to 20 million Catholic Americans. He lauded Hitler and his Third Reich in an attempt to mobilize Catholic America against war with Germany. John Kennedy Sr. (father of JFK) bought political power after making a fortune in organized crime during prohibition and was appointed US ambassador to the Court of St. James in London. As American Ambassador to Britain this Roman Catholic gangster urged President Franklin Roosevelt to curtail support for Britain's stand against Hitler's onslaught while even Catholic countries in Europe such as France, Hungary and Poland were under Nazi occupation. The rum-running activities of Kennedy, corrupt Boston politics which linger to this day, and Roman Catholicism, all went hand in hand. The relationship between the Italian and Sicilian Mafia and the Catholic Church in both Italy and the USA was, and many say is, endemic.

As always, the corrupt banking families of Italy such as the Borgias and the Medicis vied to get their family members into the papacy to advance banking interests in the Middle Ages. This corrupt history of Vatican banking endures to the present day as was seen in the Calvi murder in London. Dozens of people were murdered in the Ambrosiano Bank scandal, with the Vatican paying hundreds of millions of dollars in compensation to fraud victims. Meanwhile John Paul II refused to hand over the president of the Vatican Bank, Bishop Paul Marcinkus, to the Italian police authorities who wanted to question him in connection with the scandal. John Paul II instead gave him refuge from the law in the Vatican where he headed the Vatican's bank as head of "The Ministry of Religious Works."

The Vatican remains a holding company for a chain of Italian banks such as the Catholic Bank of Venuto and, if one can believe it, "The Bank of the Holy Spirit." According to the Catholic Church, the Holy Spirit is in the business of usury and filthy lucre. This appears to be fine with some of the leading ecumenical Protestants such as Chuck Colson, Pat Robertson and J. I. Packer who signed *Evangelicals and Catholics Together*. Indeed, why should Robertson not sign? He, too, misuses Christianity for political aims and, after beginning a Christian broadcasting empire with the contributions of Evangelical donors, sold it to Rupert Murdoch and legally finagled a way to pocket the money.

Religion, to such people, comes down to politics and money. It is a game the Vatican has played for years. By its own actions the Vatican admits to political and financial corruption combined with religious hypocrisy of a proportion that would have made the Sanhedrin blush.

As we have already noted, under John Paul II, the same religious institution that protected war criminals and gangsters within its ranks remained true to itself and its history by protecting child-molesting priests and nuns within its ranks. In the inferno of the *Divine Comedy* in the Middle Ages, Dante placed popes in the deepest crevices of hell. Looking at Pius IX, Pius XII and John Paul II, it is easy to understand why.

They say they have changed? They cannot change! Babylon cannot be healed. (Jer. 51:9)

> *I heard another voice from heaven, saying, "Come out of her, my people, so that you will not participate in her sins and receive of her plagues; (Rev. 18:4)*

The Practice of Roman Catholicism is Sin

It is not possible to practice Roman Catholicism without sinning, whether consciously or not.

There are sins which in Hebrew are called *buruth*—"without knowing," or inadvertent or unintentional (Lev. 4:1, Heb. 9:7). All the sins that were covered by the blood of animals in Leviticus were unintentional sins. For intentional sins you were stoned. But once you understand that something is sin, then it becomes deliberate sin to continue to do it.

Understand that the Holy Spirit in Hebrew is the *Ha Ruach HaQodesh*, the "Spirit (literally 'breath') of Holiness." He will never lead someone to sin. He cannot do that. That is not how the Holy Spirit operates. It follows, therefore, that when people say that Roman Catholics should stay in their church, or that the Holy Spirit led them to stay in their church, it is the same as saying "The Spirit of Holiness led me to sin."

The Dilemma of Laodicea

When someone bows down, bending the knee, worshipping an image, even to one representing "anything in heaven" (Ex. 20:4, the Second Commandment), but particularly to one they know does not represent the living God, they are committing idolatry. Likewise, when they take the Roman Catholic Eucharist, eating food that has been worshipped, they are committing immorality.

All idolatry is sin. No one can be a Roman Catholic without taking the wafer. Not only that, but they are participating in idolatry with those who believe a different gospel. The Roman Catholic Church teaches that salvation comes through the sacraments ministered by their priests, not through trusting only in Christ. This can be read in their own catechisms. Which of the two gospels should be believed?

Praying to the dead is a sacrilegious abomination. It is called necromancy and is akin to calling up the spirits of the dead, as King Saul did with the witch of Endor. God killed Saul for that faithless deed—for inquiring after a witch and not inquiring of Him (1 Chr. 10:14). No one can practice this religion without sinning.

Is it going to change? Well, if Francis of Assisi could not change the Roman Catholic Church, people today are not going to change it. They put Madame Guyon in prison, the charismatic Catholic of her century. They put John of the Cross in prison for 13 years. He tried to change it from within and he was the charismatic Catholic of his century. If Vincent de Paul could not change it from within, nor Erasmus, nor Luther, nor Calvin, nor Zwingli, nor all the martyrs—Tyndale, Latymer, Ridley, Hooper, Cranmer and thousands more—then who can? None of them set out to design a Reformation, they all began by trying to change the church of Rome from within.

We are not saying that Madame Guyon, John of the Cross, Vincent de Paul, or Frances of Assisi were doctrinally solid in all of their beliefs—they most certainly were not—but they knew from common sense and even the rudimentary knowledge of the teaching of Jesus that the Roman Catholic system did not abide in that teaching. Thomas a Kempis almost certainly was a regenerate believer, and many of the Humanist scholars such as Erasmus, John Colet, and Lefevure certainly understood the deviation from the New Testament they witnessed in the church of Rome, as did the "Common Life Brethren" and Staupitz who helped inspire Luther and the Reformation. None of these however, could change Rome from within as desperately as they tried. Neither will anyone truly change it today. Roman Catholicism is *semper eadem*—"always the same."

Repent, Those Who Commit Adultery with Her – She Misleads My Servants

"He who has an ear, let him hear what the Spirit says to the churches."

God's Spirit is the Spirit of Holiness and He will never contradict His Word. Out of love for one's friends in Babylon some may long to see Babylon changed. But whoever ceases to eat and drink with her at her idolatrous mass will be thrown out.

The Word of God says, *"Come out of her, my people."* Nothing in the Word of God suggests that Babylon will ever change. At the end of the day everyone must decide whose people they are. It is a decision which each person must make for himself. He will either walk with the harlot of Babylon or with the Lord and Messiah, Yeshua of Nazareth. Each and every individual must make this choice. As Moses put it in Deuteronomy 30, "Choose life."

Yeshua's sacrifice is once and for all (Rom. 6:10, Heb. 7:27, 9:27, 10:10, 10:14, 1 Pe. 3:18). No further sacrifice or penance or Purgatory or indulgence is necessary, only faith in Yeshua, and thanks to Him for His wonderful sacrifice. If perfection could be improved on it would not be perfection.

There is no place for a truly saved Christian in Roman Catholicism because it is a deep thing of Satan. And it was taught by Jezebel. Those in ancient Thyatira had no place else to go so the Lord put no further burden on them beyond keeping themselves from the corruption within their local church. Those in the age of Thyatira such as the Lollards, the Waldenseans and the Bohemian Brethren, found a place to go, but they paid a high price for it. Those in such an abominable church today not only have a place to go but it costs them nothing to leave in comparison to the price paid by others in the past. They need to get out fast.

Jesus calls them "My *servants*" even if they who have been seduced by Jezebel's dark secrets of the occult and those in Babylon He calls "My *people*."

"Come out of her, My people." (Rev. 18:4)

Chapter 5
Sardis: "Incomplete" – The Reformation
Mainly 16th Century Onward

1st	2nd	3rd	4th	5th	6th	7th	8th	9th	10th	11th	12th	13th	14th	15th	16th	17th	18th	19th	20th

Apostolic Church
Pre-Nicean Church
Rise of the Institutional Church
The Dark Ages
The Reformation
Great Awakening
Apostate Church

The Message to Sardis

"To the angel of the church in Sardis write:

"'He who has the seven Spirits of God and the seven stars, says this:

"""I know your deeds, that you have a name that you are alive, but you are dead. Wake up, and strengthen the things that remain, which were about to die; for I have not found your deeds completed in the sight of My God. So remember what you have received and heard; and keep it, and repent. Therefore if you do not wake up, I will come like a thief, and you

will not know at what hour I will come to you. But you have a few people in Sardis who have not soiled their garments; and they will walk with Me in white, for they are worthy. He who overcomes will thus be clothed in white garments; and I will not erase his name from the book of life, and I will confess his name before My Father and before His angels.""

"He who has an ear, let him hear what the Spirit says to the churches." (Rev. 3:1-6)

Hate evil, you who love the LORD *(Ps. 97:10)*

The City of Sardis

Sardis was the provincial capitol of the region of Lydia, first evangelized by Paul the apostle and his colleagues in the book of Acts, although there is no record of him having entered the city itself. Sardis had a temple to Artemis which in its size and grandeur easily rivaled the temple to Artemis at Ephesus. Because of its topography it was naturally fortified and easily defended, and it was a city in which Greek, Roman, Jewish, and Persian influences converged. It had a healthy and thriving appearance giving not only its citizens but its Christians a false sense of security and achievement when in fact it was not quite what it thought it was. And neither was its church.

Future Historical Prophetic Antitype

Typologically, Sardis prophetically reflects the development of Protestantism. In the character of Sardis, Protestantism is largely self-deceived and wrongly assured. As we shall observe, just as there were convergent cultural, religious, and philosophical influences in the ancient city of Sardis, the Reformation would see such a convergence of influences. These included Greco-Roman with a rediscovery of Greek biblical texts alongside the Latin Vulgate (favored by John Calvin), and Judaism with a rediscovery of the Old Testament. As well, there were various philosophies that included both Greek and Roman. And like Sardis with its historical link to Persia (present-day Iran), with a trace of Aryan identity ("Iranian" is the Persian word for "Aryan"), so too the mainstream Reformation began among Germanic Aryans such as Luther and Zwingli.

The constellation of events brought together the end of feudalism and the birth of capitalism, and with it the beginning of the end of agricultural economy and the prelude to an industrial economy catalyzed by developments in science and technology. This paved the way socially, politically, and economically for the Reformation. This is crucial in our final understanding of Laodicea that we shall encounter toward the end of this book, but the foundation to properly understand this must be laid here in the age of Sardis.

The astronomy of Galileo and Copernicus dispelled the old astronomy of Ptolemy which the Hellenized Roman Catholic system held sacrosanct, even at times excommunicating and imprisoning those who accepted the increasingly irrefutable scientific conclusions of Galileo, Copernicus, Keppler, and Tyco Brahe with the invention of the astrolabe, discoveries of new worlds, and trade with the Far East. That which had remained so much a mystery until Marco Polo now became reality. Christopher Columbus, Frances Drake, and Ferdinand Magellan pioneered a transoceanic transport not attempted since the Vikings in the West and Zhang He in the East. Genghis Khan had nearly brought the East to the West, but no one had ever brought the West to the East. And the Americas, Caribbean, Oceana, and the South Pacific had been unknown to the Western world. The explorations of Prince Henry, Vasco De Gama, and the Spanish Conquistadors such as Cortez, Balboa, Pizarro, Coronado, De Soto, and Ponce De Leon revolutionized people's perceptions and perspectives of their world. The new horizon was lifted in an age when most people rarely traveled more than 25 miles from where they were born, apart from once-in-a-lifetime religious pilgrimages to Canterbury, Rome, or the Holy Land. To the people who had come out of the Dark Ages and the Crusades through the Renaissance their experiences were what the Space Age was to the 20th century when people were forced to view their sphere of existence beyond all previous parameters.

From the Renaissance with its rebirth of Greco-Roman learning came a rediscovery of the Greek language and an increased literacy. The literature of Dante and the political audacity of Machiavelli shocked people's thinking about the established political and ecclesiastical orders. With Savonarola in Florence, the shadow of the true Gospel was once again cast upon the idolatry, superstition, immorality, and corruption of papal Rome and its tentacles. Gutenberg's printing press now made the Scriptures more widely available and no longer the nearly exclusive propriety of monastic communities where debased levels of immorality were flourishing wildly.

The Holy Roman Empire was forced to yield to nationalism as feudalism was left with no choice but to yield to market-driven capitalism. Change was on the horizon. This change would become a process that continued until the end of the Industrial Revolution at the end of the 18th century. The cultural, political and economic transformation of Europe that followed the move from an agricultural to a manufacturing economy was as much a paradigm shift as the contemporary change from an industrial to a high-tech economy has been in modern times. World views changed and governments changed. People were no longer socially and politically identified as subjects of the Holy Roman Empire controlled by mainly German emperors in league with Italian popes, but began to be known as Englishmen, Frenchmen, Germans, Spaniards, and Scots, most with their own culture, language, and royalty to match their ethnicity and newfound political identities.

While the papacy could more readily stop the spread of the Gospel before Bibles could be mass-produced and when Europe had a central government, the papacy now floundered in its efforts to stop a Luther or a Zwingli as it had stopped a Huss or a Wycliffe in earlier periods.

By his own admission Luther preached no new truths but simply reiterated what Huss had proclaimed a century earlier at the expense of his own life. Protected by German princes, unwavering by John Eck, and reinforced by the brilliant scholarship of Erasmus, Luther was able to get away with what others had been martyred for in previous times. Indeed, the Reformers were but Roman Catholic clergy who themselves were second generation humanist scholars and political nationalists—Luther (identifying with Germany), Cranmer (with England), Bucer (with France), and Zwingli (with Switzerland). This would eventually result in wars that were as much religious as they were political and economic, such as Protestant Francis Drake stripping Catholic Spain of its dominance of Atlantic trade. Catholic governance and Protestant governance readily used the church as propaganda and justification in pursuit of their political, economic, and strategic rivalries. Much of this climaxed with the sinking of the Spanish Armada and with the Seven Years' War.

Catholic dynasties such as the Hapsburgs countered the challenging Protestant competition. While without doubt religious freedom was a factor and a very complex equation, it became impossible to say where political and economic reasons for armed conflict ended and where religious liberty began. Worse still, when the persecution of the Anabaptists of Europe by the Lutheran and Reformed churches, and of the later Puritans and Non-Conformists in England, mainstream Protestantism fully demonstrated its act at denying freedom of religious conscious to others just as Rome had denied it to them. Protestantism, like Sardis, had a name for "being alive," but in fact it was dead. It indeed had a faithful remnant and began with the truth, but it ended in a moral depravity and level of apostasy and corruption that rivaled that of the Roman Catholicism.

Sardis, as with Thyatira, must likewise be properly understood in order to correctly discern and grasp the final nature of the church in the age of

Laodicea. Scientific, technological, and cultural changes will always result in social and political changes that will alter the prevailing world view, creating both a challenge and an opportunity for the church to properly present its message of salvation to a changing world where the more it changes, the more in another sense it remains the same. The Gospel is to *always* remain the same. But as with the changing world views in the eras of Augustine, Aquinas, and Calvin, Laodicea will instead seek to modify the Christian message itself along the lines of the new philosophies instead of merely repackaging their method of its presentation. What should be an eternal Gospel becomes an evolving one.

This parallel would be seen nowhere more clearly than in the United States, whose models of government and economy were the most predicated upon biblical principles and guided by what Max Weber interpreted as the "Protestant Ethic." In post-Christian America, liberal Supreme Courts have relabeled the Constitution as an "evolving" document instead of the immutable cast iron set of principles based on Judeo-Christian concepts of justice and morality it was designed to be. This directly parallels the liberal higher critical theological establishment of mainstream Protestantism that likewise reinterprets the Scriptures as an "evolving" body of documentation where moral prohibitions of homosexuality, abortion, and arbitrary divorce are simply interpreted away. Thus the U.S. Constitution is disconnected from the biblical principles that were in large part responsible for its inception. This constitutes a cornerstone of the modern crisis in faith confronting the church today. But to understand how we arrived at this we must understand the errors of the Reformation and of the Reformers. Like the constitutional democracy it helped engender, Protestantism began right, yet ended badly. Once again, there is a proverbial paradigm shift accompanied by the emerging world views of post-Modernism, and even theoretically Evangelical churches are becoming emergent under the tutelage of false teachers and spiritual deceivers such as Brian McLaren, Dan Kimball, and the agendas of Bill Hybels, C. Peter Wagner, and Rick Warren.

The consequences of this are obvious. The end result of emergence in the church, the Purpose-Driven agenda, and the Ecumenical Movement is a return to Thyatira where labyrinths, contemplative prayer, the *Lectio Divina*, and iconic mysticism are misrepresented as an authentic expression of Christianity. As in Thyatira, the true Scriptures are removed from people who instead read badly doctored paraphrases such as *The Message* by Eugene Peterson, often bearing no resemblance in translation to the original meaning of the original Greek and Hebrew. It becomes a "welcome back" to Thyatira where the true Word of God is displaced as the anchor of Christian faith.

As Europe regresses to a re-confederated Roman Empire in what amounts to a non-democratic, multi-cultural, multi-racial federal Europe, sovereignty and national identity revert to the insignificance they were prior to the Reformation. Europe again needs one government with one church to bring about this artificial unity that the Hebrew prophet Daniel warns against and describes as an ultimately futile effort to make iron stick to clay (Dan. 2:41-43). What a citizen of the European Union in Ireland (a Celtic country), in Poland (a Slavic country), in Austria (a Germanic country), and in Portugal (a Latin country) have in common is neither language, history, culture, or cuisine. The only possible uniting factor they have is Roman Catholicism. Hence the Reformation must be reversed for a return to Thyatira. The ecumenical agenda is vital to the survival of mainly unelected Eurocratic government.

In the British Isles, Celts and Anglo-Saxons have never been friends. The uniting of Scotland, Wales, Northern Ireland, and England as the United Kingdom were a direct result of Protestantism and a common fear of the papal threat that came against Britain with the Armada, Napoleon, and the Gun Powder Plot. In post-Protestant Great Britain, Northern Ireland, Scotland, and Wales all once again have their own parliaments. With the moral disintegration of the Church of England, conservative members are returning to Roman Catholicism (or in some cases to Eastern Orthodoxy) with the expectation that they will find a more solid moral base for their religious expression. The destination is logical because the Church of England never fully broke with Rome theologically, ritually, or with its "high church" sacramentalism.

Evangelical church growth in the modern world is largely a phenomenon of the developing world that is seeing incredible growth in Africa that threatens the traditional dominance of Islam in certain areas of the Far East, and Roman Catholicism in Latin America and other places such as the Philippines. What happened in Europe with the Reformation in the 16th century is now taking place in Mexico, Central America, and Brazil. Pentecostalism and Baptist churches are expanding in Romania, Italy, Spain, and other countries that never had the Reformation, while Britain, Holland, and Germany are witnessing the self-inflicted death of their Protestant heritage with declining population, declining church attendance, a moral landslide, and full-blown theological degeneration as bad or worse than Roman Catholicism.

Sardis

It is ironic that as Chuck Colson struggles to push Protestantism and to urge born-again Christians toward Rome, Pope Benedict XVI openly enunciates the illegitimacy of all churches *except* Rome. While millions are converting *to* born-again Christianity *out* of Roman Catholicism in Latin America, in French-speaking Africa and the Caribbean, and to an appreciable degree in both Europe and North America, as well as in pockets in Asia such as the Philippines, Chuck Colson and his cohorts are ushering the Roman Catholic population of the developed world back in the direction of the Vatican and its popes.

While homosexuality and lesbianism are indeed widespread among the Roman Catholic clergy, homosexual ordination is not the official policy of the Vatican. Yet the largest Protestant denominations in Britain, Europe, and America—including Anglicans, Methodists, Presbyterians, Lutherans, and various Reformed denominations—are *all* actively ordaining homosexuals, and this trend is now beginning to make headway among Evangelical Protestant churches.

One would not find a Roman Catholic theologian authoring a book or document bearing the *imprimatur* or *nihil obstat* of the papacy denying the historicity of the virgin birth of Christ or His resurrection. Among liberal Protestants however, such views are promulgated commonly. As Erasmus predicted would happen, Protestantism, in short, has become worse both morally and theologically than what it set out to correct and reform.

Refusing to either embrace Protestantism or defend the papacy, Erasmus declared himself as preferring to be an observer of what he described as a "travesty." Considering that it was Erasmus who proverbially laid the egg that Luther merely hatched, it was of interest that Erasmus, in a letter to the pope, defended the Anabaptists as being more biblically Christian than either main faction. Realizing that Protestantism had *not* gone back far enough to purely Scripture, Erasmus allowed for believers' rebaptism in the preface to the Gospel of Matthew in his famous translation of the New Testament from where we obtain the *Textus Receptus* (not a source manuscript, but a composite of four earlier Byzantian texts). Ironically it was Erasmus, denounced by the Protestants for not supporting the Reformation and condemned by the Catholics for precipitating it, who most realized the inherent short-comings of Protestantism as well as that of the papacy, and whose views theologically appear closest to the expressed views of Christ. It was only over a hundred years later in the 17th century when the Anabaptists became known as the Mennonites and the Baptists, that Protestant doctrine began to infiltrate their thinking and that they began to be identified as Protestant.

Protestantism arrogantly behaved as if it rediscovered the Gospel, forgetting that there were those such as the Waldenseans who still existed in areas of Italy and France who never lost the Gospel. It was not until the 17th century, with the patronage and protection of benevolent Protestants and the influence of Cromwell, that Waldenseanism was included within the ranks of Protestantism. To this day Waldensean (Valdesi) churches exist in Italy, as do landmark Baptist churches claiming to derive from the same Waldensean tradition still exist in areas of the United States. Even the Mennonites were eventually considered a Protestant sect, not because they came from the Protestant Reformation, but because by popular colloquial definition Protestantism had simply come to mean "not Catholic." Hence, non-Protestant Evangelical groups were almost uniformly swallowed up culturally and, in some cases, institutionally by a broadly defined Protestantism. The radical return to the New Testament envisioned by non-Protestant Evangelicals now became the pursuit more of individuals than of movements.

The demise of Protestantism however, was in the DNA of its very roots; it did not go far enough back to the Word of God from its very onset. As Jesus said to Sardis, their deeds are not complete in His sight; while imagining themselves to be alive, Christ says they are dead.

Background to the Reformation

Some people may think there exists in this book a grudge against the Roman Catholic Church. But what is actually being expressed is a grudge against the devil! Believers should have a grudge against *all* false religion and *all* cults. Believers should have a grudge not against Jehovah's Witnesses as people, but against the JW cult. Believers should not have any grudge against Mormons, but a grudge against Mormonism. Believers should not have any grudge against Freemasons, but a grudge against Freemasonry. Believers should not have any grudge against Eastern Orthodox people, just a grudge against Eastern Orthodoxy. Believers certainly should not have any grudge against Jews, but a grudge against the false Judaism of the rabbis that denies its own Messiah. Believers should certainly have no grudge against Roman Catholics. On the contrary, believers should love Roman Catholics. And because they love them they have a grudge against that false religion that is leading them into the way of perdition. Why take the time to express this so emphatically? Because this is a construction, a panorama of church history, the history of the faithful remnant, and of the devil in his many disguises.

It is impossible to review this panorama in the Western world without devoting the lion's share of the time to Roman Catholicism simply because

Sardis

for over twelve hundred years it was Satan's principal instrument and principal corrupter of the Gospel. When teaching in the Eastern world, in Israel, or in the Middle East, the focus is more on the Eastern Orthodox Church because in the East *that* is the false religious system, although it came out of a break with Rome. Time is running out for throwing rocks at the Church of Rome, and in this chapter begins the rock throwing at the Protestants, also known as "The Reformation"!

"Sardis" comes from the Greek word "*sards*" meaning "flesh." Sardis has to do with being "of the flesh" in the original Greek. Things began getting really bad towards the end of the Dark Ages as was seen when dealing with the church at Thyatira. By the 12th century the following doctrines had been instituted:

- Penance;
- Mandatory auricular confession to a "priest";
- Mandatory attendance at the mass.

The popular propaganda is that these things had been around since the time of the Apostles, but they were not made into doctrines for a thousand years.

What is more, during the Dark Ages the leadership of the Western world under the Roman Catholic religious system went not only into moral decline, but also into cultural and intellectual decline. And while Europe was in the Dark Ages, the Eastern Empire and the Islamic world were having their Golden Age, particularly the Islamic world.

Do not ever underestimate the Arabs. Islam keeps them backward but Arabs are very intelligent, clever people. For over a thousand years they occupied the cultural center of the world. Not only the best merchants and traders were Arabs, but by far the best physicians, architects, engineers, scientists, writers—everything. Similarly, the Byzantine Empire maintained a lot of its Muslim culture, and when the Eastern Orthodox Church split from the Church of Rome and reached its apex in the 1100's, there was the big split between the East and the West.

The problem again is, Babylon cannot be healed—*semper eadem*. Once a doctrine has been proclaimed, they cannot get rid of it. Roman Catholicism has two kinds of doctrine: *Proxima Fide* and *De Fide*. A *Proxima Fide* doctrine, how one practices the faith, can be changed. For instance the mass can be translated from Latin into English. But no one can change *De Fide* doctrine, a doctrine of the faith, such as Transubstantiation or the doctrine that Mary co-redeems people. Or that followers should pray to the dead (to saints) or that they go to Purgatory to pay in part for their own sins. People who think that the Roman Catholic Church can be changed from within do not know anything about Roman Catholicism. It cannot change because of what they call *semper eadem*. The Moslems first called it *idj t'had*.

When the Crusaders saw tremendous architecture, art, magnificent literature, science, medicine and pharmacy, the seeds were planted for what became known as the Renaissance.

The Renaissance had two halves. In those days, even today to a degree, Europe was divided into two halves by the Alps. The Southern Renaissance was Florentine, seen mostly in Italy. The Northern Renaissance was more characterized by Gothic architecture as seen in Britain and France. But the flying buttresses that are seen in the cathedrals were all copied from the Muslim world. So basically there was a rediscovery of Greco-Roman culture, ideas from ancient Athens and ancient Rome rediscovered. Renaissance means "reborn." But they were actually rediscovered at a time of increasing idolatry with statues, images and pilgrimages.

A Return to the Word

During the Renaissance literacy began to increase and people began to read the Bible. Most people could not read it, but the Vulgate was in Latin and priests began to read it more. This created a problem because priests began asking questions. Wycliffe and then Tyndale produced English Bibles and in Germany Guttenberg invented the printing press, on which the first book printed was the Bible in German. A mighty saint of God in Florence called Savonarola (1452 – 1498) saw from reading the Word of God the idolatry and corruption for what it was, and began preaching the true Gospel, telling the truth for what it was. Savonarola, a Dominican monk, aroused the hostility of Pope Alexander VI and was burnt at the stake as a heretic.

Cardinal Raoul, the great Cardinal who was famous during the days of Michelangelo, Bernini and Leonardo da Vinci, said that the writings of St. Paul were immoral and decadent, and that Christians should instead read the Greek and Roman classics such as Cicero. Even to the present era the curriculum in Roman Catholic seminaries is dominated by Greek and Roman classics, not by the Word of God.

But at the beginning of the Reformation, organized groups of people began to emerge. They tried to go back in some way to a simpler Christianity, the Common Life Brethren being the main ones. Once again, remember that before the Reformation there were people trying to get back to the basic Gospel.

In time, there grew out of the Reformation a movement called Humanism. Not secular Humanism as it exists today, but Christian

Sardis

Humanism. It was an academic movement among people who began reading the Bible in the original Greek and Hebrew languages, studying it as history and literature. People began to look at the plain meaning of the Bible, and this movement was born. In the UK Thomas Moore was a Humanist scholar. He was another guy who saw the corruption of Rome for what it was, but did not want to do anything about it. He was loyal to the institution. Many people are like that today.

By far the most important of the Humanist scholars was Desiderius Erasmus (1466-1536) of Rotterdam. Forget about Calvin, Luther, Zwingli, John Knox—the *real* brain behind the Reformation was Erasmus. The others got their ideas from him. In the Counter Reformation, when the Roman Catholic Church began burning all the books it did not like, they not only placed the Bible on the list of banned books and burned Bibles and those who had one as witches, but they saw Erasmus as the cause of the problem.

But people's view of the world began to change; the New World was discovered. What the papacy and the Roman Catholic Church did to the Incas and Aztecs, the sheer robbery, was incredible. The genocide was unbelievable. They stole their gold in the name of Christ and so on. The astrolabe was invented, exploration increased. The astronomy of Ptolemy from the ancient world was replaced by that of Galileo and Copernicus, who the popes tried to excommunicate as heretics because they said the earth moved around the sun. (The Bible expresses it from the earth's perspective when it says the sun rises and sets and rises again. But actually the sun does not rise and fall; it only appears to do so as the earth rotates.)

So a scientific view of the world began to be born. Superstition began to diminish and people became more and more literate, more educated, with a wider world view beyond their little farming village. Also the priesthood, the clergy, began to be exposed for what they were. The clergy were rife with corruption. Many were mendicants who were so totally uneducated that they did not have the intellectual wherewithal to effectively debate the claims of Protestantism. Indeed even John Eck, who did have the intellectual capacity to take on Luther, could not refute him effectively. And finally Erasmus, who Henry VIII (originally an opponent of the Reformation) tried to persuade to enter into a disputation with Luther refused to do so. The pope had no academic weapons left in his arsenal, so as usual, beginning with Pope Julius, the Vatican resorted to its usual weapon of burning at the stake.

As this movement began to take place the Humanists tried to change Christendom from within. As a scholar, Erasmus thought that the church could get back on the right course through education.

The Dilemma of Laodicea

In the 16th century people began to study the Bible for themselves and increasingly saw that the meaning was often simple and straightforward. At the same time they also saw that under the papacy it had become totally corrupted from the influence of the Gnostics (the false teaching that you had to have additional special knowledge to be able to interpret the Bible) and Greek philosophy which sought to allegorize the Bible. However, because the Reformers reacted against allegory, they tended to throw *all* allegory out the window. This was a replay of the ancient patristic conflict between the allegorical and Gnostic Alexandrian school of hermeneutics and the literalist Antiochan school. While the latter was plainly much better than the former, neither represented the Jewish hermeneutics of the original Apostles.

The problem with the Protestants and the Reformers, maybe their *first* problem, was that they liked to pretend that they rediscovered the Gospel. In fact, there were always people who never lost it. There was never a time when God did not have a remnant of faithful, true, Bible-believing Christians. Long before Luther, Calvin and Zwingli there were always sects of true believers. Not only that, there were always individuals within the Roman church who were trying to get back to the Bible as best they could. But the political and social circumstances were not opportune.

(The Book of Daniel reveals that one of the things that will make the Antichrist so dangerous is that the lordship of history is going to be given into his hand for two times, a time and half a time: three and a half years. It will be given to the devil. That is what will make the Great Tribulation so potent. God is the God of history and He establishes kings and He removes kings. The only thing that people like Luther and Calvin and Zwingli did was they managed to get away with things that faithful Christians had always been saying, only the social and political circumstances were not opportune for their predecessors to live to tell about it. The Reformers were able to get away with things that other people died for saying because the papacy lost its power to suppress the Gospel in many countries.)

Trying to Change from Within

Zwingli began his Reformation before Luther began his by nailing his *95 Theses* to the door of the cathedral in Wittenberg in 1525. Zwingli was trying to reform the church in Zurich. Zwingli and Luther, like Erasmus, were Roman Catholic clergy who read the Bible and tried to change the Roman Catholic Church from within. But not only were the Reformers and the Humanists Roman Catholic clergy, they were the intelligentsia of the Roman Catholic clergy. They were the scholars, the top people. Luther was a great scholar. St. Paul was a great scholar! God required people who not

164

only had a right heart but also could read the original languages of the Bible and get back to the original ideas.

Luther learned from a French Humanist called Lefevure the original meaning of the Greek word *metanoia*. The Church of Rome said it meant "to do penance," to go to confession and then do whatever the priest tells you. Luther found out from Lefevure that it meant "to repent," to turn back to God and to stop doing whatever you were doing that was wrong in the eyes of God. His was simply the natural conclusion of what had been building up and building up and building up. Erasmus was the real cause. He was the one who went to the heart of the issue. But Luther rose like a meteor because he took action. He did not expect it to go as far as it did. When he nailed his *95 Theses* to the door of the cathedral the only thing he thought he was doing was calling for a theological debate. But the whole thing exploded like dynamite. They never wanted to begin another church; they all began as people trying to change the church from within.

Regardless of what some people claim today, Babylon cannot be healed. This fundamental point must be understood. Anyone who stands up at the front and corrects them as Jesus did in Nazareth (Luke 4), or as Stephen did in the synagogue in Jerusalem (Acts 7), will experience the citizens of Babylon having them thrown out. Or like Barnabas and Paul did in Antioch in Acts 13:51 where the Jewish leaders stirred up the people and "expelled them from their region." George Fox tried it, John Bunyan tried it, and they were jailed.

The early Christians never wanted to create another church, but they would not compromise the Gospel, so they were forced out of the synagogue. Similarly, the Reformers never wanted to create another religion. But they would not compromise the Gospel, so they were forced out of the Roman Catholic Church. John Wesley never wanted to form another religion, but he was forced out of the Church of England. Believers reach a point where they will either compromise or be thrown out. If they are not willing to be thrown out, their works will have no long-term benefit. Who is it better to listen to, God or man? That was what Jesus kept saying over and over. Peter and John said this in Acts 4:19. Jesus, Peter and John never compromised whatever the cost.

Problems in Sardis, Problems in the Reformation

So the Reformation began, but look at its problems.

"'I know your deeds, that you have a name that you are alive, but you are dead....

That does not sound very nice!

The Dilemma of Laodicea

...Wake up and strengthen the things that remain, which were about to die, for I have not found your deeds completed in the sight of My God."

In other words, they went this far and no further. To reform the church, to really get back to the teaching of the Apostles, they had to radically get back to the New Testament.

"So remember what you have received and heard; and keep it, and repent."

They had heard the Gospel and they should keep on remembering it and not add to it. But in the end, in verse 4, only a few of them really believed it and had not "*soiled their garments.*" Then an insight is provided into what happens after so many evangelistic campaigns today:

*"He who overcomes ... **I will not erase his name from the book of life**, and I will confess his name before My Father and before His angels."*

A man may make a confession of faith one day, apparently being "saved" that day, but he is warned not to fall from that faith but to hold out to the end—quite a test during persecution.

"He who has an ear, let him hear what the Spirit says to the churches." (Rev. 3:1-6)

Why did this thing called the Reformation become something like Sardis, something of the flesh? What was wrong with it? Something was about to die. Things had become very bad during the late Middle Ages but the Gospel was heard. And then in effect Jesus said, "Remember what you heard, keep it, and repent. If you will not wake up, you Protestants, I will come to you like a thief." Mainstream Protestantism is going to be greatly surprised when Jesus comes back.

This can be understood another way. How many people in a group of about a hundred true believers are reformed Presbyterian? One? How many are Anglican, from the Church of England? Five? How many are Lutheran? None? In such a gathering there may be six Protestants. The overwhelming majority of born-again Christians in the world are from non-conformist churches. They are churches that in no way trace their lineage or their identity back to the Reformers. They are Pentecostals, Baptists, independent.

How many in this same group believe only in immersion baptism, and for believers only, and do not believe in baby baptism? Practically everyone. The Reformers had a cure for such people. Zwingli would have cut a hole in the ice in Zurich. Someone wants to get baptized again? They would go under the ice but they would not come back.

How many people believe in the gifts of the Spirit? Oh, the Reformers would have loved them. They look like good firewood! How many believe in the authority of Scripture alone and think that tradition is not essential? A couple of years in the galleys will straighten them out! The Reformers persecuted people like this. It was not they who personally did it, but certainly their followers did. In reality most believers today are much closer to the Anabaptists than to the Protestants.

Anabaptists, Quakers and Experiential Theology

The Anabaptists became hyper-charismatic and hyper-Pentecostal. Not all of them, but enough of them to give the movement a bad name. They began to get into Experiential Theology. There were people called the Zwickau Prophets. They were very similar, both in message and in character, to the Kansas City Prophets of today. One can read what the Zwickau Prophets were saying, and then watch the video of the Kansas City Prophets, and it is amazing. The same things the Vineyard people were saying, the Zwickau Prophets were saying—the same "Kingdom Now" message, the triumphant church, the amillennial/post-millennial position. The whole movement disintegrated into chaos.

Nevertheless, the Anabaptists were much closer to the Bible than the mainstream Reformers. What the Anabaptists said to the Reformers is said to evangelical Protestants today: *"You are born again, you are my brother or sister in Christ, but you do not 'walk in the Spirit'"* (Gal. 5:16, 5:25).

It is also said, "There is a lot more in God's Word"—"We do not need that formal structure; we can meet anywhere—houses, schools"—"We do not ordained clergy; we can just appoint elders from our own leaders; anybody can be a minister"—"Things are too structured; the early church was not like that."

Those are the kinds of things many are saying about the mainstream Protestant denominations. That is what the Anabaptists said to the Reformers and their followers. Only the most trouble someone gets into today is to have a neighbor who will pleasantly disagree with them. The Anabaptists had neighbors who would disagree with them until they were burnt at the stake!

Every charismatic movement in the history of the church has been sabotaged by Satan the same way. The Quakers under George Fox were a charismatic movement in this country. Experiential Theology was their demise. The Anabaptists? Experiential Theology was their demise. The Montanists in the early church? Experiential Theology was their demise.

Those saved in the Jesus Movement, people in the drug culture who became Christians, had a lot of radicalism and a lot of zeal. They would go on the streets witnessing for eight or ten hours a day in order get as many people saved as they could because Jesus was coming tomorrow. And they said the established church was like Laodicea, which was basically true. The trouble with the Jesus Movement was that it lacked knowledge, experience, and a lot of things needed for maturity.

Those groups from the Jesus Movement who combined with the established churches and took their zeal into the established churches produced *Calvary Chapels* and *Jews for Jesus*; they went on to become mainly good things. But the groups of "Jesus freaks," as they used to be called, who stayed on their own tended to become cults. On the other hand the established churches that embraced the Jesus freaks found a new life-blood and a new vitality. But the ones who closed their doors, and most of them did, went where they were going before—nowhere. They were two very different kinds of Christians who needed each other desperately, and when they found each other God brought something very positive encompassing the best of both worlds.

It is like that today. Pentecostals and charismatics have something that Baptists and Brethren need desperately. They need a broader openness to the Holy Spirit without compromising their dependence on the Word of God. But the Pentecostals and charismatics need just as desperately what the Baptists and Brethren have got: dependence on the Word of God. They know the Book a lot better than most. They are two kinds of believers who need each other. The devil wants to keep them apart because he knows what happens when they find each other.

Lessons from the Reformation

If the church is going to get back to what the Apostles taught and what the followers of the Apostles believed, the source of the problem must first be identified then they could get rid of it. It is no good trying to get rid of the symptoms of the disease, they must rid themselves of the disease; then the symptoms will go. The symptoms can only be treated when somebody is beyond cure to alleviate the person's suffering, but ideally they try to get rid of the disease. The Reformers fundamentally failed to go back to Jeremiah...

> *"Behold, days are coming,"* declares the LORD, *"when I will make a new covenant with the house of Israel and with the house of Judah, not like*

the covenant which I made with their fathers in the day I took them by the hand to bring them out of the land of Egypt, My covenant which they broke, although I was a husband to them," declares the LORD. "But this is the covenant which I will make with the house of Israel after those days," declares the LORD, "I will put My law within them and on their heart I will write it; and I will be their God, and they shall be My people. (Je. 31:31-33)

For many people that would automatically suggest some kind of Replacement. The new covenant would not be made with the church, or the Baptists, or the Pentecostals, it would be made with the Jews. All the Reformers believed that the church had replaced the Jews—that they have provided Abraham's seed and fulfilled their lot in Scripture. The Jehovah's Witnesses believe this.

Paul said in Romans 11:18 that *they* do not support the *root*, the *root* supports *them*. But the Reformers did not go back to the root in Romans 11. By not going back to the root as Paul said, forgetting that the root was there and the root was Israel, straightaway they set out on the wrong foot. To reform the church they had to go back to the root and understand this Jewish root. Just as the early church knew that their root was Israel, in the same way all believers have to know that their root is Israel. Not fallen Israel, but *true* Israel. That was one of the first mistakes the Reformers made, ignoring their Hebraic root.

But even today it is found that people who are wrong about the Jews are invariably wrong about other things. Just because someone might be right about Israel does not mean they are automatically right about everything else. There are some people who are right about Israel and off the rails on just about every other subject under the sun. But it is necessary to go back to the root.

Their second mistake was this: *"It will not be like the covenant which I made with their fathers."* What Jeremiah is about is what Paul picks up in Romans. The Jews thought they had an automatic relationship with God because they were part of the state church, the national religion. This was Covenant Theology. John the Baptist was warning, *"God can raise up children of Abraham from these stones"* (Mt. 3:9) as easily as to say you are not special just because you are a Jew.

Paul was dealing with the same thing. He is not a Jew who is one outwardly, but who is one inwardly (Rom. 2:28-29). They were *culturally* Jews, *socially* Jews, but they were not *spiritually* Jews. Paul goes on to say that they were cut off from their own olive tree because of their unbelief.

And Gentiles who are not Jews outwardly are grafted in if they truly believe in Jesus (Rom. 11).

The state church is always a problem. It was a big problem in Jeremiah's day, in the days of John the Baptist, in the days of Jesus and in the days of Paul. But the New Covenant is not like that. "*I will make a new covenant, not like the one I made with your fathers. I will write My law on your hearts.*"

But instead of circumcision the church made baby sprinkling the rite of initiation, whereas the true rite of initiation is a personal saving faith in Jesus. That true faith will cause a person to want to be baptized, like the Ethiopian eunuch of Acts 9:37. As Jeremiah said, "*It will not be like the old covenant.*"

This went well until Constantine made Christianity the religion of the state. And then Augustine came up with the doctrine of the visible and invisible church—that the church is made up of the saved. Therefore, they let everybody into the church and baptized the babies. That is Augustine; the Roman Catholic Church comes from this.

To properly reform the church the Reformers should have thrown out two things:

- the unscriptural marriage between church and state (Erastianism);
- the unscriptural doctrine of the visible and the invisible church.

Only born-again believers, circumcised in heart and confessing faith in Christ like the Ethiopian eunuch, should be initiated through baptism. But instead the Reformers put back the Old Covenant, the promise to the people collectively, not recognizing that Jesus died to get rid of it. First, Constantine put it back, then Augustine put it back, then Luther put it back, then Calvin put it back, Zwingli put it back. Jesus died to get rid of it, but they all put it back. Everyone is therefore baby sprinkled and a member of the church. But not everyone truly believes in Jesus. This brings about Nominalism and makes the unconverted full members of the church.

The Church of England's baptism card even tells babies that they are now full members of the church into which, in the name of the Father and the Son and the Holy Spirit, they have been baptized. It is just so obvious that babies have no understanding, no faith, they have not come to repentance and they are not born again. Not only are they not immersed in the Holy Spirit, they are not immersed in water. Therefore, members of the ruling elite who were never immersed by John the Baptist cannot understand where Jesus is from unless, like Nicodemus, they come to faith. There are a number of things neither Jesus nor any man can do for others, and one of them is to repent.

Look at the result. Britain has a Parliament with atheists, Hindus, unsaved Jews, and Muslims deciding who should be the bishops of the Church of England. It is fundamentally wrong. To reform the church one must get rid of this unscriptural marriage between church and state because if there is one thing that anybody could point to as the turning point toward the downhill for Christianity that was it. They failed to get rid of the unscriptural marriage between church and state.

That is not to say that every church that baptizes babies is full of false believers or unsaved people. Catholics and Anglicans can and do grow in the faith. We all do. But the Church of England declared a few years ago that 4 percent of baptized English Anglicans attended church regularly. The rest are apparently lost sheep without a shepherd. God help a shepherd who has lost so many sheep!

It is fair to say that God's standard for being part of the true church is to be born again, to be saved by one's faith which, Paul explained in Galatians 2:20, is actually the faith of Jesus living in each believer. This should lead into a personal relationship with Him.

When believers fully understand John 1 about the *logos* in Greek, the *mamre* in Aramaic, and *d'var* in Hebrew, there is no question that Jesus was God who became a man to die for their sins. Conversely, those who have not put their faith in Him have a big problem because there is nothing to look forward to except a grave, and that is only the beginning of their problems. But there is something much better on the other side of the hill for those who put their faith in Jesus.

Is it clear what went wrong with the Reformation, and why it was partly of the flesh like Sardis? That is one way it went wrong. They preserved the state church, and the idea of the invisible and the visible church, going back to Augustine instead of to the Bible.

But it also went wrong missiologically in terms of mission. "Go forth and teach all nations." There was one obscure figure known as Justinian Wells who went forth from out of the Reformation to convert the heathen. Luther said that the command of Jesus to preach the Gospel to all nations was already fulfilled because Europe was already "Christianized." The Reformers did not understand world mission. To go back to the original church, it is necessary to return to the idea of mission and evangelism. The Reformers basically did not do that.

Faulty Hermeneutics

Another way the Reformation failed was regarding hermeneutics—the way they interpreted the Bible. The early Christians taught midrashically, thematically. Jesus used the method of the *mashal* and the *nimshal*, teaching through parables as used by other rabbis. The Roman Catholic Church, beginning with Philo in the East, began looking at the Bible much too allegorically due to the influence of Greek philosophy. The Reformers wanted to correct this and so they rejected *all* allegorical interpretations.

There is a proper way to use allegory hermeneutically when interpreting the Bible. The caveat is that doctrine must never be *based* on it; it must be used only to *illustrate* doctrine. But the Reformers, wanting to correct the Roman Catholic error, began using the methods of 16th-century humanism instead of going back to the original Jewish methods of interpreting the Bible.

John Calvin was a second generation Reformer. He was not first generation along with Luther or Zwingli. He used the same method to interpret Scripture that he used to interpret classical literature. However, because Protestantism became so nominal from the beginning, and unbelieving people were invited into the Protestant church, it was only a matter of time before Protestantism became liberal. By the 19th century there were people in Germany such as the Tubegin at university who said they were going to study the Bible not only as history and literature that was inspired, but also as ordinary human history and literature. So liberal Protestant hermeneutics is simply the degeneration of humanist hermeneutics. But in fact no humanist model is the way to interpret the Bible. That is not how the Apostles interpreted Scripture. Examine Galatians 4:24-34, or the Epistle to the Jews (Hebrews): they used midrash, pattern, the thematic approach.

It is not wrong to look at the Bible as literature and history, but that can be only the first step. What the Protestants did was make it the be-all and end-all approach, largely rejecting the spiritual nature of God's Word. With Protestant hermeneutics one does not see midrash, or the way the New Testament quotes the Old.

The New Testament actually quotes the Old out of all reasonable context if one were to use Protestant hermeneutics exclusively. It is only if one interprets the Bible a Jewish way that one can say Matthew was justified in quoting the Old Testament in the context he did when he said, "*Out of Egypt I called My son*" (Hos. 11:1). That is obviously about Israel and the Exodus, but Matthew says it is also about Jesus. Protestant hermeneutics would not affirm that Hosea was talking about Jesus. Matthew appears to have been wrong—unless he was using a method of interpretation different from what Protestants propose. But He was using the Jewish way of interpreting the Bible and the Reformers used the Greek way.

The only good thing of note was that the Greek model used by the Reformers was at least better than what preceded it. They were trying to correct the errors of medieval Roman Catholicism so they did not consider any kind of allegory or deeper spiritual insight at all.

Remember, the Jewish concept of prophecy is not prediction; it is pattern. For example, Abraham came out of Egypt, then the children of Israel came out of Egypt, then Jesus came out of Egypt, and we in our salvation come out of Egypt in 1 Corinthians 10. And the ultimate example will be the rapture of the believers to be caught up in the air on the last day. This is all prefigured by the Exodus. That is the Jewish way of interpretation.

So Matthew could say that Hosea 11 was all about Egypt. But the Humanist/Greek approach of the Reformers would declare that Matthew did it wrong. The deeper things of God, such as Genesis and Revelation will never be interpreted properly using Protestant hermeneutics; they will only be understood by using Jewish hermeneutics. It is, after all, a Jewish book.

Nonetheless, the Reformation did correct the errors of medieval Roman Catholicism to an extent. The Reformers were able to rediscover the plain meaning of the Gospel. Now their Gospel may have been better than what they set out to correct, but once the liberals got hold of it the result was even worse than before.

A Dead Church

"You have a name that you are alive, but are dead."

No one can find any Roman Catholic bishop denying the resurrection or the virgin birth, but one will find Protestant bishops denying those biblical tenets. Also, very few, if any, Roman Catholic bishops are Freemasons, but one will find Protestant bishops who are. It has to be handed to Protestantism—it took the Roman Catholic Church centuries to get to that level of deception and debauchery, but the Protestants did it practically overnight!

Ever hear Luther's last sermon?

"Every Jew should be herded into a coral and forced to confess Christ at the point of a knife. For we should burn their synagogues. Indeed, we the German people, we do not slay them to prove that we are Christians ..." – Martin Luther.

Some people call him the great hero. He began right. "Here I stand, I can do no other." He began as a man of God if ever there was one. God took him away a week after he delivered that sermon, but unfortunately Hitler quoted it 350 years later to justify genocide against the Jews. John Calvin created a theocratic police state in Geneva, imitated by John Knox in Scotland. An actual police state.

They got it fundamentally wrong in a number of very, very basic areas:

- the marriage between church and state;
- the use of violence;
- they did not understand about mission;
- they did not know how to interpret the Bible correctly as a Jewish book; they did not go back to the apostolic approach.

What does Jesus say?

'I know your deeds, that you have a name that you are alive, but you are dead. Wake up, and strengthen the things that remain, which were about to die; for I have not found your deeds completed in the sight of My God. (Rev. 3:1b-2)'

The Reformers' work was never complete, but they did do two things. First, they rediscovered the Gospel in terms of justification by faith in Jesus and grace alone, not by sacraments. There were others who never lost it, but the Reformers rediscovered it. And second, the authority of Scripture. But that is all. Nominalism, false traditions that were merely teachings by men, and unbelief, were rife in Protestantism almost from its inception.

Look at what happened. Hooker, the man primarily responsible for putting together the theology of the Church of England, said, "A member of the British Empire is a member of the Church of England, and a member of the Church of England is a member of the British Empire." Hooker defended the state church.

Luther did the same thing when he wrote in Latin, *Cuius regio, eius religio*—"Whatever your government, that should be your religion." If your government is Catholic, you should be a Catholic; if your government is Protestant, you should be a Protestant. That was Luther. The whole Reformation went off the rails practically at the very beginning.

None of this should dismiss the faith of the martyrs who were burned alive in England even before Luther for simply being in possession of an English text translated by John Wycliffe. In France there were those who would not bow down to the "host," the wafer, and the images, and were burned for their faith, for standing against the monster that is Babylon disguised as Rome. Many recanted. Others would not recant and bow the knee in idolatry. For this they were burned alive.

But what happened as a result? Just as people had tried to reform the Roman Catholic Church from within, so in less than 100 years there were people trying to bring reform to the Protestant church from within. Count Zinzendorf and the Pietists in Germany were one main group. Later in Britain there were the Wesleyans and the Methodists. It became a charismatic movement that was trying to change and restore the Church of England from within.

The main character from the second generation of Reformers was John Calvin. He wrote a massive volume called *Institutes of the Christian Religion*. Calvin was influenced by Martin Büsser, the Reformer of Strasbourg, and by another person in Switzerland called Farel.

Erasmus faded into obscurity, but, significantly, in his preface to the New Testament he wrote at the beginning of St. Matthew's Gospel that there should be anabaptism, a rebaptism (or a first immersion) of believers. He even wrote to the pope and stated that the Anabaptists were the ones who were the true Christians. He looked at the Reformation and said, "This is what I caused. I would rather be a spectator to this tragedy."

He knew the Anabaptists had it right. *Both* Catholics and Protestants wound up showing him a great deal of animosity and hostility.

Calvinism

Because the Roman Catholic Church had *Suma Theologia* by Thomas Aquinas, Calvin tried to write a Protestant alternative to it, *Institutes*. To understand Calvin we have to understand what he was reacting against. Today most people who call themselves "Calvinists" do not even read Calvin. The key doctrines attributed to him are identified by the acronym TULIP:

- **T**otal Depravity
- **U**ndeserved Grace
- **L**imited Atonement
- **I**rresistible Grace
- **P**erseverance of the Saints.

That was how Calvin's followers interpreted Calvin. But the problem did not begin with *Calvin*; it began with *Calvinism*. His Bible was the official Roman Catholic Vulgate. Calvin was a Humanist scholar who first authored a commentary on the Latin *De Clementia* by Seneca, a pagan Roman. A cursory reading of Calvin's secular work shows that he handled Scripture by the same rules of exegesis with which he handled pagan classic literature. Yet to this day adherents to the Reformed tradition treat the grammatical-historical approach to Scripture of Calvin, which derived from Humanist scholarship, as if it derived from Scripture itself. This is not to say this approach is wrong; in fact, on a primordial level, it is right. But it is *not* the way that Jesus and the Apostles handled Scripture and their interpretations of the Old Testament in any exclusive sense, even though Jewish midrashic exegesis included a literalist approach known as *Peshet* in addition to the deeper *Pesher.*

We must also recall that Calvin himself had nothing to do with the Reformation. He was an infant when Erasmus planted the seminal influence of reform, and a small child when Luther and Johannes Oecolampadius in Germany, Zwingli in Switzerland, Patrick Hamilton in Scotland, Caspar Schwenckfeld in Silesia, William Tyndale in England, commenced it. Calvin was not even counted among the second generation Reformers such as Philip Melanchthon, Thomas Cranmer, the eminent Coverdale, or John Calvin's own mentor Farel. Like John Knox and the Bloody Mary exiles from England, Calvin was a third generation Reformer (assuming we wish to consider him to be one at all).

Calvin never preached or wrote a personal testimony of regeneration or second birth. In practice he denied that we are saved through justification by faith through grace, teaching rather a spontaneous regeneration as a divine gift, only followed by faith; at least this is how his followers define and explain his beliefs. Ignoring the straightforward teaching of 1 Timothy 2:4 and 4:10, Calvin's followers such as Beza, from the Remonstrance of Dort and onward, said that Calvin's doctrine was that Christ was not the Savior of *all* men, but as if God were the author of evil, created certain people with the intention of eternally torturing them in hell.

Philosophically Calvinism is in fact not Christian, not Jewish, and not Scriptural, but is, rather, Islamic, fabricating a pseudo-Christian equivalent of the Islamic doctrine of *Inja Allah.* Thus we see that Calvin's theocratic police state in Geneva, imitated by the Puritans in England and Colonial Massachusetts, in essence follows the same model as Islamic Sharia complete with a *Mutawa*—a religious police dictatorially enforcing legalist codes of religious behavior in which women were disproportionately victimized, and in which slavery was allowed to continue as an institution. Calvin's Geneva had more in common with the Taliban's Afghanistan or with the Wahabist's Saudi Arabia, or Ayatollahists' Iran than with Protestant democracy.

The English Puritans took Calvinism to a new level based on theonomic Reconstructionism and Reformed Erastianism where the state became a tool of the church as the church had been a tool of the state. The Puritans had faced terrible persecution under King James, son of Mary Queen of Scots, who authorized the King James Bible. Denounced by multiple historians, including Winston Churchill, as a moral reprobate and homosexual, King James persecuted all non-conformists in England as they would later be persecuted in Scotland, forcing the Puritans to come on the Mayflower, arriving in Massachusetts as the Pilgrims.

While we may justly accredit the Puritans for their role in establishing a model of democracy based on scriptural principles, with their witch hunts, religious oppression, and Calvinistic *kulterkampf* ("war against culture"), they recapitulated a nightmare of cruelty from England to Salem, Massachusetts, together with an unspeakable genocide against the Irish peasants. The Calvinistic concept of Covenant Theology was that God made only two covenants: one with Adam, one with Abraham. Thus the importance of the New Covenant was degraded and Calvinists lacked, and still lack, a single verse that exegetically and inductively establishes their doctrinal conclusion. They argue that (in their opinion) it is implied. The theological madness of basing one's view of *heilsgeschichte* ("salvation history") on something not even stated in Scripture is a theological madness. But as always, theological madness results in mad behavior.

Later, John Wesley, seeing the legacy of atrocity bequeathed by Cromwell's Puritans in Ireland, remarked, "If this is the way Protestants have treated Catholics, it is little wonder that Irish Catholics are so resistant to the Gospel."

Wesley's views were shared by Protestant Irish patriots such as Napper, Tandy, Wolftone, Charles Parnell, and Protestant clergyman Jonathan Swift, famed author of *Gulliver's Travels*, who sought Irish independence from the British crown

More insane was how Calvinism went on to affect both Britain and America. In the USA the Wesleyan Arminian followers of John Wesley were Abolitionists, while the Calvinist denominations of the American South were pro-slavery, resulting in sects such as "Southern" Methodists, meaning that they were in favor of the institution of slavery as was the otherwise noble Calvinist preacher George Whitfield who actually owned black slaves.

In Britain the English Puritan Calvinists and the Scottish Presbyterian Calvinists massacred each other in a Protestant *jihad* ("holy war"), again in the philosophical character of the Islam that they imitated. This slaughter was carried out under the advice of Puritan theologian John Owen, the personal chaplain and spiritual counselor to Oliver Cromwell. Like Sunni and Shia Muslims killing each other in a jihad, the Calvinists did the same.

The Dilemma of Laodicea

In Scotland it was no better. The Covenanters, who themselves had been brutally persecuted to a relentless degree under their leaders Alexander Piedon and later Samuel Rutherford, ended with Rutherford writing that anyone who was not Reformed (Calvinist) in their theology should be killed.

Calvinistic treachery reached its apex in England and in Salem, Massachusetts, with "spectral evidence." There people could stand up in court and claim that God showed them in a dream that another member of their community was a witch. The accused could be convicted and executed based on this kind of so-called evidence. This was Puritan "justice."

In England, Cromwell's witch hunter, General Cotton Mather, was particularly fond of tying women, young and old, to the end of a pole and dipping them under the ice of a frozen lake based on spectral evidence or birth marks on their bodies superstitiously believed to indicate demonic possession. If the victim drowned, it meant they were innocent; if they did not drown, it meant they were a witch using satanic powers, for which they would be either hung or possibly burned.

Drowning under the ice was a Protestant tradition started by John Zwingli in his murder of the Baptists in the Limmat River in Zurich. The Calvinist followers of John Knox likewise carried out such a reign of terror in Scotland while the Massachusetts Puritans of Salem brought the practice to the New World.

In the end such leaders of Protestantism were historically revealed to be little more than sadistic murderers like the popes before them. The diabolical repression and unjust execution of innocent people by Calvinistic Protestants was not visibly different than the Inquisitions that had been carried out by the Roman Catholic Dominicans in Spain a century before, and which were still being carried out by the Jesuit order of Ignatius Loyola during the Counter-Reformation.

Very quickly Protestantism had become much the same as what it set out to correct and reform. This was true of Anglican and Lutheran alike, but of the Calvinists in particular. From the slavery of the American South to the apartheid of South Africa blessed by the Dutch Reformed Church, to the plantation period of Ireland, the cancer of Calvinism spread the curse of violent injustice practiced in the name of Christ. It was not only no visibly better in many cases than Roman Catholicism, but neither did it appear to differ much from Islam.

Just as we can point to positive figures even within Roman Catholicism as individual beacons of light and good intention within a dark system, we can likewise cite John Bunyan, Richard Baxter, William Gurnall, and Miles

Standish among the Puritans. We would also note that other Reformed figures, such as Jonathan Edwards, were more moderate and more biblical. It should also not be forgotten that the founders of the American colonies-turned-states of Rhode Island and Connecticut, Roger Williams and Joseph Hooker respectively, realized the spiritual mess of Puritanism and left the Commonwealth of Massachusetts to establish more just and more biblical societies elsewhere.

TULIP

This record of shame all derived directly or indirectly from the influence of a John Calvin who rewrote Protestant Christianity as a philosophically Humanist (albeit not secular Humanist) religion in so many of its tenets closer to both Roman Catholicism and Islam than to the New Testament. The resulting downward spiral of deterioration degenerated further following the Remonstrance of Dort, which to some degree reinterpreted Calvinism as well as expanding it with the infamous "TULIP." We must remember that Jesus said, "You will know them by their fruits" (Mt. 7:16). The more than two hundred burned at the stake in Calvin's Geneva, and the legacies of Apartheid and slavery, can hardly be considered "the fruit of the Spirit" (Gal. 5:22-23). The Apostles taught the fruit of the Spirit; the Calvinists taught the TULIP.

Total Depravity. Augustine said man is fallen but his intellect is not. So Calvin had to say that man is fallen in every aspect of his being.

Undeserved Grace. No one can do anything to earn their salvation so God offers it to them even though they do not deserve it. Of course, the Roman Catholic Church was teaching sacramentalism—that one could earn grace by keeping the sacraments. By definition, grace is undeserved favor. Consider the Hebrew word *hessed*, God's "mercy" (literally "lovingkindness") in the covenant, and the Greek word *charism*, meaning "gift." The English meaning is undeserved favor but the Roman Catholic Church had redefined it, changed it, to mean something which could be earned.

Limited Atonement or, as some people call it, *Particular Redemption.* Jesus, they said, did not die for everybody; He died only for the elect, for the predestined. That is Calvinism.

Irresistible Grace. Therefore no one has any choice. If they are predestined, they are going to be saved. No one can backslide if they are saved. And if not, that is it, there is nothing they can do—they are going to hell. God has already decided their case

179

Perseverance. Now that is scriptural. Yes, persevere! However, Calvinism redefined perseverance as something that is unavoidable in the elect. The "elect" will persevere regardless of their own will.

World views were changing. Science was in its early days and people had a black-and-white view of the world. Calvin said you cannot understand something beyond the extent that God chooses to reveal it in His Word. But then he went on and tried to reveal it anyway. Some verses say that people are predestined and others say that God wants no one to perish but all to come to repentance. These two things must be held in tension. What Calvin did was try to come down on one side. Arminius later tried to correct hyper-Calvinism.

But this is not the issue. As we have previously mentioned, it all goes back to the Sadducees and Pharisees. The Pharisees said all is foreseen but the choice is given. The Sadducees said no, it is all predestined. They were fatalists. Jesus agreed with the Pharisees. He said, *"The Son of Man must be betrayed, for it is written."* It had been prophesied. *"But woe to him by whom He is betrayed"* (Mk. 14:21). Jesus held the two things in tension without coming down on one side or the other. Calvin made the mistake of coming down on one side. Part of the reason is that he went back to Augustine.

Reactions & Intentions

Augustine reacted against a heretic in England called Pelagius, a monk who denied original sin. So to Calvin the whole thing was grace: mankind is fallen, and only God can save men. That is true, but because they were reacting against an error, they overstated a truth to the extent that they introduced *another* error. These two things must be held in tension.

The opposite to Calvinism is the Pelagianism against which Augustine originally reacted, and that is also an error. Arminian held the middle position; he tried to hold the two in balance. Calvinists do not like to think in those terms; they like to think everyone is either a Calvinist or an Arminianist. But look what happened anywhere there was a kind of hyper-Calvinism. Today even Calvinists debate whether or not Calvin was a Calvinist—whether or not he believed this whole TULIP doctrine.

Something is known by its fruits. Look at those places that hyper-Calvinism permeated the social fabric of the country and what is the inevitable result? A police state. It began in Geneva; it came to Scotland with John Knox. In South Africa, the Dutch Reformed Church—what did you have? Apartheid. Why? Calvinism. Northern Ireland? They are predestined to be white or Protestant so they can keep the black people, or the Roman

Catholic people, as an under-class. This was Calvinism. The church in America split over the issue of slavery. The American Baptists were Arminian—they were against slavery. The Southern Baptists, Calvinists, believed God made these people to be their slaves! This was Calvinist predestination.

In Britain the Calvinist influence came into the Church of England. That was partly responsible for the tremendous social injustice that was prevalent in Wesley's day in the 1700's. As will be seen in the church at Philadelphia, Wesley's revival was an Arminian reaction against Calvinism. Wesley was a strong Arminian who reacted against the evils of hyper-Calvinism.

Not only did Calvin over-emphasize predestination, but he was heavily invested in Augustine and the concept of the state church. He developed something called *Covenant Theology* and he called the church the "new Israel." The Puritans, under Cromwell, were Calvinists. How did God give Israel victory? They killed all the men, women and children. So what did the Calvinists do when they invaded Ireland and Scotland? They killed all the men, women and children. This was the effect of *Covenant Theology*, believing they were now the people of the Covenant, the new Israel. Of course God told the Israelites to kill the Canaanites who were in the Land He had promised to Abraham, but He told the church to make disciples in all the nations. They were not to be His followers' victims. He said, *"Vengeance is mine"* (Rom. 12:19). Vengeance is not mankind's.

When the Puritans went to America they began burning women as "witches." This was the state church. Instead of the state controlling the church, the church began controlling the state. The whole thing became a formula for disaster. That is the negative side.

On the positive side, it can be said that the early Puritans such as Joseph Alleyne, Richard Baxter, John Owen and John Robinson were high-caliber people theologically. They had a higher sense of justice than many other Calvinists and, even though they killed the real Libertarians, they played a role in the establishment of Parliamentary democracy.

As Feudalism declined, monarchies and autocracy declined with it. And as societies became more capitalist and industrial they became more democratic. What is happening today in South Korea, Taiwan, Malaysia and Singapore is an industrial revolution for these countries now. And what do they want? They want to get rid of their kings and have democracies like the West. What is happening in these countries now is what happened in Europe in the 16th century. And they also have big revivals in many of these countries, Korea particularly.

This is not to say that the Puritans and the Calvinists were all bad. Rather it is an application of Christ's admonition, *"Wake up, and strengthen the things which were about to die; for I have not found your deeds completed in the sight of My God."*

They did not go back to the Bible deeply enough. Later on, as it will be seen, the Puritans tried to go back further and the Protestant ethic developed. In the Middle Ages the Roman Catholic Church said the only way to truly serve God was to be in the clergy. But after the Reformation people said one could be a mother and serve God, a housewife, a doctor, an engineer—anything. Every Christian is a minister, a priest, and they can serve God in whatever they do. That was total rebellion against the thinking of people in the Middle Ages.

For the church to really go back to what the Apostles were teaching it is necessary to go back to the root, as Paul says in Romans 11. The Reformation was only partial, and it was not alive as they thought. That is why Jesus said, *"You have a name that you are alive, but you are dead."*

It must be understood that the root cannot be seen, because it is underground. The "root," Jesus, is not the "state." The idea of a state church is totally blasphemous. The Antichrist will get power through that kind of marriage, the marriage of religion and state. It is an Antichrist doctrine.

Henry VIII

When Henry VIII caused the split with Rome he knew the pope would not give him a divorce from Catherine of Aragon who was from Catholic Spain. Thomas Moore knew the Catholic Church was corrupt but he would not stand with Henry VIII. This was not because he disapproved of the divorce. If the pope had approved it, this would have been fine with Thomas Moore. And the papacy frequently granted divorces if it considered them politically expedient. So instead of a church where the head was the pope, there was a church where the head was the king of England. Henry VIII actually tried to stop the Reformation. He was given the honorary title *Fidei Defensor*—"Defender of the Faith," by the pope. And he tried to persuade Erasmus to oppose Luther.

In the Counter-Reformation, when the Roman Catholic Church was killing all the believers it could, particularly the Huguenots in France, it was absolutely brutal and unbelievable. Yet Henry VIII killed over 70,000 of his own people, and he was the **founder** of the Church of England!

Whatever mistakes Luther and Calvin and Zwingli made, and they made mistakes, they could all say that their actions were born out of integrity. They stood up to Rome and put their necks on the line for godly principles. The

Church of England can never say that. The Church of England was not born out of integrity; historically it was born out of whoredom, political ambition and expediency. Henry VIII was seeking a male heir by manipulation and ungodly means instead of by trusting in the Lord and living according to the Word of God. One would think he would have learned from Abraham. The Church of England can make no claim to any moral foundation in its origins as an institution. The Church of England had its Reformation later with Hooper, Latimer, Ridley and Cranmer, the people burned in Oxford by Queen Mary. They were the ones who tried to reform the Church of England.

Later, under Elizabeth I, the Elizabethan Settlement temporarily delivered an interim peace between Catholic and Protestant. And although Edward VI (groomed by Thomas Cranmer) died in his youth, Protestantism survived despite later efforts to bring Catholic Stuarts back to a combined throne of England and Scotland. This attempt was made through Bonnie Prince Charles who was born in Rome and sent by France, but was finally defeated by a coalition of English troops and Scottish lowland Presbyterians. With the fall of Charles I after the Battle of Naseby the Puritans gained control of England, and this continued until the restoration by Charles II. Once more, secular politics and the politics of war continually remained inextricable from the ecclesiastical politics of the church. But institutional reformation does not equal doctrinal reformation, and the institutional breaking with Rome was effectuated by the ambitions and marital issues of Henry VIII.

Today in Ireland if you mention Protestants or Anglicans, they just say Henry VIII wanted a divorce in order to take another woman; that is why the Church of England came into being, and they are absolutely right. The Church of England has no moral pretext for its foundation, and admits it. At least the other Protestants had a moral foundation where they could base their actions on Scripture to some degree.

Subsequent Repercussions

To the chagrin of Protestantism the often tragic history of Ireland testifies even more to the debacle of intertwining church and secular politics. To the present generation with a history of violence and terror, Ireland has existed in the ugly repercussions of that history, particularly the 1690 Battle of the Boyne with King William of Orange from Holland opposing King James of England. Two foreign Kings had a battle on Irish soil, and the Irish people are still fighting the battle centuries after the English and Dutch had long ago made friends. History moved on but not in Ireland. The series of ironies in Irish history are staggering.

As we have stated, not only did the English first invade Ireland at the behest of the pope, but the founders of Irish Republicanism before Daniel O'Connor were ardent Protestants, not Catholics, who led the 1790s rebellion against England and founded the Home Rule Movement. More astounding, the wife of King William, Queen Mary, was a Catholic; King James was an ex-Protestant. Dutch-Catholic troops actually fought with King William against James, and the pope blessed William, not James, with a Roman Catholic celebration replete with bells ringing in Catholic Vienna. The Catholic Church was rejoicing at the victory of Protestant William because the battle had more to do with the interests of the pope's power play in France and continental Europe than with anything to do with Ireland, England, Scotland, Catholicism, or Protestantism. Yet to this day the Protestant Orange Orders of Ulster ridiculously ignore the realities of history and hideously march with bowler hats and pounding drums.

It is little wonder that Jesus, who entered a politically charged environment, refused to identify His cause with any political movement or party, but confined His political statements to issues related to morality and prophecy. To this day, from the religious right identified with the American Republican Party (Pat Robertson, the late Jerry Falwell, Chuck Colson) to the religious left (Jesse Jackson, Al Sharpton, Jeremiah Wright) identified with the Democrat Party, Protestantism, like Catholicism, has failed to imitate Jesus' example and emulate His priorities.

As we shall focus on in our treatment of Laodicea, the unscriptural association of the Christian message and church with temporal political parties is falsely justified by nothing more than human opinion. Building a Christian position on opinion, or anything other than correctly exegeted scripture, is dangerous ground. Bear in mind that Jesus condemned the religious establishment of His day for establishing doctrinally-related positions on the basis of nothing more than the often abject opinions of the Sanhedrin.

What the Reformers Forgot

The Old Testament or Hebrew Scriptures are called in Judaism by the acronym "TNK," pronounced *Tanakh*, and meaning a combination of *Torah* (Pentateuch), *Nevim* (Prophets) and *Ketuvim* (Writings—the Psalms, histories, and wisdom books.) Born-again Christians generally accept that the primary aim of the Old Testament is to point to the coming New Covenant that would be implemented by the promised Messiah. How then, if the covenants are different, is the New Covenant intended by the Lord to be understood?

How did the Reformers correctly understand the differences, and where did they fail to understand the differences? Above all, what can be done to adjust the repercussions of their misunderstandings today?

Luther rejected the book of Revelation as useless and not canonical, reasoning that Revelation's message was partially for an appointed time. The Swiss Reformers saw Revelation as having had a total, instead of partial, fulfillment in the early church, and a continuous meaning throughout church history. They simply spiritualized away the elements that had no parallel or historical fulfillment in the early centuries of Christian history.

It is ironic that since a cornerstone of Reformed theology was a stoic approach to biblical interpretation, taking a strict grammatical-historical line, Reformed Theology departs from its own principles and automatically "spiritualizes" anything about Israel as being for the church. Luther regarded Romans to be the very heart of Scripture and its message, yet his thinking virtually omitted the plain teaching of chapters 9 to 11.

What exists in the United Kingdom today is a kind of regal papacy in which the next titular head of the Anglican Church, Prince Charles, is a divorced New Ager with a combination of Buddhist, Hindu and Islamic beliefs. For all of its errors, the Continental Reformation was the result of Christian conviction. In England however, the Church of England was born out of the whoredom of a despotic womanizing king who murdered 70,000 of his own subjects. Henry VIII, in collaboration with Cardinal Wolsey, burned William Tyndale. Absurdly, the British Monarchy still retains for itself the title "Defender of the Faith," a title awarded by the pope to the Roman Catholic Henry VIII for persecution of Protestants!

Today, members of the British Royal family convert to Catholicism and the Archbishop of Canterbury marches in a procession to Mary in Walsingham calling for reunion with Rome. Meanwhile the Queen visits the pope dressed in black in a sign of subjection to his whiteness, and she has even appointed a Roman Catholic priest as Court Chaplain. Anglicanism was born from Rome (not from Scripture); it never fully broke with Rome doctrinally and ecclesiologically, and to Rome it is now returning. The root of this dates back to the shallow doctrinal foundation laid by the Reformers, and that foundation is now caving in.

Many errors result from this for Anglicans and other mainstream Protestants that are avoided by non-conformist churches holding to believers baptism. When a young Anglican, who has been pronounced "Born Again" as a baby, actually becomes "Born Again" by accepting Jesus personally, which new birth proclamation does his church wish him to believe is valid? Was his vicar telling the truth when he told him he was a Christian and born again as a baby, or is he actually born again when he believes? Telling people they are Christians when they are not, when they still need to become Christians, is a lie of the devil. "Did God really say, 'You must be born again'"?

Anglicanism is but one expression of the errors of the Reformers. Presbyterian, Lutheran and Reform churches all have the same built-in error—a state church where people become members not by repentance, faith and second birth, but by their first birth, by being born into a state church and culture, having an initiation ritual performed on them as babies. Under the New Covenant this is just not biblical.

And what did they do wrong? They twisted the parable of Matthew 13:38-42 out of context to say that the field where both wheat and weeds were planted was the church, when in fact Jesus said it was the world. Thus instead of allowing the saved and unsaved to grow up together in the world for Jesus to sort out upon His return, true and false Christians would be together in the church for Jesus to sort out upon His return. And the error? They did not go back to the Bible. Jesus said His Kingdom was not of this world; Constantine, the Medieval popes, and the Reformers said it was. Central to the popular Jewish rejection of Jesus was His refusal to accept temporal political power before the Millennium (which the Reformers rejected).

Therefore the Reformation was a theologically incomplete event, and thus a spiritually incomplete event. It must be viewed as an aborted effort to restore biblical Christianity as opposed to an authentic reintroduction of it.

The Baptists, who tried to return to the genuine *sola scriptura* faith that Luther only thought he had, were terribly persecuted and not infrequently murdered by the Protestants. Even today, such Evangelicals as Baptists, Pentecostals, Brethren and Free Church are not, by classical historical definition, truly Protestant They do not hold to a state church or accept infant baptism. Rather, they are the doctrinal heirs of the Anabaptists whom Catholic and Protestant alike persecuted.

The source of all of this tragedy once more relates back to the Replacement Theology that makes the church the new Israel. The endless arguments of Systematic Theology and Dispensationalism versus the Covenant/Reformed divide among Evangelicals all stems from this same failure to grasp Jeremiah 31:31 and what it is addressing.

Abraham is indeed "Father of All who Believe" (Gen. 12:1-3; Gal. 3:8; Is. 63:16). Tremendous expressions of God's grace are seen in the Old Testament (as with King Manasseh) and tremendous expressions of His wrath in the New Covenant (as with Ananias and Sapphira). Dispensational Theology understates the continuity between the two covenants, but the hyper-Dispensationalism of Darby is flat-out erroneous. Still, more moderate expressions of Dispensationalism do more justice to Jeremiah 31:31 and the eschatology and ecclesiology that derives from it than does Covenant Theology. Dispensationalism (for all the faults of its more extreme expressions) rightly sees a spiritual and theological relationship between Israel and the church, but keeps the distinction between them.

The Reformers simply failed to restore the idea of a Kingdom that is not of this world. Thus they failed to retain the idea that Christians are to be *in* the world but not *of* it. As a result, instead of the Last Days being as the Days of Noah with a remnant saved as Jesus taught, the church is to be triumphant. Kingdom Now, Dominionism, and the like come from this. The over-realized eschatology of Dominionism (as opposed to the inaugural eschatology of Scripture) is no more biblical on one extreme than a defeatist bunker mentality is on the other.

The return of Jesus depends upon His prophetic purposes for Israel as well as for the church (Mt. 23: 39; Zech. 12:1-10), and upon His plan for global salvation bound up with His prophetic plan for the salvation of Israel and the Jews (Rom. 11:15-25). But instead, Kingdom Now Theology teaches that His return is dependent upon a church that tramples Satan under its own feet without Jesus present, instead of Jesus trampling him under our feet as Scripture teaches (Rom. 16:20). According to Dominionist adherents, instead of the Seed of the Woman crushing the serpent as the Word of God teaches (Gen. 3:15), the woman crushes the head herself.

Three times in the text of Romans 11 it is reiterated that God is not finished with Israel and the Jews. While individual Jews may accept Jesus (remaining grafted into their own olive tree), most reject Him (being cut off from it, to be replaced by Gentile Christians who accept Him). However, some reject Him but then come to accept Him (being re-grafted into the olive tree). But the tree itself remains the same. Believing Gentiles replace Jews who are not believers, and those Gentiles are incorporated into Israel in a spiritual sense, but the tree is still Israel with its final branches (the last Christians) being Jews once more just as the first ones were.

After this, in Chapter 12, Paul exhorts the readers, "*be transformed by the renewing of your minds*" and "*be not conformed to the world.*" Paul next deals with the issue of spiritual gifts in the life of the body. These include not only ministry gifts of leadership, service and teaching, but charismatic gifts such as prophecy (verse 5). Thus, Romans 11:29 serves as a natural transitional link from what precedes it to the things that follow. The exegetical context of the verse reveals a clear thematic progression of inter-related aspects of church life, one leading into another. Hence, the theme introduced in the opening chapters of the letter to the Romans that all men (both Jew and Greek), being fallen, require salvation, logically and neatly leads in the middle chapters of Romans to the issue of the purpose of the Law. Its purpose is to illustrate man's fallen nature and his need for a Savior. Then, with the Law fulfilled in Jesus, the question necessarily arises about the purpose of the Jews now that the Messiah has arrived to fulfill the Torah. Thus Romans 9-11 form the next natural step. Following this, he speaks of body life and the role of individual members with individual gifts.

The bogus view that God is finished with the Jews is just as faulty as the bogus view that He has finished with the gifts. Both errors have the same source: an incipient hyper-Dispensationalism claiming that a new set of rules now exists that is different from the rules that existed in the time of the apostolic church. This view sees apostolic Christianity as primitive and "the perfect" as having come in the form of a book (the New Testament) in the same way as Muslims believe the Quran and Mormons believe the Book of Mormon. Because this faulty view resembles Islam and Mormonism in a qualified sense (this is not to suggest that Cessationism denies the Gospel or is fundamentally heretical but simply that it shares this one characteristic), it becomes in essence a belief in a kind of third covenant. This is in some way distinct from the previous ones, yet it claims an essential continuity with them by borrowing on their motifs, but nonetheless with certain elements of the Old having passed away.

This position is arrived at by an eisegesis, an incorrect re-reading of 1 Corinthians 13, wrongly claiming that "the perfect" to come was the New Testament Canon. If "the perfect" has already come, then according to that "perfect" text, hope and faith must have also passed away and are no longer necessary either, only love. Cessationists of course would not reject the need for faith or hope, so it is hard to believe their argument can do anything other than collapse. Even today there are Cessationists like Peter Masters reading things into Scripture which are not there with the same eisegetical license as proponents of the Toronto Experience. They get things out of Scripture that God did not put into it. "The perfect" in 1 Corinthians 13 refers, of course, not to the New Testament canon, but to the return of Christ.

While the many failures of the Reformation cannot be overlooked, neither can the Reformers themselves be lambasted for their failures. They were mainly well-intentioned but, like everyone else, fallible men in complicated and difficult times who at least began trying, as best they could for the most part, to do what they believed to be best "as unto the Lord." It is hard to believe that in their place anyone would have been immune to the same errors that they can so easily, in retrospect, be criticized for. Yet when it comes to Israel and the salvation of the Jews, it is lamentable on the one hand what the Reformers forgot, and on the other praise God for what so many today are finally remembering. After all of these many long centuries, it should be remembered what God has in store for the Jews:

> For if their rejection is the reconciliation of the world, what will their acceptance be but life from the dead?
> – Rabbi Shaul of Tarsus (St. Paul), Rom. 11:15.

So to get to the truth a return to the root is required by which one must:

- remember believers are living under a new covenant not like the old covenant;
- break the unscriptural marriage between church and state;
- get rid of this visible and invisible church idea;
- get back to this sense of mission, that believers have to reach the entire world;
- learn to read a Jewish book like a Jewish book.

The Reformers did none of these. Their works were considered by Jesus to be incomplete, and they were dead.

Revival?

Is revival going to come to the Western world? God has started pouring out His grace on the poor countries and back towards the Jews, but is there any more hope for the white people? For Britain and America and Canada and the Continent? In England 8 per cent of the people go to church at least once a month. It is mainly a Middle Class thing apart from the African and Asian immigrants. In Germany it is 2 per cent. Is there any hope for revival? Is there any hope at all?

Frankly, at this time the church in the West is on the road to nowhere. There has been no revival, there will be no revival, and there can be no revival as long as they continue on that road to nowhere. If there is any hope at all for this society and for Western Civilization it is massive revival. And if there is any hope for massive revival it has to begin with Christians.

Remember, revival is not a lot of people *getting* saved—that is the **result** of revival. Something that was never alive to begin with cannot be brought back from the dead. Revival is the Body of Christ being what it is supposed to be and doing what it is supposed to do. *That* is revival. Half-way measures do not work; renewal movements do not work; reformations do not work. There is only one thing that is going to work: go back to this Book, *The* Book, back to the root.

The future of the Christian world is no longer in the hands of white European and American Protestants. It is in the hands of black, yellow and olive-skinned people of the world. A time came when the future of Christianity was given into the hands of the Gentiles. What does the Protestant Reformation mean to a Korean? Nothing. What does it mean to an African? Nothing at all! Where are white people getting saved today? Mostly in Eastern Europe, but they never had a Reformation.

The Reformation has been described by many people as Augustine's doctrine of salvation reacting against his doctrine of the church. He believed in one church and that church being organized, but he also believed in salvation by grace. The Reformers emphasized the grace against the institution of the church. But in the East, in the Russian Orthodox Church, Augustine is not even one of their church fathers. Chrysostom and the Capadocian people are their church fathers. They have never had a Reformation; they never even had an Augustine. Even today most white people are Pentecostals or Baptists or FIEC (Fellowship of Independent Evangelical Churches). They have not come from the Reformers.

Protestantism is finished. Not only is it finished, it never was to begin with; it was a non-event. The Reformation of the church never happened. It was a *historical* event, but it was not a *spiritual* event.

Protestantism has a name for being alive, but it is dead. Tell that to Ian Paisley! More Roman Catholics are coming to genuine faith now in Northern Ireland than Protestants. What does Protestantism mean to a Roman Catholic in Ireland? His grandfather being starved off his land—that is what it means. The future is no longer in the hands of the white Protestant world. The future is going to be in the hands of people who have not been touched by the Reformation. The sooner the Body of Christ wakes up to that fact the better off it is going to be. Many are hanging on to a dead corpse of history that was stillborn anyway. The whole thing was an aborted attempt to restore the church.

The Message of Jesus to Philadelphia

Sardis falsely believed it to be what it was not, just as is the case with modern Western Protestantism.

In the Dark Ages Christianity was about to die in the clutches of a false church of Satan. Protestantism had many deeds but was stillborn, thinking

190

itself to be alive but spiritually, theologically and in the final analysis morally, dead. Jesus urged those listening to Him in this church to strengthen the vestiges of scriptural Christianity that still remain that the popular wisdom foolishly believed to be flourishing.

The mainstream Protestant churches in the World Council of Churches , The National Council of Churches, and the Ecumenical and Interfaith movements are dominated by unsaved theological liberals and are mostly populated by the unsaved. Much of popular Evangelicism is absorbed into this dead system. Yet these churches did hear the truth. The Church of England was evangelized by courageous martyrs like Ridley, Latimer, and Hooper under the cruel reign of Queen Mary. Lutheranism, Presbyterian the Reformed churches and others, were initially established on the grounds of scriptural beliefs just as this church indeed received the Gospel of justification by faith and salvation by grace and professed to elevate the authority of Scripture over tradition.

Yet Calvin, in defining his doctrine, repeatedly reiterated "by the authority of Augustine," went back to Patristic tradition and not to God's Word, reaffirming the Erastrian church-state union of Augustine, infant baptism, etc. Those in this church are urged by Jesus to repent, for the church itself as a whole will not be prepared for His return. While they professed salvation, it was either false and cultural or they were backslidden and He warned their names would be blotted out of the Book of Life unless they repent. Yet Jesus concludes by making it clear that there is a faithful remnant in Sardis just as there is in Protestantism. They are His and He will confess them as His before His Father and the angels in eternity. This is what Christ said to Sardis and is what He says to mainstream Protestantism.

But then there was another church in Philadelphia. Jesus told Sardis, I am going to come to you quickly, like a thief, and you are not going to be ready. But He had a very different message for Philadelphia. And we should all want to be found like Philadelphians when Christ returns.

Chapter 6
Philadelphia: "Brotherly Love"
18th Century Onward

1st	2nd	3rd	4th	5th	6th	7th	8th	9th	10th	11th	12th	13th	14th	15th	16th	17th	18th	19th	20th

Apostolic Church
Pre-Nicean Church
Rise of the Institutional Church
The Dark Ages
The Reformation
Great Awakening
Apostate Church

The Message to Philadelphia

"And to the angel of the church in Philadelphia write:

"'He who is holy, who is true, who has the key of David, who opens and no one will shut, and who shuts and no one opens, says this:

"''I know your deeds. Behold, I have put before you an open door which no one can shut, because you have a little power, and have kept My word, and have not denied My name. Behold, I will cause those of the synagogue of Satan, who say that they are Jews and are not, but lie–I will make them *come and bow down at your feet, and make them know that I have loved you. Because you have kept the word of My perseverance, I also will keep you from the hour of testing, that hour which is about to come upon the whole world, to test those who dwell on the earth. I am coming quickly; hold fast what you have, so that no one will take your crown. He who overcomes, I will make him a pillar in the temple of My God, and he will not go out from it anymore; and I will write on him the name of My God, and the name of the city of My God, the new Jerusalem, which comes down out of heaven from My God, and My new name.'"*

"He who has an ear, let him hear what the Spirit says to the churches."
(Rev. 3:7-13)

The City of Philadelphia

The city of Philadelphia is located on the banks of a river in a valley along what was the main road between Laodicea and Pergamum. It was established by a regional king who reigned in Pergamum, and named after his predecessor in the 2nd century BC. The city was badly damaged by a major earthquake and aftershocks, and in its day it existed in the shadow of more prestigious cities in the province of Asia that had more architectural grandeur such as Pergamum and Ephesus, or were more prosperous like Laodicea. It did not have the political importance of the capitol of Lydia, nor was it a site of pagan pilgrimage for the temple worship of Artemis cum Diana.

Jesus spoke well of the believers who lived here as having but little power yet remaining faithful and noted mostly for their love. What is most curious about Philadelphia is that its description is the most Hebraic and features a Davidic motif. Laodicea also had a largely unbelieving Jewish community with a synagogue, and the persevering Christians of this church were promised to be spared from the coming hour of temptation corresponding to eschatological events of the future set to take place globally.

While not having the colossal temples of the other main cities, Jesus promises them to be pillars in the temple of God and assures them that the unbelieving Jews will one day acknowledge them, indicating that there were also a considerable number of ostracized Jewish believers. As it had never been a regal capitol, the kingship aspect of Christ as the Davidic King is promised to them much the same as is the alternative temple of God to those of the pagan world in the more celebrated cities of the region.

Future Historical Prophetic Antitype

The character of Philadelphia, as with each of the churches, is contained in its name and was known for its love. Sardis was a carnal pseudo-

194

improvement of Thyatira; it was a church that did not go far enough in returning to the Word of God; Philadelphia was a church that did, despite its lack of power. Indeed the power of Christ is always manifested in our weakness. This principle is midrashically as true for a church as it is for an individual, and is based on *qal wahomer*–the "light to heavy" principle of biblical interpretation from the Midot of Hillel that St. Paul learned from his mentor Rabbi Gemaliel and used in his own writings. What is true in a light situation (in this case a person) intensifies in the weightier one (in this case a local church). Hence the message of Christ is both to this church corporately and to the individuals in it.

As Protestantism sought but failed to reform Catholicism, the movements of God's Spirit that followed would seek to reform Protestantism. These included Moravian sects in Germany and their British equivalent, the early Methodists in England and her colonies. Many of the things that the Reformers forgot were remembered by the early generations of revivalists. An early pioneer was Justinian Welz who realized the Reformers overlooked the reason d'etre of the church itself: missions and evangelism. He would be followed by William Carey who went to India, Hudson Taylor who went to China, and George Whitfield who earlier went to America. This was a missions-oriented church focused on its Christ-given mission of fulfilling the Great Commission as opposed to the Reformation which already saw the Western world as sufficiently evangelized, even counting Roman Catholic and Eastern Orthodox countries as Christian, howbeit in a heretical sense described by Luther in his *Babylonian Captivity of the Church.*

These intended Reformers of the Reformation, however, discovered the truth that new wine cannot be put into old wine skins. The Methodist followers of Wesley who first endeavored to reform the Church of England from within found themselves ostracized from the Church of England, while the Moravians found themselves ostracized from popular Lutheranism just as the Jewish believers in ancient Philadelphia found themselves ostracized from the synagogue that they, too, tried to reform with the Gospel message. Thus unbelieving churches and denominations rejecting the true Gospel and persecuting those who believe it are likewise the "synagogue of Satan," as the Greek term *sunagoge* simply means "assembly" and is used for the church in the Epistle of James.

The Wesleyans of England and Count Zinzendorf and Pietous groups of Germany emphasized holy living in their concept of discipleship. Wesley himself had come from a group known as "Enthusiasts," and first met Moravian missionaries on his way to be an Anglican missionary in Georgia, stating he came to convert the Indians but "Who will convert me?" It was under the ministry of Moravian missionaries in England that John and Charles Wesley were born again in Aldersgate, London. The Pietism of the German-speaking world had become the Methodism of the English-speaking world.

While France had descended into a revolution that began as populist but turned into a blood bath that devoured the population, England witnessed an avalanche of socio-economic disorder ignited by the Industrial Revolution that began in the Severn River Valley and in the coal mining communities that fueled the machinery of manufacturing. Displaced economic refugees from the old agricultural economy saturated the cities in swelling slums. Oppressive sweat shops exploited the working classes brutally with monotonous tasks performed 18 hours per day, 6 days per week. Children as young as 4 labored in coal mines under dangerous conditions, often dying from cave-ins and black lung disease.

Once more a new world view was born. The Gospel message became irrelevant to the average person whose Christian faith was mainly cultural to do with mere rites of passage while they took respite from their misery in gin mills where fisticuffs and two-part harmony vocal choruses provided a form of entertainment. Wesley recounted the story of "Bruising Peg," the bare-knuckled female boxer noted for decking other women whom she fought topless outside of gin mills as the sport of the working classes. The Methodist hatred of poverty was not simply because of the hardship of social injustice itself, but because Wesley believed poverty and ignorance fanned the flames of immorality and decadence even though it did not light the fire which Wesley attributed to the fallen nature.

His brother Charles adopted the same 2-part vocal harmonies sung in the gin mills, giving the choruses Christian words, while he and George Whitfield preached on horseback to the crowds not uncommonly over 20,000 in the factory and mining towns and cities of England and beyond. Their Gospel preaching was frequently interrupted by rioting and mob violence organized by the Church of England clergy. In his home church in Epworth near Doncaster, England, where his father had been the vicar, Wesley was forced to preach the Gospel while standing on his father's sarcophagus in the church graveyard because he was not permitted inside the church.

Again, these champions of the Gospel had but little power, yet Christ set before them an open door. They did not have the grandeur of the cathedrals or elaborate church buildings, but commonly preached in fields and in whatever churches would allow them in, settling for the chapels they established to disciple the converts. The early Methodists recognized that without discipleship evangelism would prove to be futile because Jesus said to make "disciples," not "converts."

Unlike the Reformers, the Methodists began to disassemble the clergy class, not by abolition of ordained clergy, but by commissioning lay preachers and circuit preachers in a return to the priesthood of all believers. Early Methodism then turned its focus to expansion external and internal. Externally they sent missionaries to Ireland, North America, and to the British colonies; internally they attacked social injustice with the power of the Gospel from which would come social reform that included literacy and education plus healthcare for the working classes. They did this without much by way of government help or sponsorship from the mainstream religious establishment represented by the Anglican bishops in the House of Lords who often opposed them just as the synagogue had done to the believers in Philadelphia.

The seminal influences of Methodism permeated the social fabric and played a role in everything from a health system to a school system with literacy for the working classes. The Methodists saw education as necessary so converts could read the Word of God. The ripple effect had socially transforming ramifications. Trade unions and labor unions that would later become left wing were at first instituted under the guidelines of biblical principles by organizers who believed the Gospel. There were similar effects not only in education and public health, but in the mass media of the day where publications such as *The Guardian* newspaper (today a biased left wing propaganda sheet) gave voice and expression to the disenfranchised working urban classes.

Wesley understood that to change society we must change the people in it, but that we cannot change them; only God can by second birth. Once people were transformed spiritually by the power of God, society and its institutions, including government, would likewise change because of a church that was "salt" and "light."

Paramount to this was the reform of child labor laws in England and the Abolitionist Movement later championed by former slave trader John Newton (composer of *Amazing Grace*). British Abolitionism gave root to early American Abolitionism, but such social activism was always the result of the Gospel of salvation that the Methodists preached.

While transforming society dramatically, the early Methodists did not preach a "social" Gospel as they do today. In the modern environment that has seen so many evangelistic welfare organizations degenerate into non-evangelistic social organizations, we see little that the founders of such organizations as Christian Aid, Bernardo's, World Vision, and increasingly the Salvation Army would even recognize. All of these and others began as Gospel-preaching, but once a ministry ceases to be evangelistic it will soon no longer be biblically evangelical. Bernardo's Homes for Children founded by Dr. Bernardo and the incredible ministry of George Mueller in Bristol, England, were all born out of the Gospel. William Booth preached his first sermon at Mile and Wastes in the same neighborhood as Dr. Bernardo began his ministry to children. It is conspicuously noteworthy that the same areas of London, at that time the main city of the world and the "New York" of its day, where Radicalism, Fabianism (Progressivism), and Marxism began, are the same neighborhoods where Bernardo, Booth, and other evangelists brought an authentically scriptural solution to the urban problems of poverty and social injustice.

In time, these influences reached the corridors of power where benevolent aristocrats and Christians in Parliament, motivated by their faith, pursued courses of reform. This was the era of William Wilberforce, the Earl of Shaftsbury, and Florence Nightengale. But the tide of the Gospel and its ramifications even swelled up to the entertainment industry where the hymns of Isaac Watts, Charles Wesley, John Newton, and Augustus Toplady were matched by Sir Arthur Sullivan. Prior to his Evangelical conversion Sullivan had been the carousing and womanizing musical partner in Gilbert and Sullivan, famous for their penny operas such as *Mikado* and *The Pirates of Penzance* in the early Victorian era. But now the 19th-century equivalent of a major pop star had become a Christian, and composed *Onward Christian Soldiers*, the marching theme for generations of street preachers, missionaries, and evangelists.

What had begun in the mid-18th century went on, going from growth to growth, until the time of Spurgeon in the late-19th century when American evangelist D.L. Moody first preached in England and the epicenter of biblical Evangelicalism began to shift to North America. Prior to this the USA, having first been evangelized by missionaries from Britain, progressively produced a string of powerful evangelists beginning with Jonathan Edwards. This was temporarily interrupted by the unfortunate influence of Charles Finney, who denied original sin and bordered on Pelagian heresy. Finney paved the way for the "cheap grace"/easy believism of compromised evangelism that would reach its modern climax in such unscriptural delusions as Rick Warren's *Purpose Driven* agenda.

In reaction to liberal theology at Princeton, Yale, and Harvard universities, Benjamin Warfield unfortunately polarized the church with his stoic Calvinism and Cessasionist rejection of charismatic gifts. These setbacks, however, were eventually remedied and the tradition of Dwight Moody, R.A. Torrey, and dynamic preachers such as Harry Ironside ultimately prevailed. These were powerful men of God, as strong in their faith and as diligent in their faithfulness as Wesley, Whitfield, and Charles Spurgeon had been in England.

Back in Britain, however, John Wesley's belief in biblically-based charismatic experience and his Wesleyan Arminian doctrinal position were a lynchpin in preventing the false doctrines of Cessationism and hyper-Calvinism from gaining strong momentum except residually in Scotland and Northern Ireland and in certain areas of Wales. Yet even in the Celtic areas of the British Isles there were formidable revivals under Billy Nichols, a short-lived revival in Wales under Evan Roberts (which did not last due to its lack of discipleship), and finally the last of these moves of God in the Hebrides off the coast of Scotland under the preaching of Duncan Campbell as late as the 20th century.

At this time there was a further restoration in the church of the historical and theological connection between the Body of Christ and Israel and the Jews. The church turned its mission back towards evangelizing the Hebrews with the establishment of a number of ministries such as Christian Witness to Israel, the Church's Ministry Among the Jews, and Mildmay Missions. Jewish Christian scholars such as Alfred Edersheim, David Baron, and Franz Delitzsch began to re-explore the New Testament as a Jewish book, looking at the original Jewish cultural and theological background. While this tradition continues to this day with the ministries of Dr. Arnold Fruchtenbaum, Dr. Michael Rydelnik, and others, it is a far cry from the pseudo-academic lunacy and legalism of most of the modern "Hebrew Roots Movement." Delitzsch, who translated the New Testament into Hebrew, Edersheim, who authored *The Life and Times of Jesus the Messiah,* and Brother Rabinowitch—the dynamic evangelist to Jews in Eastern Europe—were serious scholars. It was at this time that Jews began to be saved again in significant numbers, including leading rabbis such as Isaac Lichtenstein and Leopold Cohen who founded the American Board of Mission to the Jews (today called "Chosen People").

When the British Empire was at its absolute political, strategic, and economic peak in early Victorian England, Great Britain even had a Hebrew Christian Prime Minister Benjamin Disraeli, while Britain's greatest classical composer of the 19th century was indisputably another Jewish Christian, Felix Mendelssohn.

After her meeting with D.L. Moody, Queen Victoria was moved to fascination with Scripture and prophecy. While Cromwell allowed the Jews to return to England because he saw in Scripture that Jews would need to return to Israel from every nation, Victoria likewise prophetically believed in the re-establishment of the Jewish state and pressed Lord Balfour as Prime Minister to issue a declaration promoting the return of the Jews to their biblical homeland. Initially the Zionist cause was ardently promoted by the British government when the Holy Land came under British control during the First World War. The first Evangelical bishop of Jerusalem, Bishop Alexander, was an ethnic Jew who built an Anglican church within the walls of Jerusalem's Old City opposite where the palace of Herod had stood and the trial of Jesus took place. Yet he designed and constructed this large house of worship to resemble a Jewish synagogue.

Not least of all, the early Plymouth Brethren began to study the Scriptures using exegetical methods that were in essence midrashic, illuminating New Testament truths with Old Testament typology. Even Hudson Taylor sent from distant China the first of his tithes, donated to Jewish evangelism, back home to England stating that the Gospel is by covenantal promise still available to the Jew first.

In accordance with the character of Philadelphia, this was indeed a church very much in tune with its spiritual identity deriving from the fact that salvation comes through the Jews. It was also at this time that there was an increased interest in the subjects of end-time prophecy and the return of Christ, likewise in tune with the eschatological remarks of Jesus to the church of Philadelphia. This was indeed an incredible age with an incredible church for which Christ had no complaint, but much commendation. Sadly, only pockets and vestiges of this noble tradition still exist today.

History and Martyrs

"Philadelphia" means "brotherly love," but there were those present *"from the Synagogue of Satan, who say that they are Jews, and are not, but lie."* Strong words from Jesus. This was examined under Smyrna where Jesus also used this phrase.

Philadelphia was renowned for being a divided church. Ignatius, shortly after the death of John, tried to heal the rifts, telling them to "Give heed to the minister, and to the presbytery and to the deacons." Later in the 2nd century the church had a highly charismatic lady leader called Ammia. She was a fine preacher and trusted prophetess. Further persecution broke out and there were martyrs from this church including Germanicus, a man of noble birth who was terrified of physical suffering but refused to deny Christ. When faced with martyrdom, he found the grace of God and actually encouraged the wild beast to come after him, doubtless influenced by Irenaeus as previously discussed. Others were tortured and none yielded. Philadelphia birthed good teachers and eternal martyrs.

In later days, when Islam swept across Asia Minor, Philadelphia was one of the last bastions of Christianity. The Christians of Byzantium, who were jealous and desired its honor for themselves, ultimately betrayed it. Today the town of Philadelphia is called "*Allah-Shehr,*" meaning "The City of God." If "Brotherly Love" was a misfit it was nothing compared to the lie assigning its Muslim name!

'I know your deeds. Behold, I have put before you an open door which no one can shut, because you have a little power, and have kept My word, and have not denied My name (Rev. 3:8)

The Reformers got certain things right and they achieved this by going back to the Bible – but only *certain* things. The Protestant church was filled with "nominalism" from the onset.

The name of God is very precious to Him. It is so good that He swears by His own name. There are those who come from a family with a good name. So does Jesus! At Philadelphia they had "*kept ... not denied*" the name of the Lord. That is to say, once a year, on the Lord's Day, they had refused to say, "Caesar is Lord."

And So to Philadelphia

The 18th century, represented by Philadelphia, was the time of George Whitefield, John Wesley, Charles Wesley and the Methodist revivals. It began as a charismatic movement within the Church of England with signs and wonders, gifts of the Spirit, healings, people slain in the Spirit, etc. But then there were the anti-enthusiasts, the Liberals and the Catholics, asserting their episcopacy, their hierarchy under the bishops. What occurred in the 18th century? The Liberals became more liberal, the Catholics became more Catholic, and out came the Methodists.

And what took place in the 19th century? There was tremendous Evangelical revival within the Church of England led by William Wilberforce, the Earl of Shaftsbury and many more. But what eventually happened in the Church of England? The Liberals became more liberal. By this time English theology in Oxford and Cambridge was invaded and overwhelmed with ideas from Germany such as Higher Criticism and Rationalism. The Tractarian Movement, which became the Oxford

Movement, was led by John Henry Newman. Many people think he was a Jesuit even when he was an Anglican, but in the end he became a fully-fledged Roman Catholic and a Cardinal. The Liberals became more liberal, the Catholics became more Catholic. And, as a reaction, out came the Plymouth Brethren.

What transpired in the 20th century? Evangelicals again appeared to be on the ascent. But there were reactions such as George Carey's book *The Meeting of Waters*, his call to go back under the papacy. Yes, this was the call of the head of the Anglican church, the Right Honorable George Carey. It gives one pause when looking for something either "right" or "honorable" since he became Archbishop.

What is happening presently? Dr. Runcie acquiesced and kissed the pope's ring, acknowledging his position. When David Jenkins said no one is required to believe in the bodily resurrection of Jesus or the virgin birth to be a Christian, two-thirds — note, **two-thirds** — of the Anglican Bishops took his side. The Liberals got even more liberal.

The phenomenon of *Pax Romana* was discussed as part of the church at Ephesus. The reason the Gospel spread so quickly during the 1st and 2nd centuries was because of *Pax Romana*. The Romans provided a system of roads, trade routes, and relative political and economic stability. The Jews were in the Diaspora, the Scriptures were in Greek (the Septuagint) and everything was in place for the Gospel to spread quickly. Similarly, everything was set up for the Reformation to happen quickly when it arrived. The printing press produced the Bible, and as it spread with the increase in trade, people's view of the world changed.

Nominal Christianity

But the onset of the Reformation produced nominal Christianity, and Protestants were at war with Catholics all over Europe. By pure chance two foreign kings, William of Orange and James—a Protestant who became a Catholic, engaged in a war in Ireland. The war had nothing to do with Ireland; it was between two foreign kings. As we have again noted, the ramifications of that conflict continue to this day. They speak about the Battle of the Boyne (1590) as if it were a recent event.

The Puritans were like Calvin, Replacementists who believed in Reformed Theology. And, rightly, Calvin was afraid of the Roman Catholic Church. What the Roman Catholic Church has done even to this day is tell people that their first loyalty is to "Holy Mother Church," and it is their obligation to practice subterfuge to undermine non-Catholic governments.

In his book. *Fifty Years in the Church of Rome*, Charles Chiniquy (1809 – 1899) argued that President Abraham Lincoln was murdered by a Jesuit with the full knowledge and support of the pope because Abraham Lincoln was a Protestant and his death might have led to a Roman Catholic government in America. To this day they have engaged in such practices.

Cromwell's fears of the papacy were justified but he actually began engaging in open genocide. No one should intentionally discredit the positive things to be said of the early Puritans, and the fact that Joseph Aileen, Richard Baxter and John Owen are well worth reading in many respects. However, the police state that Calvin created in Geneva was duplicated in Scotland and again in England by the Puritans. They openly engaged in war crimes. The popular stance is to associate the Puritans with the establishment of parliamentary democracy, and that is true, but the *real* Democrats, the *real* Libertarians as Libertarians are thought of today were killed by the Puritans!

Although the Anabaptists slid into Kingdom Now theology and Montanism, just as the late John Wimber's people have done today, and began predicting things that did not happen—the way that the Kansas City Prophets and others have done today—they were not all crazy. For example, Menno Simons (1492-1559), a converted Roman Catholic priest, represented the best of that movement. The Mennonites had a tremendous influence. They kept the Bible and politics separate and evangelized much of Europe at a turbulent time. Terribly persecuted, disliked by both Catholics and Protestants, they were shown grace even in Russia where Catherine the Great welcomed them. To this day it is not uncommon to find Mennonites who frequently name one of their daughters Catherine in memory of her.

Initially, before the Reformation, the chief murderers for the papacy were the Dominicans. They sold indulgences and tortured people with their inquisitions. But after the Reformation the Counter-Reformation was led by the Jesuits (the "Society of Jesus" of all misnomers) founded by Ignatius Loyola. Loyola used exercises, copied in part from Eastern Shamanists, which was a form of brainwashing using visualization techniques. Going through these guises under a sort of spiritual guru enables the practitioner to reach a point where if it is daylight outside, should the pope proclaim it is instead night, they must believe it is night.

It is shocking to read books by the likes of Joyce Huggett espousing the use of the exercises of Ignatius Loyola as a guide to Christian prayer. She does a lot of strange things including breathing techniques which come from yoga. The name-it-and-claim-it techniques and visualization techniques are all rooted in shamanism and traditional African religions. They are pagan influences coming into Evangelical churches just as they originally came into Roman Catholic Churches. But they are totally unscriptural and very dangerous. The Jesuits became the chief agents as missionaries spreading to the New World, Roman Catholicism with all its idolatry and tortures, accompanied by forced conversions or death. But the Jesuits also became the agents of political subversion, trying to overthrow governments to bring them under the papacy. And regardless of assertions to the contrary, they are still very much in the same business.

John Wesley

Ultimately in Britain the movement to change Protestantism from within was introduced by the Methodists. John Wesley (1703 - 1791) was the son of a preacher from Epworth near Doncaster and he had gone as a missionary to the American Indians in Georgia. On his way there he experienced a storm at sea, and on the same ship encountered Moravian missionaries. Wesley was struck by the faith shown even by their children who showed no fear during the storm but trusted completely in God. Even during this very dark period in the history of the church there existed this very noble sect of people who for over one hundred years maintained a non-stop prayer chain.

Wesley knew the Anglicanism he had grown up with could not satisfy the spiritual hunger within his soul. But later he and his brother Charles were baptized in the Holy Spirit in the city of London in Aldersgate, and he gave his testimony of how his heart was strangely warmed. (Note that the Wesleys already had *some* faith. The mystery of the Holy Spirit is that God can fill a person at conversion, or at baptism, or subsequently.) On that ship, in that storm, John Wesley saw the faith of the Moravians when even their children showed no fear, such was their complete trust in God. Wesley knew he did not have their faith and that he lacked something, but did not understand what. Later in life he accepted that it is possible to serve God truly, in faith, whether or not one has had the experience of a baptism in the Holy Spirit. Many great servants of God cannot testify to any such experience and many charlatans can. But no one should set off to convert the American Indians without *any* faith at all!

Wesley realized what had happened, that he had simply been born again, and then understood what had happened to Protestantism. So he again set out to try to change the Church of England from within, although as we said initially he was not received very well. He went all over the country on horseback, at which time Anglican vicars all over England organized to oppose him. Wesley's own soul searching began when as a child the family home caught fire and he referred to himself as "a brand plucked from the fire" (like the Priest Joshua in Zechariah 3:2). His whole life was a preparation for what he faced. The church was organizing riots against him.

Wesley married, quite probably outside the will of the Lord, and his wife used to follow him and shout, "He's no good, do not listen to him!" As if he did not have enough problems! That is, until the Lord took her.

When he went to Epworth, the church where he grew up and where his mother had over twenty children, they would not allow him into the church, the very church where his father had been the vicar. So he went into the churchyard, stood on his father's grave and preached the Gospel! He said this was consecrated ground where his father lay buried, therefore he had the right to stand there and preach the Gospel, and that is what he did! But there was tremendous opposition and persecution.

John Wesley had a brother Charles who wrote hymns. But instead of composing Latin chants he heard what sort of music these people listened to as the only respite from their poverty and misery and adapted it. The pub patrons used to drink cheap, distilled gin and get horrifically drunk, yet sing two and three-part vocal harmonies. That was the only entertainment the working classes had.

When Charles Wesley began writing hymns to the melodies he had heard in the pubs, the established church did not like it. Presently they are held to be sacrosanct hymns, but in their day they caused a lot of controversy. *O For A Thousand Tongues To Sing. My Chains Fell Off, My Heart Was Free.* And later Isaac Watts: "At the cross, at the cross, where I first saw the light." Where did they get these melodies? From drinking songs in pubs. Wesley and George Whitefield came to the mining towns and began preaching the Gospel to those people. The haves became the servants of the have-nots. Wesley found a way to take the unchanging Gospel and recontextualize it. He adapted it in the appropriate context for a new culture.

At the same time, along came George Whitefield (1714 - 1770). He was somewhat Calvinistic, but at heart certainly a man of God. These people went all over Britain and something happened; people began having serious prayer meetings. This is what was happening at the time of the Wesleyan revival.

Social Conditions

The Agricultural Age was coming to an end and the Industrial Revolution was in its infancy. People who had always made their living from farming began to find themselves in towns and cities, unemployed, and socially and economically displaced. There was unbelievable social injustice, with children as young as four digging in coal mines, working twelve to sixteen hours a day. The conditions were horrible and crime was astronomical. Children were born out of wedlock, widespread immorality was rampant, and the Church of England was at an all-time low. It was the end of the agricultural society and the onset of the Industrial Revolution.

It was against this background that Wesley's revivals began, but they were largely composed of educated, middle class people who had a heart for the poor. One of the reasons why revival has not come to Britain in recent times is because practically every Evangelical church in Britain, apart from those in the inner cities where there are a lot of immigrants, is a middle class institution. The Gospel has always spread most rapidly among the poor. It is when the affluent, educated middle class have a heart for the poor that things begin to happen.

Jesus, by the standards of His day, was not working class but a lower middle class carpenter with a trade. Even Peter, the fisherman, was lower middle class. Working class people owned nothing and used to work for other people in their fields for very long hours. That was what the majority of the people were. Trades people were a step above that in the lower middle class. Matthew was middle class. Barnabas was from the aristocracy. Paul was from the religious theocratic elite. Right from the beginning God's economy has always consisted of the haves taking care of the have-nots, the rich taking care of the poor, the educated taking care of the uneducated, the clever taking care of the simple, the strong taking care of the weak. That has always been His economy. Until middle class Christians begin going into the inner cities there is not going to be any revival. This is not to say that this is the sole key to revival, as revival is a sovereign act of God's grace and a sovereign outpouring of his Holy Spirit, but there *are* guiding principles. And one principle in revival has always been the haves ministering to the have-nots. It begins with people praying for it and, when God's Spirit is subsequently outpoured, there is that attitude of servanthood.

This is what happened. Wesley began having a dynamic impact to the point that the Church of England was shaken to its foundations. The church was a somber, dead, Calvinistic corpse being kept artificially alive because people were somehow expected to go to church and for some reason they kept going. Sometimes an employer made them go, or expected them to go—things like that—and for whatever reason, people went. Wesley's revivals were an Arminian reaction against Calvinism and the social reaction it bred. It should not be forgotten that Arminius said God is **NOT** the author of sin, whereas Calvinism led to the belief that God predestined—foreordained—who was to be saved, which resulted in its adherents becoming fatalists. Evangelism was blunted because one's fate was purportedly already decided by God.

When revivals did not take place in Ireland Wesley again concluded that this was due to the mistreatment of Catholics by the Protestant establishment, figuring it was little wonder that the Irish wanted to stay under the pope. However, a few years later and as a result of his revivals, slavery was abolished in the British Empire. Child labor was also abolished in the British Empire. Prison reform took place in the British Empire. Schools for the working classes were set up in the British Empire. The mission movement began. Building societies and housing schemes were initiated so that ordinary people could own their own homes. Even the British Labour Party was born out of the influences of early Methodism.

But Wesley knew that repentance had to come first before revival. He saw social injustice as a sin, but the real reason he hated it in its own right as sin is because he said it produced the onset of additional sin. He saw the crime and the decadence and the immorality as something that was bred by poverty, and he asserted that to get rid of the sin one must get rid of the things that engender it, which are sins in themselves.

It all began this way, but once Jesus is taken out of these things, what follows? Things go the way of the world. That is what happened to the Labour movement, the Building Societies, everything. Each of these things began right, but when Jesus was taken out of the movements they turned into sources of oppression themselves. The state of such things return to the mentality of the world.

Understanding this background is very, very important. Just as in Wesley's day Britain was at the end of an agricultural economy and the beginning of an industrial economy, so today Britain is at the end of an industrial economy and the beginning of a high-tech service and information economy. The change is just as radical.

In Wesley's day people who made their living harvesting crops and driving teams of horses had no place in a coal mine or working a lathe or machine; they did not know those skills. Today someone who built ships on the Clyde or who worked in a textile mill in Leeds does not know what a microchip is. It is the same thing. People are totally, socially, and economically displaced on a massive level. When such middle-aged people are laid off in these smoke stack industries, it is inevitable that most of them will never work again. This is exactly what happened in Wesley's day. The new capitalists became tremendously rich and other people possessed nothing. And that is the sort of world that exists today. The pressing question is, however, is there going to be revival?

Whitefield and Wesley

George Whitefield went to the United States. Although moderately Calvinistic himself, Whitefield said the Calvinists and the Puritans failed in their mandate, so the Lord sent him to evangelize America. Jonathan Edwards felt the same way. The Methodists did very well, but eventually the High Church of England would not have any more of it and a split ensued over ecclesiastical polity and church government. Because of this the Methodists separated themselves.

Wesley realized toward the end of his life that he had made a mistake trying to put new wine into old wineskins. And he realized that by trying to change the church from within instead of taking a more radical stance in the very beginning, he had saddled himself with things he could not change. One was the decline of Scripture reading, the decline in the emphasis on teaching the Word of God. He said, "If this is what happens to Methodism when I am alive, what is going to happen when I am dead?" And in hindsight the result is well known and *exactly* what he knew would happen: it died.

Several years ago while visiting Wesley's chapel on City Road in London, I was astonished to discover no Christians in attendance there. There was a church in Acton Town in London where it was proclaimed, "Wesleyan and Reformed Church." Well, "Reformed" is Calvinist and Wesley was an Arminian! How could a church be Wesleyan *and* Reformed? Very simply. The Wesleyans no longer believed what Wesley did and the Calvinists no longer believed what Calvin did. Problem resolved!

To this day a point of interest is London's Bunhill Fields on City Road in the Borough of Islington. There will be found a cemetery where John Bunyan, who wrote *Pilgrim's Progress*, is buried, as well as Daniel Defoe who wrote *Robinson Crusoe*, John Wesley and his mother Susanna, George Fox (the founder of the Quakers), Isaac Watts the hymn writer and others. They are all buried in this non-conformist cemetery because the Church of England would not allow them to be buried in their own, very special, "consecrated ground"!

Bunyan, the Quakers and Wesley

This period was preceded by different attempts to get it right. Even in Cromwell's day, and shortly thereafter, John Bunyan ministered in Bedfordshire. There was a charismatic movement called the Quakers that preceded the Methodists. The Quakers began as an Evangelical movement, but the devil got to them the way he always gets to most charismatic movements, through Experiential Theology. They would meet in a room and wait for the "inner light," the prompting of the Spirit. No leadership, no agenda, no structured worship as such, just waiting for the inner light and prophetic revelation and what God wanted to say to them. That was the mainstay of their meetings. Eventually the inner light began telling them all manner of crazy things, such as refusing to participate in the Lord's Supper and who knows what else. They began getting into wrong doctrines. The Quakers, although they began right as most charismatic movements do, quickly went off the rails because they were not well-grounded in Scripture.

The Methodists initially were based around the simple preaching of Scripture. But Wesley was shocked when people began being "slain in the Spirit" in his meetings. There are those who will assert it is not biblical to be slain in the Spirit, but in Revelation 1 the apostle John was *"in the Spirit on the Lord's Day"* and he *"fell at His feet as a dead man."* (Rev. 1:17) The warning of the counterfeit is in Isaiah 28:13, *"That they may go and stumble backward, be broken, snared and taken captive."* This is in the context of priests and prophets who stagger from beer, not from the presence of the Holy Spirit. Also "counterfeit miracles" get a mention in 2 Thessalonians 2:9. The phenomenon of being slain in the Spirit can be found in other places in Scripture but the term occurs in Revelation 1. Whitefield was astounded when he saw this happening in Wesley's meetings. But then a few days later he was even more astounded when it began happening at his own meetings!

Wesley traveled a quarter of a million miles in England in all weather on horseback. This shows Wesley was some traveler. He instituted clinics for the poor and many such things. His brother Charles wrote 6,000 hymns, 60 of which are still sung, and their theology is sound. He wrote them to convey the Word of God. They gave almost all their money away to the poor—almost all. Wesley's stipend was £100 a year. He received vastly more in gifts but ensured that he never spent more than this modest stipend on himself and his family. These were mighty times.

After this, God began working even in the established churches. Similar movements of people imitating Wesley sprang up even in the Church of England. Aristocrats such as William Wilberforce and the Earl of Shaftsbury began caring for the poor. Florence Nightingale was a Christian. And the Gospel's influence began permeating all of society. In music it influenced Handel who wrote *The Messiah*, as well as Felix Mendelssohn, a Jewish Christian and composer. Sir Arthur Sullivan of Gilbert and Sullivan wrote

Onward Christian Soldiers. This whole Christian influence began going into all areas of Britain and into other parts of the British Empire. Righteousness exalts a nation (Prov. 14:34). (This was when God blessed and used Britain.) But it was always a moderate Arminian reaction against strong Calvinism.

William Carey, Colonialism and Mission

The equivalent for the Baptists was William Carey (1761 - 1834). As the story goes, he was told at the Baptist Convention, "Brother Carey sit down and be quiet. If God decides to convert the heathen He will do it without your help or mine." He was a Northampton shoemaker who learned multiple languages and translated the Bible into East Indian languages. He founded the Baptist Mission Society. It is alarming not only that a lot of the Baptist Mission Society today is liberal even though the leaders are Evangelical, but that to commemorate their anniversary they asked Archbishop George Carey to write the prologue to their book. It is quite shocking what has become of the Baptist Union. Britain evangelized nation after nation after nation.

The bad side of Colonialism and exploitation is common knowledge, but there are two sides to the coin. While the Church of England was popularly engaged in turning people into Christians in order to turn them into subjects of the Queen, there were other mission societies in the country that were only out to turn them into followers of Jesus. Whatever mistakes they made, God still blessed this country and Empire for 200 years as a result of these revivals.

The Plymouth Brethren and the Salvation Army

But then something else happened in the Church of England. As the Catholics got more Catholic and the Liberals got more liberal, there were those who could not stand it and out they came: the Plymouth Brethren. What does Philadelphia mean? "Brotherly love." That was their defining characteristic.

Hudson Taylor founded the China Inland Mission in 1866 and went to China. He was way ahead of his time. He knew that it was not appropriate to turn African or Asian people into Englishmen. He saw that he must bring them the Gospel in their own culture, so he went to China and lived like a Chinaman. He dressed like a Chinaman, ate with chopsticks, and even married a Chinese woman.

Dr. Barnado in the East End of London found a little child asking for help. He could not help the child, and the next day found the poor little chap frozen to death. Out of that tragedy was born a mission to children named after Barnado. In 1999, for the first time, Barnados has abrogated its statement of faith. It is now a social organization and no longer a Christian organization. Yet it claims to be following Dr. Barnado who was a 1,000 per cent Bible-believing Christian. George Muller in Bristol did the same thing with the street children. The main hallmark of this church, Philadelphia, was its name: brotherly love. Their sense of mission was always to bring the Gospel but never without bringing people practical help just as Jesus did.

We have taken note of the repeated mistake that exists today where organizations such as Christian Aid and World Vision that began as genuinely Christian later began meeting people's human needs without giving them the Gospel of salvation. That is not what Wesley did and that is not what Jesus did. He met their human needs, but He also met their greater spiritual need. These organizations begin right, but over time digress from their own heritage. When such a divergence occurs God calls someone else. There were terrible slums in East London, Mile End Road, Bethnal Green, and along came General Booth, the founder of the Salvation Army, a real *Onward Christian Soldier*! Once again the Gospel not only had the power to change lives, but to change society. That was the church at Philadelphia, one movement after another.

Philadelphia

Of the seven churches there were only two for which Jesus offered no criticism. One was Smyrna who was anointed for burial—it was persecuted—but the other was Philadelphia. That was the greatest age the church had known since the days of the apostles. Of the seven churches it was also the most Jewish in its description: the key of David, the synagogue, the pillar of the temple, the New Jerusalem. The imagery Jesus used is the most Jewish, the most Hebraic, because it was the least Hellenistic of the seven churches.

The Plymouth Brethren's method of Bible interpretation was probably the closest that any Gentile church has ever been when it comes to doing it correctly. The typology of the temple, looking at how the New Testament is in the Old concealed, the Old is in the New revealed. Having little power, just like the early Christians, they nonetheless through faithfulness possessed the power to triumph. Jesus said,

> *"By this all men will know that you are My disciples, if you have love for one another." (Jn. 13:35)*

That was the defining characteristic of the Philadelphians. And it happened at a time in history very, very much like the time of history currently being experienced.

The Dilemma of Laodicea

Something true even today is that people come along claiming to be the followers of the founders of American and British Evangelicalism. They will claim a heritage or doctrinal link with John Wesley or George Whitefield. But John Wesley and George Whitefield believed in the gifts of the Spirit. They will claim a link in America with D.L. Moody or R.A. Torrey or Jonathan Edwards or Charles Finney, but those people *all* believed in the gifts of the Spirit!

While considering enrollment in Moody Bible Institute, the prospectus at that time stated that students were not allowed to have beards, but on the front page there were pictures of Moody and Torrey with great big beards. They could not have gone to their own school! On the first page it stated, "We do not endorse the tongues-praying movement." Compare this to either D.L. Moody's or R.A. Torrey's biography. They *both* testified to having received the baptism in the Holy Spirit and subsequently speaking in tongues—*both* of them!

The arch-problem at this time was Charles Finney. Finney began with a mighty anointing on his life, believing in holiness and in power, but bordering on full-blown Pelagianism. Pelagius denied original sin, something Augustine opposed. Finney, too, denied original sin. He said man is not fallen and that salvation can be obtained by choosing Christ instead of being chosen by Christ. Nonetheless, God used him. A book called *Finney on Revival* opens with the words, "Revival is nothing less than a wholesale repentance and turning to God."

But there was a reaction not only against Finney but against the growth of Liberalism. Rationalism began in Germany with Wellhausen and the theory of Pentateuchal sources. It is called "JEDP." They proposed that Genesis was originally five books which were later fused together. It comes from the names of God in the Hebrew language: Jehovahistic, Ellohistic, Deuteronomistic and Priestly, the last source being from Babylon. That is what Liberal Protestantism teaches.

Additional people came along such as Rudolf Bultmann, the German existentialist theologian, who said that the resurrection was not literal but merely a principle. They said a distinction must be made between the Jesus of faith and the Jesus of history. They taught that the Jesus of faith was an invention of the early church to engender belief, and that it is the Jesus of history everyone must be concerned with, and therefore not much more can be known about Him.

In reaction against these things, as we have stated, Benjamin Warfield arose in America totally opposed against the gifts of the Spirit. He basically redefined Western Evangelicalism in cessasionist terms. Whatever the reason, the gifts of the Spirit fizzled out in Britain but continued in America. Finney's ministry was concentrated in New York and New England. From there D.L. Moody came preaching, and instead of Britain sending missionaries and evangelists to America, America began sending missionaries and evangelists to Britain.

in her old age Queen Victoria was led in prayer by D.L. Moody to receive Jesus. It was, once more, based on his influence upon her and what she observed in Scripture. As a result, she supported what became the Balfour Declaration to allow the Jews to return to Israel. When the Jews began returning to Israel in the 19th century, D.L. Moody went to Jerusalem, stood across the street from the Damascus gate presiding over the Arab cemetery where Golgotha is found, and preached the Gospel, causing a riot among the Muslims.

The Bible Belt of America shifted from the Northeast around New England to the Midwest. Subsequent to Moody there appeared the likes of A.B. Simpson and A.W. Tozer. They founded the Christian Missionary Alliance. Another was Harry Ironside. These were the men of God for their day. Billy Sunday was another. Then the Bible Belt shifted to the South. The place to study in Finney's day was Yale, but Yale became liberal. Subsequently the place to study became the Moody Bible Institute in Chicago in the Midwest and eventually came to reside at the Dallas Theological Seminary in Dallas. In the 1960s and 70s the Jesus Movement came along and the Evangelical center of America became California, the West Coast, and everyone wanted to go to Fuller Theological Seminary. But even in America Evangelical Christianity is in decline. It is in decline because of the phenomena associated with Laodicea, the last church, the lukewarm church. Under the unfortunate influences of C. Peter Wagner, Fuller Seminary has become an infected boil, oozing out the poison of ecumenism, psychology, and market-driven formulas of church growth which have infiltrated most of Western Evangelicism. This however, is not how this institution and others like it began.

But in reference to the church at Philadelphia, once again at the present time there is a cataclysmic change being experienced by the social and economic fabric of society. People are totally displaced and cannot make a living doing the things they, their father, or their grandfather did. There is urban decay, poor people crowded into the inner cities, crime rates rising through the roof, social injustice. It is socially acceptable for children to be born out of wedlock; everything is breaking down. People are saying, "What is happening to our country?" The crime, the moral decay, the diminished importance of church—it is dead. Everything is dead. People do not respect the government or the church any more. A few make fortunes while everyone else goes to the wall, and everyone wonders what is happening. That is what was happening then, and that is exactly what is happening now.

But God had a plan. His plan was to take people who really had a heart for Him, educated middle class people who had a heart for the poor, who cared about what was happening to their country and their society. They cared about it so much that they were willing to put their lives on the line and turn their backs on everything else except the Gospel, except Jesus. That is what happened.

God had to send foreigners, the Moravians, to bring the Gospel, but then God began raising people up in Britain. He raised up the Methodists and then other groups who similarly followed the ideals of Philadelphia. This was the church that was the least Hellenistic of any of the seven churches, and the closest to the Jewish church in its philosophy and structure, even in its hermeneutics. The Philadelphia movement as an era started in Norwich with a person named Jane Leed and people in her church began to see how these churches were representative of events in history.

God was looking for people who were willing to emphasize repentance, holiness, self-sacrifice, and not only a loving word but a loving deed. He was looking for those with a love for the people in the inner cities, the unemployed, the children in single-parent families. God was looking for people who were willing to take their Middle Class affluence and education and become servants of those people. These were the kind of people God was looking for then, and He found them. And they are the kind of people He is looking for now.

Chapter 7
Laodicea: "People's Opinions"
1950s Onward?

1st 2nd 3rd 4th 5th 6th 7th 8th 9th 10th 11th 12th 13th 14th 15th 16th 17th 18th 19th 20th

Apostolic Church

Pre-Nicean Church

Rise of the Institutional Church

The Dark Ages

The Reformation

Great Awakening

Apostate Church

The Message to Laodicea

"To the angel of the church in Laodicea write:

"'The Amen, the faithful and true Witness, the Beginning of the creation of God, says this:

"'"I know your deeds, that you are neither cold nor hot; I wish that you were cold or hot. So because you are lukewarm, and neither hot nor cold, I will spit you out of My mouth. Because you say, "I am rich, and have become wealthy, and have need of nothing," and you do not know that you are *wretched and miserable and poor and blind and naked, I advise you to buy from Me gold refined by fire so that you may become rich, and white garments so that you may clothe yourself, and that the shame of your nakedness will not be revealed; and eye salve to anoint your eyes so that you may see. Those whom I love, I reprove and discipline; therefore be zealous and repent. Behold, I stand at the door and knock; if anyone hears My voice and opens the door, I will come in to him and will dine with him, and he with Me. He who overcomes, I will grant to him to sit down with Me on My throne, as I also overcame and sat down with My Father on His throne.""*

"He who has an ear, let him hear what the Spirit says to the churches." (Rev. 3:14-22)

The City of Laodicea

Laodicea was a wealthy city known for dyed fabric. It was so wealthy that when the city was damaged extensively by an earthquake the people declined financial assistance from the Roman government because they did not need it. It also benefited from being located near some mineral springs where the water could be either hot or cold. Approaching the source they were either hot or cold, but by channeling the water into an aqueduct they drew some of it away making it lukewarm and horrible to drink. The city was also in close proximity to the ancient equivalent of an eye hospital. This is what Jesus drew on for His message to this last church.

Biblical archeologists have in recent years excavated much more of Laodicea, uncovering much more than was available a generation ago. Although the same would be true for Ephesus (and to a lesser degree of Sardis) the sheer size of Ephesus still leaves much buried beneath the silt, placing the heart of the existing ruins a full mile inland from the Mediterranean shore containing the original port and densely populated residential sectors. In Laodicea however, more than enough has been excavated in fairly recent times to fully confirm the description found in the text of Revelation 3. The ruins of the Roman aqueduct delivering mineral water from the cascading white stone springs of Pamukkale above, and the system of Roman public fountains, are on open display. And some of the structures are remarkably well-preserved. While nearby Colossae and Heliopolis largely remain unexcavated, Laodicea has become one of the finest examples of archeological discovery and the unearthing of Greco-Roman ruins that both validate and illuminate the scriptural record.

Here again the issue of "the mixture" is plainly illustrated by the archeology. Before the hot springs had sufficiently cooled to become cold, the lukewarm mixture poured out of the third set of fountain faucets. Once again, God always hates the mixture. From the outlawed combination of garments made from wool and flax (typologically meaning that the garments of salvation and robes of righteousness must be from the Lamb and not from anything that man produced) so too we have Peter's warning of "paraxousin" (2 Pe. 2) combining true prophecy and true doctrine with false. The ensuing mixture is spiritually deadly. More problematically it is a homogenous package where the one cannot be extricated from the other. We ought not to seek the true things out of Jehovah's Witnesses or Mormon belief or the church of Rome any more than we should from the Word-Faith money preachers or the Emergent Church or the Purpose-Driven agenda, as well as from books like *The Shack*. Any elements of truth are merely there to camouflage a trap—a trap which is a snare not of Rick Warren or Brian McLaren, but of the devil who uses them. We may enjoy hot tea or iced tea, but no one likes lukewarm tea. Christ hates the mixture, and the good cannot be separated from the bad. Nothing I have seen more superbly illustrates this fact than the excavations at Laodicea.

Future Historical Prophetic Antitype and the Meaning of the Name

As each of these churches has a name that indicates something describing its character, Laodicea is no exception. The name Laodicea comes from two Greek words, *Lao Dictaomi*, meaning "people's opinions," or "judgments," sometimes with an emphasis on people's rights or what they think their rights to be.

"*The Amen.*" Jesus always has the last word. He was "*the faithful and true Witness,*" not someone who could be characterized as lukewarm. He was "*the Beginning of the creation of God.*" By these three titles Laodicea is vividly reminded of just who He is.

Laodicea said, "*I am rich.*" Jesus said, "*You are poor and blind and naked ...*"! They were spiritually bankrupt but thought themselves spiritually rich under the delusion of their affluence. And it was crucial for them to wake up to the fact and see it. Although they may have been rich in worldly wealth, yet they were naked spiritually because they were not clothed with good deeds. This church, like the modern church of Western Civilization, ran on the ideas and opinions and men that were not subordinated to God's Word. This was, again, a practice of the Sanhedrin condemned by Jesus in Matthew 15 where He castigated the teaching of inventions of men as divine precepts.

The Dilemma of Laodicea

Like the modern church also, material affluence becomes the bogus barometer of blessing and the counterfeit gage of one's standing before the Lord.

Laodicea's chief problem was that it did not know it was Laodicea, due to its blindness much like the modern church does not view or comprehend itself for what it actually is in the all-penetrating sight of God. There have been those such as the late Dr. Francis Schaffer who authored *The Church at the End of the 20th Century* who understood the relationship between history, philosophy, theology, and ecclesiology. Too much of what he wrote, and what the late A.W. Tozer warned of, has been too easily forgotten. In a better age, figures such as Bishop J.C. Ryle in the UK saw even in his day what was coming, but his message too has been so readily ignored. John Wesley warned that true revival would bring higher degrees of social justice and, as a result, would produce affluence. But once the church became affluent and was not persecuted, the danger was that it would become lukewarm, lazy, and backslide. Yet even the Methodists largely discard the caveats of their founder. This is today's Laodicea.

To understand it we must revert back to the geography and topography of ancient Laodicea. Devastated by an earthquake, it required no imperial assistance financially to rebuild. Its nearby cities of Colossae and Heliopolis (which also had churches named in the New Testament) formed an upscale metropolis. The churches in these three cities being so proximal to each other can in one sense due to their proximity be, to at least some degree, regarded as one. It is of little coincidence therefore, that in writing to the next door Colossians, Paul the apostle even then warned of the dangers of the vain philosophies of the world entering into the church. What may have been retarded in the first century has become the norm in the 21st century.

To this day the excavated remains of the Roman aqueduct bringing mineral water from the mountain top spa at Pamukkale with its ivory white cliffs down to Laodicea remain visible. The water feeds into a system of springs and water tables with some of the Roman fountain wells still visible to this day. There are the hot, the cold, and where the two mix, the lukewarm. Scripturally God has always hated the mixture. The ancient Hebrews were forbidden to make a garment of wool and flax. Wool came from sheep, flax was manmade; thus salvation had to be purely from the Lamb of God and not by the work of man.

In his second epistle Peter warned of the false teachers and false prophets who would *paraxousin*–mix truth and error side by side in their false doctrine. Elements of truth would be used to camouflage the false. For God's people the mixture was always to be detestable. As one could not separate the fabrics in a garment sewn from wool and flax mixed together, or extract the hot water from warm water to make hot tea and use the cold water from the same mixture to make iced tea, it is impossible to spiritually or theologically separate the good from the bad where doctrine is fundamentally wrong or heretical. The mixture is a deception and will eventually lead to the judgment of Christ and rejection by Christ. Once the bread is baked, one cannot segregate the leaven from it. This too is the problem of modern Laodicea; it seeks to hold a mixture of right and wrong, biblical and unbiblical, truth and error, in a balanced tension oblivious to the warnings of Christ.

Insight on the Sightless

This final church is characterized by being lukewarm and fully engaged in self-deception. In the Last Days *understanding* becomes God's barometer of faithfulness.

When the prophet Daniel was given his vision of the Last Days, which is replayed in Revelation, Daniel concluded Chapter 12 by saying *"None of the wicked will understand"* (Dan. 12:10). But in 11:33-35 he said, *"Those who have insight among the people will give understanding to the many."* This was partially fulfilled in the days of the Maccabees when Antiochus Epiphanes came along as a major type of the Antichrist. But it also means something for the Last Days.

"None of the wicked will understand."

Wise virgins requiring oil in their lamps to see in the night is a figure of the tribulation, of those who walk in the light even when it is the hours of darkness. The bridegroom opens the door to them (Mt. 25:1-13). *"Thy word is a lamp to my feet and a light to my path"* (Ps. 119:105). The believer's understanding of Scripture is accomplished by the illumination of the Holy Spirit. In John 8 the Levites would have been topping off the lamps, and against this background Jesus said, *"I am the Light of the world"* (Jn. 8:12). It is critical to grasp that understanding and faithfulness go hand-in-hand.

"I advise you to buy from Me... eye salve to anoint your eyes, that you may see."

Remember how Jesus made salve in John 9 and anointed the man's eyes so that he could see? He counsels the Laodiceans to allow Him to open their eyes. In other words, Laodicea's first and foremost problem is that it does not recognize its own condition, that it is blind, poor and naked, or that it is lukewarm and deceived by its material affluence. It did not know that Jesus saw it as it really was.

Laodicea today thinks that because it is well-off materially and has a high standard of living, it must be blessed in God's sight. To be sure it is blessed, but it has made the blessing, the material affluence, the measure of its own spirituality. According to their reasoning if someone is prospering, they must be in God's will. After all, the Bible states, "*The wealth of the wicked is stored up for the righteous*" (Prov. 13:22). This is true. As well as, "*The meek shall inherit the earth*" (Mt. 5:5). Yes, when the time comes this most certainly will happen. But His kingdom is not of this world (Jn. 18:36). There will be a Millennial Reign and there will be an eternity.

This all fits hand-in-glove with Kingdom Now Theology which makes financial prosperity the barometer of each person's spirituality. This belief ignores the fact that it is Christians who are in prison in China or who are being attacked in Mexico and Nigeria. In reality such ones who are closest to Jesus are the ones who are the most spiritual.

Laodicea in Greek means "people's opinions" or "people's judgments." *Lao* is from the word meaning "laity"—"the people"—as was seen when discussing the Nicolaitans, the conquerors or rulers of the laity. And *dicea* means "sayings" or "judgments" or "opinions." The root of "dictation" is derived from this word. In other words, it was a church that was run on the opinions of men.

The World after the Reformation

The response of the papacy to the Reformation was predictable. The papal bull issued against the *95 Theses* of Luther refused to address the issues themselves, but condemned Luther for writing it. The ad homonym approach has always been the unmistakable signature of religious hypocrisy be it the Levitical attacks on Jeremiah or the kangaroo trial of Jesus before the Sanhedrin. If the malefactors are unable to respond to the issues, they attack the person who raised the issues.

As the Gospel spread, so did political efforts of the papacy to contain it. These resulted in a number of gruesome wars in Continental Europe claiming the lives of a high percentage of the population. Those wars continued until the end of the 17th century and even into the 18th century. Efforts to restore a Catholic monarchy in Britain resulted in everything from the exploits of bonnie Prince Charles (born in Rome) to the Battle of Culloden in Scotland. Celts did not like Anglo-Saxons, yet Protestant Scotsmen fought with the British and formed a union against the Catholic forces bent on re-establishing a Stuart dynasty in a series of back-and-forth power games of political intrigue and wars involving William of Orange,

Mary Queen of Scotts, and James II. It was a sad and prolonged aftermath for both Protestants and Catholics. Not infrequently Catholics would turn against each other and fight with the Protestants as did the Dutch Catholics in joining William of Orange. In Britain Presbyterians, Calvinists, and Puritan Calvinists massacred each other.

As the Gospel spread, so did nominal Protestantism, which was no more biblically Christian than that which it set out to reform. Yet in the age of modern Laodicea, mainstream Protestantism has become worse. Despite its hypocrisy and the widespread pedophilia of its clergy, officially Roman Catholicism does not sanction the ordination of homosexuals and lesbians; liberal Protestantism certainly does. One cannot find a Roman Catholic theologian publishing officially with the approval of the papacy who would ever deny the biblically recorded miracles surrounding Christ. Mainstream Protestant scholarship however, dismissed such belief long ago.

Yet in order to stop the advance of Protestantism the Roman Catholic Church responded with two stalwarts, one of which was the Council of Trent that extended and solidified the power of the papacy, condemning all that is not Catholic and asserting that membership of the Roman Catholic Church is central to salvation. Even in the 21st century, Pope Benedict XVI restated this position that only his church is the correct one, which did nothing to dissuade ecumenical Evangelicals led by Chuck Colson from paying the papacy homage, scarcely stopping short of genuflecting before the pope and kissing his ring. Colson and his ilk encourage Evangelicals to accept the legitimacy of a scandal-plagued church which will not accept the legitimacy of any Evangelical church. Meanwhile his predecessor John Paul II had already denounced Evangelicals as rapacious wolves on at least four occasions dating back to 1985 in La Paz, Bolivia, Santo Domingo, Mexico, and in Rome in protest of the large numbers of Hispanic Catholics turning to Evangelicism. The Vatican message is simple; it is the same message they have enunciated since the Council of Trent: "Come home to Mother Rome or there is no basis for unity. You must accept the validity of our church based on papal decree, but we will never accept the validity of yours."

The Second Vatican Council of the 1960's in fact reaffirmed all of the pronouncements of the Council of Trent. The concentration of power in the hands of the papacy continued until 1854 when through a finagled process the pope had himself proclaimed "infallible" when speaking *Ex Cathedra*. It is upon this doctrine that later popes could make wild pronouncements directly contrary to Scripture, such as proclaiming the alleged sinlessness of Mary the mother of Jesus. The quest of the papacy to re-swallow those who departed from it has, if nothing else, remained consistent. The *Filioque* dispute that finalized the final split between Rome and the Eastern Orthodox tradition based on two rival interpretations of a Platonic philosophical re-interpretation of biblical Christology has been at the center of attempts to bring about a doctrinal reconciliation between the Roman Catholic and Greek Orthodox worlds. This after the Roman Catholic *Ustashi* genocide by Roman Catholic Nazis in Yugoslavia, like the Crusades, failed to achieve it. It has been the Church of England and the Anglican communion however, that has been most amicable to crawling back to Rome and doing so on its hands and knees. The papacy was willing to make concessions on everything from the marriage of clergy to accepting Darwinism, but there could be no compromise with the monarchial primacy claimed by the pope despite the history of corruption, treachery, and moral debauchery that characterized pope after pope for centuries.

The banking families of Italy that had always been in competition with each other to control the papacy from the time of the Renaissance onward such as the Medici and Borgia families found a common enemy in Protestantism. So, too, the philosophical and theological rival factions within Catholicism that positioned the Aristotelians and Platonists against each other with the Jansenist Schism likewise had a greater common threat to each other. Even neutrally antagonistic religious orders such as the Dominicans of the Inquisition and the Franciscans were forced into a tenuous unity in the face of Protestantism. Meanwhile the Roman Catholic Church linked its political fortunes in Europe to the Hapsburg Dynasty as would later happen in America with the Kennedys.

The second weapon fashioned to stop the spread of a biblical Gospel and to oppose Protestantism however, was the institution of the Jesuits by Ignatius Loyola. Beginning as missionaries and educators they became the religious propaganda agents of the Spanish Conquistadors and the political agents of papal diplomacy. The Jesuits also formulated the philosophy of Roman Catholic education: "Give us a child until the age of seven and they are ours for life," proving that Catholic education is not about learning but rather about indoctrination, manipulation, and fear. Over the centuries the Protestant-Catholic divide remained largely intact until the age of ecumenism, but now the papacy seeks to restore itself to past glories.

The papacy finds its opportunity to do this through the encouragement of Euro-Federalism where the nation-state that allowed Luther and the Reformers to take root would be eroded in favor of a united Europe. In accordance with the prophecies of the Hebrew prophet Daniel there is a quest afoot in Europe to make iron stick to clay. A culturally, historically, and linguistically diverse European Union comprised of Slavic cultures such as Poland, Celtic cultures such as Ireland, Germanic cultures such as Austria, and Latin cultures such as Portugal, have only one common ingredient: it is not language, history, ethnicity, or cuisine; it is Roman Catholicism. Hence the Ecumenical agenda to reverse the Reformation and the socialist European agenda to reverse the nation-state into a united pseudo-democratic Europe meet each other's need. The quest is to see the resurrection of a Holy Roman Empire that once again will be neither holy nor Roman.

After the Reformation prosperity grew, but somehow increased at the expense of other people, particularly people who were not white Protestants. People therefore began to identify their Protestant culture and political ideas with their own version of the Gospel. After all, God seemed to have blessed them.

Today in Northern Ireland more Roman Catholics are being saved than Protestants. Yet the strict Presbyterians cannot understand how people can get saved out of the Roman Catholic Church, stop supporting the IRA, experience rejection by their families as a result, and still not be Unionists or Orangemen or Protestants. They can still be Republicans and believe that the country should be united! Similarly the strict Presbyterians cannot understand how it is possible to be both a Christian and a Republican.

The conservative Southern Baptists in America hold to the same notion. A now deceased American preacher, Jerry Falwell, went on television and said, "You cannot be a Liberal and a Christian." This in spite of the fact that there are a great many born-again Christians in the black community and the Hispanic community, 85 per cent of them voting liberal. When extra-biblical criteria is superimposed on salvation the very edge of something that the Letter to the Galatians calls "witchcraft" is approached. ("*You foolish Galatians! Who has bewitched you?*" [Gal. 3:1]) It is very dangerous to do that. But they cannot separate their social mentality, their perception of history and their political views from the Gospel. That became the basis of Laodicea.

Compounding this is the Calvinistic mentality that God predestines people to be this way. Thus, many such people are quite content to abide tremendous social injustice and go to church just the same. That is how it is in South Africa, Northern Ireland, the American South. People's opinions is how such things are established; they are rules taught by men, not by the true Word of God. Laodicea is like that. People have always tried to reinterpret the Gospel in the light of their own world view, and it is happening today.

Consumerism and Contextualization

Presently this is a consumer society. Everything is consumption-oriented, fueled by the advertising industry, controlled by media psychology with such powerful persuasion that they begin applying it to children as soon as they can watch a television. Consumerism. That is the current economic basis of society.

The biblical calling is to bring the Gospel of the Kingdom into the world, to meet people where they are. That is called "recontextualization." Believers are called to take the Gospel and, without changing it doctrinally, package and present it in a way relevant to a given social situation. God's calling is to bring the Gospel into the world, not to bring the world into the Gospel. Similarly, the ship in the sea is all very well, but the sea in the ship is all very bad. But that is what was happening in Laodicea. The consumerism of society was getting into the church.

Biblically, Christians should say to their Counselor, "Lord, what church do You want me to belong to? Do you want me to join the Elim church, the Baptist church, the Brethren church? Where do You want me to be committed?" It may be impossible to agree with the doctrines, but God wants committed believers there anyway. Or maybe if it is impossible to agree with the doctrines it is God's place to tell you to leave. But that is the attitude Christians should have. "Inquire of the Lord." Whenever King David inquired of the Lord he did what was right in the eyes of the Lord. But when he clapped eyes on Bathsheba and neglected to inquire of the Lord for the better part of a year, look what happened.

What do people commonly do today in place of inquiring of the Lord? "Have you heard this preacher? Have you heard that one? Have you been *here*, have you been *there*?" They engage in comparative shopping! It is the mentality of the secular world seeping into the Body of Christ. The real question should be, "Have you been to Jesus? Have you heard Christ? Do you know Jesus?" Instead of inquiring of the Lord they ask themselves what they want. It is the opposite of what is supposed to take place.

Another example is the phenomenon of the rise in feminism over the last 20 years. In the beginning it had some merit. It is hard to imagine anyone in their right mind denying that it was an absolutely outrageous injustice for a woman to be paid less money than a man for the same job just because she was a woman. Most movements begin by doing good. A lot of these things are based on biblical principles and were even founded by Christians. But when Jesus is removed it turns secular. Today violent crime, which is already astronomical among males, is rising twice as fast among women as it is among men.

Laodicea

Stress-related health disorders, peptic ulcers and cardiovascular disorders are increasing much faster among women than among men and there is a direct relationship to the emergence of feminism. What is happening in the world is the same thing happening in the churches. The move for women pastors and women leaders began coming into the church. People have always tried to redefine the Gospel in the light of their world view or culture. The distinction should always be drawn between the doctrine of the Word of God and culture. Everyone is called to introduce God's principles and God's doctrines into their culture but not to take the mentality or culture of this world into the church and into God's doctrines.

That is Laodicea, the church of people's opinions. That becomes the basis of the problem. This church is a church that has a faithful remnant that the Great Shepherd is going to rebuke and discipline. Because He loves them He will use His rod and staff to correct them and to persuade them from being led astray.

It is important to remember that only a very small percentage of Jews were ready for the Messiah to come the first time. They were God's people, they had His Word, they believed His promise, they expected the Messiah to come. But only a very small percentage of Jews were ready for Jesus to come the first time. Similarly, only a very small percentage of Christians will be ready for Jesus when He comes back because of the very same reasons.

Charismatic Pandemonium

We do not subscribe to the doctrinal error of cessationism which falsely teaches that the gifts of the Spirit ended with the Apostles. Neither do we deny that God can bless and prosper His people and that when biblical principles are applied to a society these principles of God will permeate cultural, economic, and political structures, thus bringing improvement and more blessing simply because temporal things are being seasoned with the eternal Word of God. This perspective is scriptural. What is unscriptural however, is not biblical charismata itself but rather what some have called the charismania that has dominated most of the modern Charismatic Movement. Too often Bibles went out the window followed by brains. There are many reasons why the Charismatic Movement after forty years has failed to bring revival. The first and foremost is its embrace of Experiential Theology, basing its theology on the flesh and experience instead of on God's Word. But the sociological reason why it has failed is because it has largely failed to preach the Gospel to the poor. Almost by definition, Christianity makes people upwardly mobile.

A real-life example is missionary work with illiterate gypsies. As soon as they get saved the first thing they want to do is to learn how to read the Bible. Immediately they become more educated. Within a generation the capacity to reach out to those where they came from is lost. But the Bible teaches wisdom. That is one reason why Roman Catholic Latin America and the Philippines are backward countries. Wherever Evangelical Protestantism has had an influence, people are more upwardly mobile. God's Word makes people wiser.

In today's environment, how can these truths be given to people with a new world view? As Daniel prophesied, something sinister is happening today: the countries that were in the (Un)Holy Roman Empire are reuniting. And like it or not it will surely continue on this course because this is what the Bible says will happen.

> "Thus he said: 'The fourth beast...will devour the whole earth and tread it down and crush it. As for the ten horns, out of this kingdom ten kings will arise..." (Dan. 7:23-24)

The whole earth is grouping into ten economic regions, one of them being Europe.

Who Wants to Be a Millionaire – Televangelist Style?

> 'So because you are lukewarm, and neither hot nor cold, I will spit you out of My mouth. 'Because you say, "I am rich, and have become wealthy, and have need of nothing," and you do not know that you are wretched and miserable and poor and blind and naked, (Rev. 3:16-17)

Note the affluence of Laodicea, keeping in mind that this represents the current condition of mainstream Western Christianity. They have forgotten that the affluence and freedom enjoyed in the English-speaking democracies in particular transpired as a result of the Gospel flourishing in these lands, and that such freedom and affluence were bought at the price of the blood of the martyrs who were murdered by the Roman Catholic Church and the Church of England. Those martyrs paid a price for everyone's freedom.

Market principles, democratic principles, representative government—these work very well *as long as they are based on the biblical principles which gave rise to them*. But once Jesus is taken out of equation, the principles will not work. They are, after all, *His* principles.

What is Secular Humanism? In the Western world it is largely Christless Christianity. If Christ is taken out of Christianity the principles and ideals might be there but there is no way those principles and ideals are going to last. Their removal results in going from a Christian society to a *Christianized* society, or Christendom. Britain is nominally Christian but is, in fact, post-Christian or even neo-pagan. Christians in this situation find themselves caught up in the thinking that because of their affluence and freedom they are blessed, when from God's point of view they are not.

Consider the Faith-Prosperity teaching that came from the late Kenneth Hagin and Kenneth Copeland. The devil is much, much too clever to state an out-and-out lie; he is much too smart for that. No, the lies of the devil are subtle distortions of things that are true.

In Revelation the serpent and the dragon are cast down to earth. The devil has two modes of attack: the dragon represents outward persecution, but the serpent is much more subtle. It was the serpent who beguiled the woman. The woman Eve is both a type of Israel and the church being seduced by Satan. What does Satan say to the woman in the garden? "*Indeed, has God said...?*" (Gen. 3:1). He does not tell an out-and-out lie but begins by twisting things God actually did say. It is important to understand that the symbols and typology in Genesis and Revelation go together and reflect each other perfectly. The Bible is like a loaf of bread; it looks the same from either end. When Satan tempted Jesus what did he do? Tell a lie? Yes, but what kind of lie? He twisted biblical truths.

Kenneth Hagin and Kenneth Copeland got their theology from E.W. Kenyon. The apostle Paul tells us that if somebody comes with another gospel, even he himself, even if it should come by an angel, do not believe him (2 Co. 11:4). E.W. Kenyon said that Jesus did not win the victory on the cross but secured the victory when he died "a spiritual victory for us and descended into hell." Hence the place of the cross is diminished in Faith-Prosperity preaching. Kenneth Hagin and Kenneth Copeland preach another gospel. They say God wants people rich and they should believe God for it. This is what happens with people possessing a consumer mentality and Western affluence who reinterpret the Bible. They end up inventing a surreptitiously acquired and theologically erroneous basis for doing so. These things are not out-and-out lies, but distortions of things that are true.

All one has to do to obtain the true definition of faith is turn to the faith chapter, as it is commonly known, which is Hebrews 11. This paraphrase of the climactic conclusion of the faith chapter should be attempted with an American accent from the deep South:

"Faith mah friends, yes *faith!* Hallelujah! Yes, friends I want each and every one of you to just *believe* God. Hold up yer hands—just in faith now—and make out that check for five hundred dollars and trust God to *multiply* it fer y'all *tenfold*. Make it out for five hundred dollars, payable to me and I'll put yer picture in ma Bible. *Faith* my friends, y'all need *faith*. 'If you have faith even as a grain of mustard seed,' the Lord said! Hallelujah! Can y'all say Amen? Y'all just *believe* God for that *blessin*,' brother. Y'all just *trust God* for that new dress, sister! Hallelujah!"

If you think this is a joke, then go to Texas and turn on the radio. Those same clowns are trying to get into Britain. They have made "born again" a household joke in America and they are now coming into Britain and obtaining open doors from church leaders who should know better.

That is their definition of "faith." But look at God's definition of faith:

"... and others were tortured, not accepting their release, so that they might obtain a better resurrection;"

Their faith was not in *this* world but in the one to come.

"...and others experienced mockings and scourgings, yes, also chains and imprisonment. They were stoned, they were sawn in two, they were tempted, they were put to death with the sword; they went about in sheepskins, in goatskins, being destitute, afflicted, ill-treated..."

Living in mansions? Driving Mercedes Benzes?

"...(men of whom the world was not worthy), wandering in deserts and mountains and caves and holes in the ground. And all these, having gained approval through their faith..." (Heb. 11:35-39a)

Who are people going to believe? Are they going to believe the Word of God or these scoundrels from America? Unfortunately people prefer to believe these scoundrels from America.

"For the time will come when they will not endure sound doctrine; but wanting to have their ears tickled, they will accumulate for themselves teachers in accordance to their own desires," (2 Ti.4:3)

It is all according to their *own* desires in the Last Days!

Is This Christianity or Is This Madness?

In one of the most shameful spectacles the church has endured, we witnessed Todd Bentley on YouTube and television literally kicking elderly ladies in the face in the name of the Father, the Son, and "Bam" (his name for the Holy Spirit). Those criticizing his actions were said to be of Satan according to God Channel presenters Wendy and Rory Alec. This Satyricon-esque explosion of moronic lunacy resembled more a Felini movie than anything found in the Book of Acts. The events were staged at a church in

Lakeland, Florida, run by the criminal Strader family, one of whom is in prison for life under the American RICO Act for racketeering after elderly Christians were defrauded of millions. (The father and other brother of this family were named as unindicted co-culprits by the prosecutors.) The local Arnold Palmer Hospital issued a statement claiming none of the healings attributed to Todd Bentley could be medically authenticated.

Bentley is a criminally convicted bisexual pedophile who was in prison for molesting a 7-year old boy. Bentley claimed to have become a Christian and had his body covered in tattoos from head to toe. As he kicked old ladies in the face and stomach and punched people in the mouth, something the world would have defined as assault and battery, Wendy and Rory Alec, joined by C. Peter Wagner, Rick Joyner, Bill Johnson, and Che Ahn called it a "revival." Bentley also claimed personal visitations by an angel named Emma, although there are no female manifestations of angelic beings in Scripture.

The apologist for this madness was Gary Grieg, just as Michael Brown had attempted to defend the similar fiasco in Pensacola, and as Guy Chevreau likewise attempted to defend the indefensible in Toronto. The actions of Grieg were not surprising in view of the fact he attends Jack Hayford's Church on the Way in San Fernando Valley, California. After Oral Roberts claimed a 900-foot-tall Jesus Christ was demanding that he cough up millions of dollars by the end of the month or Jesus would kill him, Greig's pastor Jack Hayford attacked those critical of Roberts, warning about witch hunters. Hayford is the pastor of Paul and Jan Crouch. How anyone can issue a defense of someone claiming that a 900-foot-tall Jesus is running a protection racket defies reason. And how anyone from the same church can defend Bentley defies sanity!

The entire time Bentley was involved in serious adultery and an unbelievably manipulative amount of money preaching, Bill Johnson, Rick Joyner, C. Peter Wagner, and Che Ahn prophesied over Bentley in God's name that he would lead a great revival. Approximately four days later he abandoned his wife and three children and took off to Hawaii with another woman. A few short months later Rick Joyner was trying to rehabilitate him and bring him back into ministry with his new wife from a marriage that Jesus called "adulterous" in the Sermon on the Mount. Joyner prophesied about dancing elephants named "Revival."

From Bentley to South Africa's Ray McCauley to Britain's Ray Bevin to Ted Haggard, morally fallen pastors are "restored" to ministry in a manner of months even where there is no repentance. In fact, the New Testament teaches that pastors must have a good name with non-believers outside the church (1 Ti. 3:2; 3:10; Titus 1:7). Hence, after a moral fall they can be restored to fellowship but not to leadership.

This biblical truth, however, is ignored in favor of people's opinions in a world where there is no fault and no blame. Just as we have no-fault divorce and no-fault accidents in the secular world, we now have no-fault divorce and no-fault moral failure among leaders in the church. King David, of course, was never "restored" to leadership because he was never removed from it after his sin with Bathsheba because David's position was not one of High Priest but of King. He was not a member of the Aaronic priesthood from the tribe of Levi, but rather a king from the tribe of Judah. Comparisons to fallen Christian leaders under the New Covenant with a morally failed king of Israel under the Old Covenant is, exegetically, an apples-and-oranges false comparison. But in a church age where people's opinions prevail over the Word of God, anything goes. Even a Todd Bentley and a Rick Joyner.

Why False Teachers?

There are five main reasons why these people have been set up by the devil to deceive believers and take their money.

First, most of these people began as honest men of God. But the love of money, religious pride, sexual immorality—or some combination of those things—overtook them. Satan wanted to destroy their ministries.

"for the gifts and the calling of God are irrevocable." (Rom. 11:29)

The issue of whether or not **some** of these healings and miracles are genuine is not in question. On that very point Jesus Himself said,

"Many will say to Me on that day, 'Lord, Lord, did we not prophesy in Your name, and in Your name cast out demons, and in Your name perform many miracles?' "And then I will declare to them, 'I never knew you; DEPART FROM ME, you who practice lawlessness.' (Mt. 7:22-23)

For His own glory, and the good of others, God may use these people, but that does not automatically authenticate them. Signs, wonders, miracles and healings only authenticate **Jesus**, not the ministry of any man.

"When the Helper comes, whom I will send to you from the Father, that is the Spirit of truth who proceeds from the Father, He will testify about Me, (Jn. 15:26)

That is the first reason that Satan wants to destroy their ministry.

In the final analysis only God Himself ultimately knows who is a believer and who is not. It is reasonable to question if men like Robert Tilton, Benny

Hinn, Kenneth Hagin, Kenneth Copeland, and Creflo Dolar were ever truly saved to begin with, but without doubt other money preachers who have so maligned the Word of God to line their own pockets began right. And on the basis of such passages as 3 John and Deuteronomy 8 they may have discovered there is a legitimate scriptural basis for God wanting to prosper His people, although they have either completely misunderstood it out of all context or intentionally distorted it out of context themselves with a nefarious intent of milking the sheep. It becomes an example of someone finding A truth and treating it as the central truth of Scripture when in fact it is not. Of course the *fundamental* truth on which all other truth is predicated is the *cross*, the resurrection, and the promised return of Jesus. That is the fundamental truth upon which all other truth is based. There are a lot of other truths, but they all have to be based on *that* truth. Whenever any other truth is made the basis for truth, everything else becomes faulty. In effect what these people have done is to take a view of faith, which is partly true, and elevate it to be foundational in their teaching. Subsequently everything else is built on it, but it is not the proper, firm foundation.

The second reason the devil raises up these people is as a subtle way of seducing Christians to trust in this world at the expense of picking up their own cross.

The third reason is to render ineffective the resources entrusted to Christians. For instance, Tear Fund needs the money to feed starving children in Africa, and the Wycliffe Bible Translators need the money to translate the Word of God to make it available to the people of Nepal. Honest Christian charities and evangelistic organizations need that money for the straightforward, honored work of Jesus. It is Satan's way to divert who knows how much (in America it must be hundreds of millions of dollars annually) away from where that money belongs and into the coffers of these scoundrels with their mansions and bodyguards.

"But if all prophesy, and an unbeliever or an ungifted man enters, he is convicted by all, he is called to account by all;" (1 Co. 14:24)

Paul puts an ungifted person and an unsaved person in the same category. The Greek word for "ungifted" is *idioti* from which we get the word "idiot."

The fourth reason is to diminish the gifts of the Spirit in others' estimation.

In this verse it is important to ask, "Why does Paul put someone who is *not* a Charismatic in the same grouping as someone who is not even saved?" Is he trying to say that if someone does not go with the Spirit or does not pray in tongues (or whatever) they may as well not be a Christian? No, that is not what is being said here. The context provides the answer as to why he puts the unsaved and the ungifted in the same category: he is talking about *practicing* the gifts of the Spirit in such a way that (a) the unsaved will be convicted and will want to get saved, and (b) the ungifted will want to get gifted.

When people who are fundamentalists or conservative Baptists or Brethren (or whatever) see Pentecostals caught up in this name-it-and-claim-it stuff and all the scandals that accompany it, they say that if such behavior is the "gifts of the Spirit" they do not want it.

The fifth reason is much more sinister and much more dangerous. When difficult times come as they are coming now, when people begin losing their businesses, their homes, their possessions, their jobs, who are the first people to lose their faith? The ones who have been fed this line of garbage. And in the Last Days when persecution comes there is going to be a massive falling away. The Bible speaks clearly of the *apostasia*—"apostasy"—falling away (2 Th. 2:3). It is almost certain that the first people to fall away will be those who have been conned by these scoundrels.

Jesus warned directly of false teachers and false prophets in the Last Days. Within the proper context of the Olivet discourse in Matthew 24 and Luke 21 it can be clearly seen that Jesus is not warning about false prophets *outside* the church, or even about sects such as Jehovah's Witnesses, Mormons, Roman Catholics, Moonies or any such similar groups; He is primarily warning about those who would "*mislead, if possible, even the elect*" (Mt. 24:24).

Satan already has the unsaved. These he has already successfully deceived. His goal is to deceive the believers in Jesus as well.

Laodicea Today, at Ease and Affluent

> *Thus says the LORD my God, "Pasture the flock doomed to slaughter. "Those who buy them slay them and go unpunished, and each of those who sell them says, 'Blessed be the LORD, for I have become rich!' And their own shepherds have no pity on them. (Zech. 11:4-5)*

Who really believes that these guys with the big rings and the big suits, going around in these big limousines, care about the sheep?

Yet some genuine ministers of truth cannot support their families. That is not right either. Anyone else with their level of experience, education, the number of languages they can speak, would make a lot more money in the secular world. It is not right to expect people, simply because they are in full-time Christian service, to have a lower standard of living than other people in the church. That is not fair and it is not right. But a middle class lifestyle should be good enough. It exceeds a level more than 75 per cent of the people in the world are ever going to achieve. The problem is when someone makes an extravagant living from their "ministry."

Throughout Scripture women are types of churches.

Tremble, you women who are at ease;
Be troubled, you complacent daughters... (Is. 32:11)

As they had their pasture, they became satisfied,
And being satisfied, their heart became proud;
Therefore they forgot Me. (Hos. 13:6)

This explains the basic problem. Reverting back to John Wesley, what did Wesley assert? If revival comes to England, social injustice will begin to decline and affluence will begin to increase. After the church becomes affluent, it will become lukewarm. And after it becomes lukewarm it will backslide and fall away. Wesley was right!

The problem is not affluence in and of itself, the problem is the heart. There was a very famous rabbi who said, "*For where your treasure is, there your heart will be also*" (Jesus, Mt. 6:21). There is nothing that is going to be more obvious in determining one's attitude toward Jesus and the caliber of their relationship with Him than what is done with their money and their time; one's bank statement and diary tell it all. In Daniel the books will be opened for our judgment, a time when God is going to reveal each person's bank statements and diaries because they document the true condition of the heart.

"*He humbled you and let you be hungry, and fed you with manna which you did not know, nor did your fathers know, that He might make you understand that man does not live by bread alone, but man lives by everything that proceeds out of the mouth of the LORD. Your clothing did not wear out on you, nor did your foot swell these forty years. Thus you are to know in your heart that the LORD your God was disciplining you just as a man disciplines his son. (Deut. 8:3-5)*

What does Jesus say to Laodicea?

'*Those whom I love, I reprove and correct... (Rev. 3:19)*

God will usually teach people to trust Him and not money, by bringing them to hardship. Then He will bless them financially. If He takes someone's money away, very frequently He will give it back to them after He has changed their attitude towards it so they will never trust money again, but trust Him alone.

> *"In the wilderness He fed you manna which your fathers did not know, that He might humble you and that He might test you, to do good for you in the end. (Deut. 8:16)*

When God brings people through difficult times financially and materially, it is to bring good to them in the end.

> *"Otherwise, you may say in your heart, 'My power and the strength of my hand made me this wealth.' (Deut. 8:17)*

Otherwise, one might say in their heart, "I am a good businessman. I am a good lawyer, a good surgeon, a good dentist. I am a good preacher, hallelujah!"

> *"But you shall remember the LORD your God, for it is He who is giving you power to make wealth....*

Why?

> *"...that He may confirm His covenant which He swore to your fathers, as it is this day. (Deut. 8:18)*

Why does God provide wealth? To have a good time in this life and to be able to squander it on individual pleasures?

> *You ask and do not receive, because you ask with wrong motives, so that you may spend it on your pleasures. (Ja. 4:3)*

Believers ask but do not receive because they ask from the wrong motives, to squander it on their pleasures. That is not why God provides wealth, to squander on one's own pleasures. The Christians whom God blesses with wealth are the ones who would not love Him any less if He took it away from them. It is true that God makes some people very rich because they are the ones who write the big checks for the poor and for missions, and yet there are Christians who were previously very rich from whom God took everything away. It is not an issue of money but an issue of attitude. The problem is not wealth, it is the problem of the old nature.

> *"He who is at ease holds calamity in contempt, As prepared for those whose feet slip." (Job 12:5)*

People who are at ease are being set up for calamity.

Before the judgments of Jeremiah there was a period of real prosperity in Israel and people would not believe that what Jeremiah prophesied was going to happen. Similarly, before AD 70, before the temple was destroyed, there was an unprecedented period of prosperity under the Romans and people did not want to believe what the early Christians were telling them was going to happen.

> "Cursed be the one who does the LORD'S work negligently,
> And cursed be the one who restrains his sword from blood.
> Moab has been at ease since his youth;
> He has also been undisturbed, like wine on its dregs,
> And he has not been emptied from vessel to vessel,
> Nor has he gone into exile.
> Therefore he retains his flavor,
> And his aroma has not changed." (Jer. 48:10-11)

Throughout Scripture Moab represents anyone who does not allow himself to be disturbed by what is happening around him. Moab was an area that always had a penchant for being totally decimated suddenly, because Moab never took notice of the signs and forebodings that were beginning to take place around him. The text begins talking about "the one who does the LORD'S work negligently." The chief characteristic assigned to Laodicea, remember, is that it was lukewarm. "Doing the Lord's work with slackness." (Jer. 48:10)

"And cursed be the one who restrains his sword from blood." That is another characteristic of Laodicea. The sword is the sword of steel in the Old Testament; in the New Testament it is the sword of the Spirit, the Word of God, the Gospel of Peace. There are Christians who do not want to go to war, to stick their necks out for the Gospel. That is a mark of Laodicea, Christians refusing to take the risk. When believers are first saved all they want to do is to tell everybody about Jesus. After a few years, however, if somebody asks them in the supermarket about Jesus they will tell them, but they lose their first love like Ephesus did.

Evangelism is like going to war. In the Old Testament the example is provided in how David had to bring the Philistine foreskins. In type, this represented people being saved! Romans, quoting Jeremiah, speaks of true circumcision being circumcision of the heart. The lack of keenness to go to war, to go on missions and see others saved, is a mark of Laodicea.

Not only that, Laodiceans show a kind of woolliness to the outrageous things that go on in the church. They are too woolly to stand up to heresy and such nonsense, so they allow things to continue on and on. This characteristic is evidenced today in the major Evangelical leaders in this country who have strayed.

Even John Stott has started teaching that there is no such place as hell; that Jesus did not die to save people from going to hell. Jesus *spoke* about hell! Actually it can be argued that there may be no permanent hell on the basis of Revelation 20:14; Death, followed by Hades or hell, go into the lake of fire. Perhaps that is what he meant.

The people who organized the March for Jesus, Graham Kendrick and Roger Forster, teach that there is no such place as hell.

Author of *The Shack*, William P. Young, states that the God who executes His own Son for the sin of others is a God who does not exist. Young denies Jesus died for sin, and rejects the existence of such a God, yet many professing Evangelicals advocate Young and his ridiculous book as being "Christian," when neither it nor he are by any scriptural definition Christian.

British youth minister Steve Chalke likewise states that if God had His Son killed for the sin of others it would make God the quintessential cosmic child abuser. Chalke also claims that Moslems and Hindus can be born again and have salvation without a saving faith in Christ because of the truths in Hinduism and Islam.

Similarly, British anti-Israel clergyman and academic Colin Chapman states that he cannot say Hindus and Moslems are lost without a saving faith in Jesus.

In this Laodicean age, propounders of such apostate views are regarded by many supposed Evangelicals as also being Evangelicals despite their avid denunciation of the most fundamental tenets of the Christian Gospel. Nobody in Laodicea wants to stand up and fight this and say it is wrong. People do not want to pick up the sword of the Spirit in Laodicea; they want to be at ease just like Moab. But then, like Moab, destruction comes and it is too late.

"*But I am very angry with the nations...*

(the Hebrew word for nations is *goyim* – Gentiles)

...who are at ease; for while I was only a little angry, they furthered the disaster." (Zech. 1:15)

Instead of repenting of being lukewarm it gets worse.

"*I spoke to you in your prosperity;*
But you said, 'I will not listen!'... (Jer. 22:21a)

It is only when things get difficult that the desire arises to remove the wax from the ears and seek God's advice.

Remember, the entire scenario that transpired in the days of Jeremiah is a paradigm for the Last Days. The whole idea in Revelation, "Fallen is

Babylon," comes from Jeremiah 51:44-45. What happened before the Babylonian captivity is a type, in some sense, of what will happen to the church at the end of the this age when following the midrash, the pattern, of Scripture.

> Then the Pharisees also were asking him again how he received his sight. And he said to them, "He applied clay to my eyes, and I washed, and I see."(Jn. 9:15)

Laodicea does not know that it is Laodicea! Christians in the affluent West do not know that they cannot see. They are not cognizant of their true spiritual state! They do not realize, because they are lukewarm, that they are not wearing the garments of salvation. They are naked! They do not know they are Laodicea! "Buy from me ... eye-salve to anoint your eyes so that you may see." Unless they buy from Jesus, they will not see this to be true.

> "I am not at ease, nor am I quiet,
> And I am not at rest, but turmoil comes." (Job 3:26)

The Book of Job continually alludes to things that are going to happen at the end of the world.

> "But Jeshurun grew fat and kicked—You are grown fat, thick, and sleek—Then he forsook God who made him, And scorned the Rock of his salvation." (Deut. 32:15)

What has happened in the Western church today? They have become fat and sleek at the same time Western Christendom has scorned the God of its salvation.

> And Ephraim said, "Surely I have become rich,
> I have found wealth for myself;
> In all my labors they will find in me
> No iniquity, which would be sin." (Hos. 12:8)

Laodiceans are very self-righteous people. They mistake their affluence for a blessing that is becoming a curse without realizing it. What did Jeremiah complain about?

> "Why has the way of the wicked prospered?" (Jer. 12:1)

God can and does prosper His people. By virtue of the fact that such live in a Western democracy they are relatively wealthy people. Even if they have a working-class job they are relatively well-off just because they live in Britain. If biblical principles are applied to a social situation, standards of living will increase, that is true, but the wicked also prosper.

Amos speaks repeatedly and continuously about things concerning the Last Days.

> Woe to those who are at ease in Zion... (Amos 6:1a)

> "And through his shrewdness...

(This is talking about Antiochus Epiphanes, pre-figuring what Antichrist will do at the end of the world.)

> "...he will cause deceit to succeed by his influence; And he will magnify himself in his heart, And he will destroy many while they are at ease..." (Dan. 8:25)

The Antichrist is going to destroy many lukewarm Christians as discussed in the character of Moab.

> They have lied about the LORD
> And said, "Not He;
> Misfortune will not come on us,
> And we will not see sword or famine. (Jer. 5:12)

Today they say, "I am not going suffer; I am blessed of the Lord, Hallelujah! I am a king's kid; I am gonna prosper, can ya say Amen?" Well, that is what they are saying in many of the American churches. And that is what people are believing. People wanting to have their ears tickled will acquire for themselves teachers after their own desires. That is what is happening and that is what God said was going to happen.

> Our soul is greatly filled With the scoffing of those who are at ease,
> And with the contempt of the proud. (Ps. 123:4)

There is a faithful remnant in Laodicea, but the faithful remnant, the zealous Christians, are going to be mocked and scorned by the lukewarm ones. It is relatively easy to be opposed by the unsaved—just read the book of Judges. It is about war from beginning to end, but the last war is the bloodiest with the most people killed. Why? Because it was a war between Jews. All the other wars were between the Jews and their neighbors. But wars between God's own people are always the most devastating battles.

Believers should never be afraid of rabbis, never afraid of the Roman Catholic Church, and certainly never afraid of the Freemasons. But whom should they fear? The born-again Christian establishment and its leaders who are compromising with the world—*that* is who they should be afraid of. Believers can handle the unsaved; it is what is happening to the Christian leadership that causes them the most grief and fear.

Laodicea

I will bring distress on men So that they will walk like the blind,
Because they have sinned against the LORD...(Zeph. 1:17a)

They are blind. In Zephaniah the whole idea about putting the trumpet to the mouth is about the Last Days. The calamity is going to come. Western Christianity is going to be devastated by an onslaught. It will begin by seduction, compromise, being led astray by its leaders, then betrayal and persecution, but there is going to be a faithful remnant that is going to overcome.

There will be a faithful remnant in Laodicea. There will be Christians in Laodicea who will listen to the counsel of Jesus. They will repent of their lukewarm faith. They will look at their bank statement and their diary and say, "I have to repent." They will anoint their eyes that they may see. They will buy gold refined with fire. That day will not overtake them like a thief.

"Harvest is past, summer is ended,
And we are not saved." (Jer. 8:20)

Lukewarm Christians are *not* going to be rescued, just as it was with the foolish virgins of Matthew 25.

In the Song of Solomon 3, the bride, representing the church, is ready, but in chapter 5 she is not. It is just like the wise and foolish virgins. The Song of Solomon was being read in the synagogue at Passover time when Jesus spoke of the wise and foolish virgins in Matthew 25. The wise virgins are like the bride Solomon meets when she is ready for the bridegroom in chapter 3, but in chapter 5 where she is lazy and does not want to get out of bed, that is like the foolish virgins. Jesus was explaining what this means for those Christians who are going to be ready for Him when He comes back, and those who are not.

But in Laodicea there are going to be those whom the Lord corrects.

Whoever loves discipline loves knowledge,
But he who hates reproof is stupid. (Prov. 12:1)

No one likes difficulties. No one enjoys hardships. No one likes having to struggle through Bible College after having had a lot of money at one time in their life; it is very difficult. They would have been better off never to have had money than to have had money and then had to go and live by faith with their family. But if that is what God has to do to prevent someone from being deceived, let God do it.

Everybody in the church today is going to be either somebody who does not anoint his eyes or somebody who does. No one can trust in the riches of this world. Things that are for *here* are not the things Christians are here

239

for. "Buy gold" from Jesus; store up treasures in His kingdom where moth will not consume. It is only a matter of time before some terrible calamity or catastrophe happens to the whole world's economy anyway. Believers can trust Jesus now and stop trusting in their affluence now, or wait until Jesus shows them His love—by rebuking and disciplining them!

Persecution for Those at Ease

Laodiceans think that because they are not being persecuted they are right. Warnings have been publicized for the past few years that persecution is going to come to the Western democracies because they have abandoned their biblical foundations.

The British Cabinet has enlisted four unashamed and unrepentant homosexuals recently, at the same time that Christian preachers are being arrested in this country. They will not arrest militant homosexuals operating in the streets, they will not arrest militant Muslims, but they will arrest Christian preachers. And it will get worse because Christians do not know their true state.

It says in Daniel 8:25 concerning the lukewarm people, that the Antichrist will destroy many while they are "at ease." In other words, lukewarm Christians who are "at ease" will be the first targets. What did the prophet Amos say? *"Woe to those who are at ease in Zion"* (Amos 6:1). There are over two dozen such references which all relate to Laodicea in the Old Testament. There is also one in Isaiah revealing that the unfaithful will persecute the faithful. The lukewarm Christians are the unfaithful who will persecute the zealous.

And why does Laodicea not know it is Laodicea? Because it runs on *people's* opinions instead of on *God's* opinions—on God's Word.

The Words of Jesus to Laodicea

'I know your deeds, that you are neither cold nor hot; I wish that you were cold or hot. (Rev. 3:15)

That is what Jesus is saying to the churches. It is not that they are openly evil, but simply that they are just not on fire. Warm water is horrible to drink.

'So because you are lukewarm, and neither hot nor cold, I will spit you out of My mouth. Because you say, "I am rich, and have become wealthy, and have need of nothing," and you do not know that you are wretched and miserable and poor and blind and naked, (Rev. 3:16-17)

Laodicea

That is precisely the current state of Western Evangelical Christianity! This is not referring to the liberals who are described as *"holding to a form of godliness, although they have denied its power"* (2 Ti. 3:5). This is instead describing people professing to be in possession of a personal relationship! The physical cold can be felt physically, but spiritual things can only be spiritually discerned.

I advise you to buy from Me gold refined by fire so that you may become rich...

This contrasts the spiritual riches of Jesus with the riches of this world.

...and white garments so that you may clothe yourself, and that the shame of your nakedness will not be revealed; and eye salve to anoint your eyes so that you may see. Those whom I love, I reprove and discipline; therefore be zealous and repent. (Rev. 3:18-19)

The remedy is repentance from being lukewarm and materialistic.

Now the next verse is one often used in evangelism, and it is perfectly valid to do that. But in its context that is not primarily what Jesus is saying.

'Behold, I stand at the door and knock; if anyone hears My voice and opens the door, I will come in to him and will dine with him, and he with Me. He who overcomes, I will grant to him to sit down with Me on My throne, as I also overcame and sat down with My Father on His throne. He who has an ear, let him hear what the Spirit says to the churches.'" (Rev. 3:20-22)

Heaven is for overcomers. On the door of who's heart is Jesus knocking and encouraging to repent of being lukewarm and of their materialistic attitudes? Are they willing to let Him do the things He needs to do to correct them, even to bring them to difficult times if that is what it takes? They must buy the gold from Him, refined by fire, and salve from Him so that they can see and be overcomers.

Most of Laodicea is not going to overcome; there is going to be a tremendous falling away, but they are still provided the opportunity. Jesus is knocking now, He is warning everyone now. There is going to be a very, very difficult time ahead for all Bible-believing Christians. If they open the door now they are going to overcome. If they do not open the door now, and if they do not repent of being lukewarm and materialistic, they are **not** going to make it.

'Those whom I love, I reprove and discipline; therefore be zealous and repent...He who has an ear, let him hear what the Spirit says to the churches.'" (Rev. 3:19,22)

Daniel said, "Those who are wise will understand" (Dan. 12:10). At the end of the age faithfulness and understanding will become very closely associated. Those with one will seek the other. "*My people are destroyed for lack of knowledge*" (Hos. 4:6). "*Come out of her midst, My people*" (Jer. 51:45; Is. 48:20; Rev. 18:4). It does not say they were ***not*** His people.

When the pope is observed at Assisi in Italy, meeting the Dalai Lama, Shinto priests, Buddhist monks, Jewish rabbis, Sufi Muslims, and others celebrating communion and not attempting to make any of them Catholics, let alone Christians, and seeking to be the head of the world's religions, then one can suspect that this pre-figures a one-world religion. It will be acceptable to be anything except a born-again, true-to-the-Bible Christian.

The Kingdom of Heaven

In Matthew 24 Jesus said, "The gospel of the kingdom must be preached." This is not simply the "good news." There already exists the Gospel of peace, the Gospel of salvation, and they are all the same Gospel, but they highlight different aspects of what that Gospel is. Jesus is the Bright Morning Star, He is the Messiah, He is the Prince of Peace. All these titles refer to the same person, but each of His titles highlights a different aspect of who and what He is. It is the same with the Gospel.

What is "the Gospel of the kingdom"? It is the eschatological Gospel; it is what John the Baptist came preaching: "Repent, the kingdom is at hand." Jesus preached it, too. The Gospel of the kingdom is seen most clearly in Matthew where Jesus warned about hell three times as much as He talked about heaven.

It may appear that the world is changing fast, but look at what the Book of Daniel offers. Those countries of the Roman Empire will come back together. In Matthew 24 Jesus said that when the Jews come back to Israel, and Jerusalem is no longer under the feet of the Gentiles, it will be a sign of the end. There are those who are presently afraid of nuclear blackmail, nuclear holocaust, Islamic countries getting nuclear weapons. But Peter, a fisherman in Galilee, said that the whole world would be destroyed that way. More accurately, he declared it would happen by fire and not necessarily by means of nuclear fire, although Zechariah 14 appears to support nuclear war. Nothing presently known but a nuclear bomb melts the eyes in their sockets while people are on their feet.

Amidst the chaos and rapid change, the Bible says that men's hearts will be failing them. There will be fear and anxiety among the nations, none of them knowing the way out. No country, no government, no leader, no unsaved person, no politician—**none** of them—will know the way out. But Christians who preach the Gospel of the kingdom will know the way out, and they will know how to show that way out to other people.

But is the Gospel to be preached? The late Barrie Smith may have been a third-rate Bible teacher, but he was a first-rate evangelist. Why have so many people been saved through his ministry in the South Pacific? Because he read the directions! He used worldly events and biblical prophecies to preach the Gospel. *The Late Great Planet Earth* by Hal Lindsey was a gross over-simplification of biblical prophecy. It is not doctrinally very solid, but it does show how world events are lining up with biblical prophecy. But Hal Lindsey was some evangelist. He preached the Gospel of the kingdom. There is no secret; they simply went to the Word of God and did what Jesus said to do.

Why is the Times Square Church under the leadership of David Wilkerson growing so fast? He is simply preaching the Gospel of the kingdom. It is no secret! There is no need for a program, no need for a gimmick, no need to psychologize it; just read it and God will do it! He has already revealed what to do.

Chapter 8
The Dilemma of Laodicea
Understanding the Problem

As with each of these seven churches, the first clue the Lord has given us to understanding both its virtue and its flaws is conveyed by the character of the church etymologically revealed in the Greek meaning of its name. Precise meanings are not exact and are subject to interpretation, but while somewhat imprecise, the essential meaning is not uncertain. As we have noted, this becomes progressively illuminated by that aspect of Christ as He appeared in the first chapter of Revelation highlighted for each specific church. A further exactitude is arrived at from the content of Christ's message to each church and is made clearer still by what can be gleaned from what is known historically and archeologically about each church. Equally important, however, is what is said concerning these churches in other areas of Scripture, bearing in mind that by the time John received his vision a margin of change had already ensued from the earlier time period covered in the Bok of Acts. Still, the epistle to the Ephesians must weigh carefully in our understanding of the words of Jesus to the Ephesians. As it were, we have two epistles to the Ephesians, the former divinely inspired and authored by Paul, and the latter not requiring divine inspiration at all because Christ dictated it Himself personally.

The Dilemma of Laodicea

Historical accounts of what transpired in Ephesus as recorded in the Book of Acts must also be given due consideration. As Ephesus is an encompassing representation of the apostolic or Ephesian age, it is obvious why the Holy Spirit has provided us with more scriptural material about the Ephesian church than any of the other churches. Concerning Laodicea, however, we have only sparse reference elsewhere in the New Testament. In the epistle to the neighboring church in Colossae Paul addresses Colossae as being part of the same local church community of believers as Laodicea in Colossians 2:1, and in 4:15-16 makes it clear that the epistle to the Colossians is co-addressed to the believers in Laodicea. On this point we again note the very close geographical proximity of these two cities together with Hierapolis. Conversely, Paul writes from Laodicea to the Colossians sometime around AD 62.

The community of believers was constituted of Greeks, Phrygians and Jews. Akin to Pergamum and Alexandria, Colossae was a city where pagan influences from the East first began to arrive at the doorstep of the church. The Lycus River Valley in which Colossae was located had the lukewarm springs of Laodicea as tributaries in subterranean channels flowing into it twelve miles from Colossae. Thus the epistle to the Colossians was not originally circulated far and wide, but was the modern equivalent of local post within the same zip code or postal code area. The same factors that applied to Laodicea applied in Colossae, and vice versa. In his writing Paul treats the message in Colossae as of equal relevance to Laodicea in a situation where they were virtually two branches of the same church within walking distance of each other. In light of Paul's references in Colossians 4 we might say that the epistle to the Colossians could also validly be named "The Epistle to the Colossians *and* Laodiceans."

Of these seven churches it is therefore the first (Ephesus) and the last (Laodicea) that have the most scriptural reference within the internal evidence of the New Testament as well as being the two churches for which we have the most extra-biblical, historical, and archeological knowledge. It is in the author's estimation unfortunate that previous treatments of the subject of Laodicea have generally, if not nearly exclusively, failed to understand that historically and doctrinally Laodicea is in essence the same as Colossae. In effect the same as we have two epistles to Ephesus, we likewise have two for Laodicea—the first written under the inspiration of the Holy Spirit by Paul which we call "The Epistle to the Colossians" and the second, once more, dictated by the Lord Jesus personally, called "The Letter to the Church of Laodicea."

The Dilemma of Laodicea

Because of its general location which furnished an avenue for the influx of Eastern religious ideas, particularly Gnosticism of a form which separated matter and substance from critical objective thought, the church in the tri-city area of Laodicea, Colossae, and Hierapolis was incipiently vulnerable to Gnostic seduction. Paul's epistle also issues caveat of the nascent danger of secular philosophy.

With these two came a hybrid of a philosophy of knowledge that was not biblical but Gnostic which Paul describes as "*epignosis*" where there is an actual participation in a mystical knowledge as opposed to a mere cognizance of what it entails. As with all heresy it became a false doctrine resulting in schismatic repercussions that ultimately challenged the church with Paul's Christology. In Colossians 1:15 Paul describes Jesus as the image of the Father (*prototokos*) which the influences of Gnostic thought filtering into the church was causing some of the Colossian and Laodicean Christians to misunderstand what Paul meant.

This also resulted in a Platonic notion of reflection based on the term "*eikon.*" These ideas would later be propounded in the 5th century and afterward to the point of becoming the icon veneration of the Eastern Orthodox and Roman Catholic Churches. After the time of the Antiochan fathers and figures such as Gregory of Naziunzus a deterioration began to ensue that was not the fault of the Antiochan fathers primarily, but rather of these secular philosophies and world views coming into the church with the end product that the icons were ascribed a metaphysical property as "windows" into the supernatural realm. Because the subject of the icon appeared Christian, the church would lose sight of the fact that the philosophy and theology of icon methodology was of pagan origin and would lead to a Christianized idolatry, today still existing in Eastern Orthodox, Roman Catholic, and various Eastern Catholic communions.

This effect was also essential in the further fostering of Monophysite heresy which saw Jesus not simply as "*homoousios*"—"one divine substance" with the Father—but one person. This developed because the Greek world view was enthralled with the language of substance while the Hebrew world view of the Apostles was concentrated on one nature and relationship.

Bearing in mind that Laodicea carries the inert meaning of "people's opinions" and "people's rights to their opinions" as well as "people's judgments," it was in the Laodicea/Colossae church we see theological truths being contorted into errors based on the misguided opinions of people within the church trying to understand the nature of God in Christ in light of the prevailing Hellenistic philosophies of the Greek and Phrygian world.

The Dilemma of Laodicea

This in part relates to what happens when the theologically and spiritually Judaic faith of Scripture is reinterpreted as a Hellenistic one and becomes further corrupted by Eastern religion.

God, wanting to bring His message of salvation to all nations of the earth through the seed of Abraham, brought Abraham to geographic Israel in the heart of the Levant so that through the vehicle of Israel and the Jews the Gospel would have a central point of dissemination. The Levant is where Europe, Asia, and Africa terrestrially converge, and with Israel at its center, the message of Jesus could geographically and culturally travel in all directions. Christianity is neither a Western Hellenized faith nor an Eastern one. Although Oriental geographically, and Occidental in its preeminence, it is theologically and philosophically an entity unto its own.

To understand this we must understand the scriptural perspective of *Heilsgeschichte* – "salvation history." The Eastern world had a circular philosophy of history based on seasons of the meteorological and agricultural year. Concepts of salvation and judgment were understood as things such as "karma," and escape from the cycle of futility was called "nirvana." New birth was, to the Eastern world of India (where Thomas the apostle went as a missionary to bring the Gospel), understood as reincarnation. In reaction to the idolatry, superstition, and social injustices of Hinduism, Taoism, and Shintoismm, moral philosophers such as Buddha and Confucius arose. Sadly, these teachers who represented themselves to be nothing more than moral philosophers were deified by later generations who turned their teachings into new religions. In fact, Guantama (the Buddha) and Confucius themselves were largely concerned with the social justice of the temporal world and to a fair degree were reacting against religion.

A blend of East and West arose in Persia where ethnic Aryans of Indo-European anthropological origin (today called Iranians) who had migrated to the east of the Fertile Crescent witnessed the rise of Zoroaster, also known as Zarathustra, who attempted to monotheize Persia and held to the same motifs of sons of light and sons of darkness seen in the New Testament and Dead Sea Scrolls. Zarathustra believed in personal sin and responsibility and, unlike the aforementioned moral philosophers further to the East in India and China, Zarathustra sought both theological and socioeconomic reform.

In the aftermath of the Babylonian Captivity, Persian civilization became strongly influenced by the Israelite monotheism of Queen Esther and the prophet Daniel, which also impacted the Medes. This without doubt played a role in the benevolence toward the Jews of Artaxerxes and Darius as recorded in the books of Ezra and Nehemiah, and also had longer term ramifications as is recorded by the saga of the Magi in Matthew's Nativity narrative in the Gospels.

On the Western front however, Socratic monotheism and certain elements of Platonic thought parodied the Christian message. The problem in both of these cases is that by the first century there was enough truth in both Eastern and Western religious philosophy to superficially appear compatible with the Gospel but also disguised the false religious beliefs and secular philosophies with which they were blended. Concerning Colossae and Laodicea, these are the things that Paul refers to as "the vain philosophies of the world," having an inherent capacity to permeate into the cytoplasm of the church and even to corrupt the DNA of its nucleus like a virus having the right RNA to get in and destroy because the cell's defenses do not initially identify it as alien and antagonistic.

Projecting this ahead to the last church of Laodicea, we again see a remarkable infusion of secular philosophies and Eastern religious thought into the Body of Christ, even among supposed Evangelicals—particularly charismatics and Pentecostals, but also among increasing numbers of non-charismatics and even some Fundamentalists. We have already reviewed with warning the Hinduistic Kundalini origins of much of the phenomena we have experienced in the failed revivals and spiritual counterfeits of Toronto, Canada, and of Pensacola and Lakeland, Florida. Such demonic infections and carnal corruptions superficially resemble effects that are biblical sufficiently enough to gain a credibility among the biblically ignorant and undiscerning. On the Western front, however, we witness secular marketing psychology and programmatic management philosophies generated by Fuller Theological Seminary, Willow Creek Church, and Saddleback Church, with Bill Hybels, C. Peter Wagner, Brian McLaren, and Rick Warren performing the kinds of parts once played by those who sought to take the church captive with their empty deception and philosophies in Laodicea and Colossae (Col. 2:8).

An additional factor that faced this church was Sabbatarian and Festal legalists surfacing from extremist factions of Messianic Jewish believers attempting to enforce on the church in a compulsory manner Old Covenant legislation intended for Israel, or outlawing free-will observances by believing Jews. Today in modern Laodicea such problems are indeed resurgent. We have been confronted by the Sabbatarian legalism of Seventh-day Adventism predicated upon alleged angelic visions that Colossians 2:16-18 specifically prohibits. Moreover, we have an extreme access of the modern Messianic

The Dilemma of Laodicea

Movement on one hand attempting to bring non-Jews under Sabbatarian and Festal observation in a legalistic manner, as well as into bondage to the Deuteronomic legislation that was juridically and ritually intended for Old Testament Israel. This is not to say that all contemporary Messianic fellowships practice this error, nor is it to suggest that non-Jewish Christians should not understand the typology and Christological significance of this legislation and of these feasts. Indeed, unless one understands the Torah and its fulfillment in Christ, one cannot with any depth properly understand the role of Christ or the full meaning of His message.

On the other hand, as in Colossae and Laodicea, there were those seeking to prohibit the voluntary and cultural observances of such feasts by Jewish believers. In fact such feasts were celebrated or commemorated by the Apostles in a Christo-centric fashion and are used by Paul the apostle in his first epistle to the Corinthians and by the epistle to the Hebrews as crucially important teaching tools to explain New Testament doctrine. In his letters to Timothy, Paul also emphasizes the importance of the Law in evangelism to both Jew and non-Jew. Unless one knows on the basis of God's Law that they are lost they will not understand the need to be found. This is because the Torah illustrates through the example of Israel and the Jews as a microcosm of the human condition for man's incapacity to meet God's standards, and hence it reveals the universal need for a Savior-Messiah.

Thus both the Sabbatarian and Festal legalists and the anti-Messianic Gentiles are rebuked in Colossians 2 (as they also are in Romans 11 and 14) just as they must be rebuked today in modern Laodicea. The heart of the emphasis of the epistle to the Colossians and Laodiceans includes a rebuttal of the confusion of legalism with holiness. Scripturally, holiness and worldliness alike have little if anything to do with temporal things, but have everything to do with the attitude of our hearts toward temporal things. It is, for instance, of little surprise that the Church of the Nazarene, with its massive rule book for Christian conduct that governed everything from circus attendance to going to films, is but one denomination that is rapidly departing from the Wesleyan roots of its primary founder Phineas Bresee. It is increasingly moving in the directly of ecumenism and theological liberalism. Such people indeed know how to strain gnats (which in some cases are not even real gnats), while at the same time ending up devouring camels (Mt. 23:24). We are told in no uncertain terms that the implication of do's and don'ts on others not specifically found in the New Testament are decrees to which Christians should refuse to submit (Col. 2:20-23). They have the appearance of self-made religion and, in fact, resemble the warped

The Dilemma of Laodicea

Roman Catholic concepts of mortification, but they are useless against carnal indulgence. Certain things not found in Scripture may indeed be inappropriate for one Christian according to the Lord's conviction, because "anything not done in faith is sin" (Rom. 14:23. But seeking to impose restrictions on others is a carnal act in itself, and is no different in substance from the oral law of the Sanhedrin condemned by Christ.

These problems of secular philosophies that are demeaned as "vain" in the epistle to the Colossians and Laodiceans have certainly gained momentum not only in the church of Laodicea at the end of the first century to whom John wrote, but to the church of Laodicea today. From *Purpose-Driven* marketing psychology programs from the Western world to the Eastern religious ontogeny of the Emergent Church, we are again squeezed between East and West. In modern Laodicea we are accordioned by secular philosophies of church growth and secular psychology coming from the Western world and New Age beliefs and practices imagined to be Christian that have their origins in the East. All of this finds place and is given leeway because of one thing: the usurping of the authority of the Word of God by people's judgments and opinions, and their supposed rights for which they contest so vigorously in most of the modern Western church.

Thus, before we can properly elucidate the second letter to the Ephesians found in Revelation 2, we must contemplate it while bearing in mind the consideration found in the first epistle to the Ephesians written under divine directive by Paul the apostle. The same principle applies to a proper understanding of the letter to Laodicea. In order to grasp the full depth of what Jesus was saying to them we must first recognize the relationship between the contents of the letter He dictated to John and the one written 35 years earlier by Paul. We can no more effectively study the messages of Christ to Ephesus and Laodicea without the first epistles of Paul to those two churches, any more than we can effectively study 2 Corinthians and 2 Thessalonians without first carefully reading and understanding 1 Corinthians and 1 Thessalonians. Until we understand what it meant for them we will fail to correctly comprehend what it means for us.

In the contemporary world we see activist legates reinterpreting the Constitution as a dynamic evolving document instead of as a fixed anchoring document around which all other juridical decisions must be docked. For instance, the original intentions of the American Founding Fathers, conspicuously evident in their confessed theistic presuppositions in both the Constitution and Declaration of Independence (as well as in their predecessor documents the Mayflower Compact, the Fundamental Orders of Connecticut, and a host of others in the Anglo-American legal tradition dating back to the Magna Carta), mean absolutely nothing to the modern American Civil Liberties Union. Such leftist anti-Christ organizations wish to divorce the Judeo-Christian deism and principles upon which the American model of constitutional democracy and the British model of parliamentary democracy are both founded. In the age of Laodicea the same has happened.

It began with liberal higher critics produced by such institutions as Tubingen, Germany, who reinterpreted Christianity as 19th-century German Rationalism, invoking a tradition dating back to Immanuel Kant with his categorical imperatives and critiques on natural and pure reason—what Scripture calls "the vain philosophies of the world." This Frankensteinization of Holy Writ, however, is no longer the exclusive domain of liberal higher critics and post-Modernists. It is now within the realm of would-be Evangelicals who are themselves not scriptural Evangelicals but Post-Modernists and New Agers using "Evangelical speak." At the forefront of this has been Brian McLaren, Dan Kimball, Rick Warren, and the author of *The Shack*, William Young. The patriarch of this change of deceivers however, has been the Jesuit Tielhard de Chardin. The marketing and psychology side of modern deception was pioneered by Robert Schuller and his mentor Norman Vincent Peale, and was compounded by the secular marketing guru Peter Drucker. The philosophical and theosophical seminal influences are indisputably that New Age Jesuit.

When Brian McLaren demands a moratorium on Evangelical debate of the morality of homosexuality and lesbianism, saying that after a moratorium the church should decide, or when Bart Campolo, son of apostate Evangelical Tony Campolo, preaches that he would spiritualize away portions of Scripture he does not agree with, what we have is a new self-appointed Christian Supreme Court with agenda-bound judges. Like the liberal theologians from the school of Rudolf Bultmann before them, these false brethren in essence maintain that "the church wrote the Bible and the church can rewrite it." It is no longer the Word of God.

Just as a Sandra Day O'Connor and an Earl Warren ignored the proven intentions of the Founding Fathers when they handed down rulings redefining the U. S. Constitution to please themselves and supplant the place of Congress, so too, in modern Laodicea, we now have the same thing taking place in the church. While many Scripture-believing, saved Christians rightly decry the rejection of the theistic and constitutional principles upon which the USA was established, it is little wonder that this departure from the America of our Founding Fathers is taking place in the U.S. while the departure from the Christianity of Jesus and the Apostles is taking place in the church. It all becomes a mere matter of "people's opinions."

This is Laodicea today. We can conclude this by considering Jesus' letter to Laodicea after examining Paul's. It happened then, and it is happening now. Newfangled meanings have nothing to do with possessive author's intent; this is the juridical philosophy of the world, and this is the theological philosophy of the Emergent Church.

Recontextualize or Redefine?

To understand this we have to understand the subject of "world views." Laodicea was viewing things in terms of its own affluence; that was its world view. When the city was destroyed by an earthquake it did not even need any imperial help or government assistance to rebuild. Whenever there is a change in world view there are going to be other changes in the society and in the church. The Word of God is immutable; the doctrines of Scripture never change. However, the way they are explained and communicated have to change even though the doctrine will not. So there are two terms we have to understand: "recontextualize" and "redefine."

The Wycliffe Bible Translators went to a certain tribe in equatorial Africa where the people had no concept of snow; they never saw it and did not know what it was. They had no written alphabet and they had no idea what snow was. They had never seen such a thing. Few of their people ever went more than 20 miles beyond where they were born, and it was tropical. So when the Wycliffe translators had to translate Isaiah 1:18, "Though your sins are like scarlet they shall be white as snow," those people would have asked, "What is snow?" They instead translated it, "Though your sins be like scarlet they shall be white as coconuts." That did not change the meaning. They merely "recontextualized" the ***presentation*** of the truth; they did not ***change*** the truth.

I do not like paraphrases but I accept the fact that in children's Bibles or in cultures where they do not have a Bible yet or even an alphabet, in order to see people saved and to get people literate enough to read a proper translation as an interim provision, I have no problem with saying "coconut" instead of "snow," although eventually that should be adjusted. All the Wycliffe translators did was recontextualize. Paul would take the same truths that he preached to the Jews in one way, and preach those truths to the Greeks and Romans in another way. He did not change the truth. Recontextualizing is good, but the history of the post-Apostolic church has been a saga of those who did not simply recontextualize it, but redefined it.

A History of Redefining the Gospel

We already looked at one case with Constantine and the Roman Empire making Christendom its official religion. Along comes a figure named Augustine and, as we observed, Augustine rewrites Christianity as a Platonic religion using Plato's philosophy. In the Middle Ages something happened.

We also considered that under Medieval Roman Catholicism Europe went into the Dark Ages. (If you ever want to know what a Roman Catholic world *will* look like, look at what a Roman Catholic world *was* like. They had twelve centuries to do exactly as they wanted, and they gave us the Dark Ages.) But when the Crusaders came back from the Middle East, the influences of Islam and the Byzantine Empire returned with them. Islam was having its Golden Age. Whatever existed from the Greco-Roman age still existed in the Eastern half of the Christianized world, the Byzantine Empire. But Islam had a burst of Aristotelian philosophy in Alexandria. As we explained, Islam had their Golden Age and was at the forefront of architecture, medicine, literature, philosophy, mathematics, science, etc. Islam became Aritistotelianized, and was mixed with a Western philosophy by Avicenna and Averroes. It was not the Islam seen today. What happened?

Following this, Judaism was also Aristotelianized by a rabbi called Rambam—Moses Maimonides. He wrote the book, *A Guide for the Perplexed*, and he rewrote Judaism as an Aristotelian religion. Then came Thomas Aquinas who rewrites Christendom as an Aristotelian religion. And those Roman Catholic orders who followed Plato were fighting the ones who followed Aquinas. The Reformation was just a natural extension of conflicts that were already going on. The Reformers were Platonic; mainstream Catholicism had become Aristotelian.

Aristotle had a warped view of reality based on a misunderstanding of chemistry and physics. The Greeks knew about elements, but they did not know about gram atomic weight, or atomic number, or subatomic particles (i.e, electrons, positrons, neutrinos). They knew about atoms, that which is indivisible; they knew about elemental chemistry. But in the Middle Ages in the ancient world magic and chemistry were the same thing called "alchemy." When they saw chemical reactions taking place they thought it was magic. They did not understand the transfer of electrons going between orbitals and atoms; they did not know about chemical reactions. So when they saw something like putting chlorine and sodium together to create sodium chloride—table salt—they had to explain this some way.

Basically what Aristotle said was that the appearance of table salt may *look* like salt and it may *taste* like salt, but that is only its appearance or "accidents." We know now that it is sodium chloride, but they did not know that then. So according to this thinking it *writes* like a pen, it *looks* like a pen, it *smells* like a pen, it *seems* to be a pen, but no, it is a cigar—so give me a light. This *looks* like a microphone, *feels* like a microphone, *works* like a microphone, but this is an ice cream cone. The "microphone" is only its "accidents." It *looks* like bread, it *tastes* like bread, it *looks* like wine, it *tastes* like wine, but those are only its accidents; it is the protoplasm of Jesus Christ.

Today a Catholic will tell you, "We accept it by faith." But originally they did *not* accept it by faith; they thought that is what it was *chemically*, which of course has now been completely debunked by modern science. But to understand Catholicism it is necessary to understand that there are two kinds of doctrine: *Proxima Fide* and *De Fide*. Once again, they can change only the *Proxima Fide* doctrine. They can take the mass out of Latin and put it into English, but they cannot change their doctrine of transubstantiation which was finally defined by Aquinas; he explained it in terms of Aristotelian philosophy—a new world view.

Examples of Recontextualizing

Other figures were more noble. When the Gospel first went to the Greco-Roman world the apostle Paul said, "Jews seek a sign, Greeks seek wisdom" (1 Co. 1:22). When he spoke on Mars Hill to the Greeks he spoke very differently than to the Jews in the synagogue. He recontextualized.

At the dawn of the Industrial Revolution the old institutions of society were breaking down. An agricultural society was disappearing. The Industrial Revolution began in England. The church was a dead middle-class institution that could not meet the needs spiritually or otherwise of the common people. As we saw earlier, children as young as four were working the coal mines, dying of black lung disease, working brutal hours in sweat shops, and the only respite the poor had was getting drunk out of their minds in cheap gin mills. In the Industrial Revolution the church was finished, society was Pagan, violence was going through the roof, everything was breaking down. Along came John Wesley and his brother Charles, and they found a method to go to these people in a factory culture, the sweat shops, and the coal mines. These early Methodists found a way to *recontextualize* the Gospel with these urban classes of the working poor and their factory culture.

The Reformers come along and get some things right and some things wrong. But essentially when there is a change in world view there has to be a way to recontextualize the Gospel, not *change* it. Some people got this right, some got it wrong.

A Change in World View

In a nutshell, the manner in which people think and look upon their world based on the presuppositions that influence them is transformed by a tide of change periodically throughout human history. This of course is the now proverbial "paradigm shift." There are changes in science. Changes in science bring about changes in technology. Technological change brings about economic change. Economic change brings about social and cultural change, and this brings about political change. Why? Because it brings about a change in world view.

Long before the Reformation, over a hundred years before Luther, a heroic personality named John Huss of the Bohemian Brethren said most of the same things Luther said. The Catholic Church invited him to a disputation at Lake Constance in Germany, and burned him alive, stating, "The holy mother the church has no obligation to keep her word to heresy." (In other words to non-Catholics.) Before him it was the Lollards in England—the followers of John Wycliffe. Before them were the Waldenseans. There was never a time in history when God did not have a people for His own name, long before the Reformation.

The Reformers in the Protestant churches were assigned this idea that they had rediscovered the true Gospel, but evidently unbeknownst to them, there were people who never lost it.

What happened was that in the Holy Roman Empire the pope always had the leverage to stop the spread of the Gospel, to wipe out the Lollards, to wipe out the Bohemian Brethren, to wipe out the Waldenseans, to wipe out the Novationists, to wipe out the faithful remnant. But along comes Galileo and Copernicus. The Roman Catholic Church excommunicates them because they say the earth revolves around the sun; a change in science. This produces a change in technology: the astrolabe. Magellan and Sir Frances Drake circumnavigate the world, opening the opportunity for people to reach the New World. Columbus comes to the New World, da Gama circumnavigates Africa. They reach India with its silk trade, and there is a new economy. How did this come about? Because with Keppler, Copernicus, and Galileo the old Ptolemaic astronomy from the ancient world disappears and produces new technology and a new economy. Feudalism declines and Capitalism is born.

With that comes political and social change: the nation-state is born. People's loyalty is no longer to the pope or their local noble, but to nationalism. "I am French," "I am Scottish," "I am German." The pope no longer had the kind of control he had in the Middle Ages.

The Dilemma of Laodicea

But with this technological change comes an increase in literacy. Now we have Guttenberg's Bible; Luther puts the Scriptures into German. Erasmus translates the New Testament, Luther puts it in German, Tyndale puts it in English. They can no longer burn someone for owning Bibles. In the Middle Ages they had to be hand-copied by monks into Latin; now they go back into the original Greek and Hebrew and they can mass-produce them! The Bible is placed on the Catholic Church's index of banned books, but they cannot stop it. Luther simply got away with things for which other people were killed earlier because German princes protected him. The world view changed. God is the God of history. In the book of Daniel it says He establishes kings and removes kings (Dan. 2:21).

One of the things that will make the reign of the Antichrist so unique is that the "two times, a time, and a half time" (Dan. 7:25), as it were the lordship of history within certain parameters, will, for a fixed period, be given into the hand of the Antichrist. Other than that, God is the God of history.

It Changes Yet Again

Neither the Reformation, the Renaissance nor the Industrial Revolution were the first times this transpired, nor would they be the last. When an originally Jewish Gospel was first taken by Paul and Barnabas, followed by Titus and Timothy, from the Hebraic world of the Jews to the Hellenistic world of Greco-Roman civilization, the Gospel had to be re-explained. Each time the world view changes the church is confronted with the same challenge, which is capable of either being a threat or an opportunity. There is a reason the Reformation exploded when it did. Ultimately, when world views change, people think differently. This happens again with Wesley; the world view changes with industrial society, people's horizons broaden. They hear about America, they hear about China, they hear about India, they hear about places that only Marco Polo had ever seen. Now they think differently and it happens again. The same as before the agricultural world and the birth of the industrial world, now we have a post-industrial world—a high tech information economy. A change in science, a change in technology, a change in world view.

When I was a youth it was amazing to go to the New York World Fair and see a computer. I had only seen them on television. "What will they think of next?" A new economy evolves where we do not need people to work on assembly lines because we have robots controlled by computer systems. Menial jobs can go to the Third World where they are having their Industrial Revolution; we are high tech. New social perspectives on things bring about political changes, even the end of the nation-state as we are going into federal Europe, going into NAFTA, forming trade blocks of nations. The nation-state is finished and is becoming obsolete as we speak. There is a new world view.

Whenever this happens, whenever there is a new world view, the church faces a impending need to modify not its message but rather the methodology by which the message is presented. If the message itself is modified the church has failed; if the method is modified it succeeds. The principles of Scripture and the truths of the Gospel are immutable. What *is* mutable is the way in which these eternal truths are presented. When the world view changes, the church will either recontextualize the Gospel or redefine it. When it recontextualizes it is taking the immutable, permanent truth of God's Word and simply presenting it in a context people can understand with their new world view. But if they redefine it there is a problem. We are called to bring the Gospel into the world, not to bring the world into the Gospel!

It is not always easy to make sense of the history of the time in which we live unless we understand it in light of what is happening spiritually in the church and with Israel and the Jews. Yet too few Christians have ever known how to properly interpret their own time in light of Scripture and church history. When we see a money preacher such as Morris Cerullo marketing "Holy Ghost miracle cloths" to take away debt from unemployed people, we are seeing the same kind of fetishism that resulted in the sale of relics to finance the projects in the Medieval church. When we see the actions of the Roman Catholic Church in its ecumenical plan for Catholics and Protestants we see a new strategy for the same old Counter-Reformation from the era of the Council of Trent. When we see the dominionist ideas of so-called "Kingdom" preachers such as Dutch Sheets we see a re-innovated attempt at age-old Reconstructionism, even though Mr. Sheets may not fully realize it himself. All of these things have happened before. Social, cultural, and economic changes will always see some change for either better or for worse in the church. When the change is for the worse it will have something to do with someone's opinion.

We see what began as Gospel-preaching organizations degenerate into mere social welfare organizations, often with a political agenda using the Christian label, even though they began as biblically Evangelical. This is the tragedy of World Vision, of Barnardo's Children's Homes. We have seen 19th-century German Rationalism produce Higher Criticism, and that in turn produced a liberal Protestantism that loves a merely social gospel simply because it does not have the true one.

When any of these things are pondered and questioned on the basis of Scripture, their defenses invariably lack an exegetical basis, but rather come down to people's opinions.

At present we are at one of those pivotal points in history and church history where the world view has changed. It is not "changing"; it is virtually "changed." We are in a post-Christian, post-neo-pagan society. The world view has changed, so what do we do about it? How do we recontextualize the Gospel for the new world view? Let us consider what this new world view is like.

An Instamatic World View

To begin with, the new world view is "instamatic," an adjective first coined in upstate New York in Rochester. Not long ago, when someone sent a letter to a cousin in Australia it took five weeks. Today, air mail takes five days, fax machine less than one minute, email one second. "Instamatic"–we need this yesterday. It is a world of fast foods, TV dinners, instamatic communication. How do we recontextualize Christianity for an instamatic society? "We'll get an instamatic church!"

The Bible speaks of discipleship, learning the Scriptures, learning to walk with Jesus–"Pick up your cross and follow Me" (Mt. 16:24). We are basket cases when we get saved, so the process of discipleship–sanctification by the Holy Spirit–molds the new creation in the image and likeness of Christ, commencing with regeneration. But in an instamatic world it is always, "We need it quick!"

Your problem with anger? Your problem with drunkenness? Your problem with lust? Your problem with greed? Pick up the phone and order a pizza; they have a "deliverance" service. Pick up the phone and order a hamburger; they have a "deliverance" service. Pick up the phone and order a Pentecostal preacher; he has a deliverance service.

They think that by getting the demons cast out of them this week it will solve their problems. Why did the Apostles never teach casting demons out of believers? Why not once, anyplace, does the Bible teach one instance of it? Unsaved people are something different. No one says they cannot have demons. They are confusing demonic **possession** with demonic **oppression** at best. Who is getting the demons cast out this week? The same ones who got them cast out last week. Did their lives change? No. An instamatic Christianity for an instamatic society. "We want it yesterday."

It takes a second to be a convert; it takes years to be a disciple. Jesus never said to make "converts." When a baby is born it has to grow, but not in an instamatic world view.

A Post-Modern World View

The new world view is post-Modern. Post-Modernism says there is no propositional truth. "Truth is relative." "Truth is experiential." "It works for me." I do not mind if people have a house church; meet in a house by all means. However, have a *biblical* house church. When they sit around and all read a chapter of the Bible and discuss it, "This is what it means to me," that is a subjective interpretation. We are told in Peter these things are not subjective; there is an objective, exegetical meaning. Truth becomes relative. "It works for me"; it is experiential.

"It's not about truth; maybe there are no answers," says Brian McLaren. Post-Modernism says there are no moral absolutes, so Satan's servant Brian McLaren once again says we should have a moratorium on debating the issues of ordination for homosexuals and gay marriage, and after five years the church should decide. As we have already seen, McLaren is saying the same thing theological liberals have always said: "The church wrote the Bible, the church can rewrite it." There is no propositional truth. This is the Emergent Church.

There are multiple threads to this movement called "Emergence." But many of the essential tenets are encompassed in Dan Kimball's book of the same title, *The Emergent Church*, forwarded by Brian McLaren and Rick Warren. Further examples of it are seen in the spiritual and theological depravity of William Young's *The Shack*, where God is an uneducated heavy-set black woman expecting a baby in a world of eternity where biblical doctrines with whom the author disagrees are omitted, such as the existence of eternal hell. (A concept finding support by Annihilationists such as England's John Stott and Roger Forster.) In Young's world (and in Warren's), the church makes a quantum leap from being ecumenical to being interfaith, following the precedent set by Peter Kreeft in his apostate book, *Ecumenical Jihad*, endorsed by J.I. Packer and Chuck Colson. In a full compromise of the biblical Gospel of justification by faith and salvation by grace facilitated by the second birth requiring repentance, a sacramental gospel, a social gospel, or any gospel will do. Once in bed with the pope, ecumenical Christians following deceivers such as Colson discover that the pope is in bed with the Dalai Lama, and on the story goes, all the way back to Babylon. Or as the book of Revelation describes it, "Babylon the Great."

In the Post-Modern world of McLaren, Christianity is no longer about objective truth, but subjective perception and relational reality. Rick Warren's gospel is no longer about a repentant faith, but about a seeker-sensitive delusion. In a quest for a hollow unity pretending to be unity of the Spirit, absolute truth is replaced by relative truth, and objective scriptural spirituality is replaced by subjective experiential spirituality where the theological becomes confused with the psychological.

While such concepts are not only alien to, but in flagrant conflict with, New Testament Christianity, they are very much compatible with the Gnostic mysticism of Eastern religion that came into the Western church during the early Dark Ages with candles, incense, icons, religious mysticism, contemplative prayers, and once more the delusional pseudo-spirituality of *Lectio Divina*. All of these made a big comeback with Satan's book of lies, *The Celebration of Discipline*, by Richard Foster, the Protestantization of the post-Reformation exercises of Ignatius Loyola by Joyce Huggett, and now a complicated maze of Emergent authors and lecturers led by the English teacher turned self-proclaimed Bible teacher Brian McLaren. It is incredible that what is supposedly contemporary Evangelicism is jettisoning the lessons of Scripture, church history, and rational thought in favor of a return to the Dark Ages that embraces the monastic mysticism of the 5th to 8th centuries that produced the debacle of medieval Roman Catholicism against which the Lollards, the Waldenseans, the Bohemian Brethren, and the Reformers all reacted.

In the topsy-turvy world view of McLaren the quest for truth is dismissed as irrelevant, even though Jesus claimed to be that Truth. In McLaren's irrational book on the parables we see his demonic distortion of both reason and scriptural revelation. McLaren argues that the key to interpreting the parables of Jesus is the use of our imagination. This is pure Gnosticism and opens the door to **any** interpretation no matter how fanciful or indeed satanic it may be. Objective truth is arrived at through exegesis in a study of the parables in light of the *Sitz im Leben* of Second Temple Period Judaism and in the original biblical languages through the illumination of the Holy Spirit. Holy Spirit revelation does not contradict exegesis, but exegesis is a key to verification that our conclusions are guided by the Holy Spirit.

A new quantum leap theology is demanded to dogmatically make possible the kinds of transformations envisioned by those pressing to abandon biblical orthodoxy for a neo-Gnostic heterodoxy and to reframe Christianity as a New Age religion. Leonard Sweet pieces together quantum ideas into a new kind of theology, while Brian McLaren likewise embarks on a new theology that in essence is no theology at all. The paradigm must "shift" in their thinking.

The "Emergent" becomes convergent with the submergent as Peter Wagner's New Apostolic Reformation uniting the forces of experiential doctrine, psychology, dominion theology, and hyper-charismatic mysticism of a nature that is more Gnostic than biblical becomes a mainstay in the "new thought." The British equivalent of Wagner's ideas of a restoration of kind of apostolic authority is called "Restorationism." Hyper-charismatic figures such as Terry Virgo, Gerald Coates, Roger Forster (whose wife Faith authored *The Femininity of God*), and the late Bryn Jones sought to restore three things that never existed, based on a distorted exegesis of Ephesians 4.

The first of these is a restoration of apostolic authority. That is not the apostolic authority Jesus bestowed upon Paul and the twelve Apostles, but rather what amounts to a mono-Episcopal heavy shepherding. The second feature they are trying to restore is a version of apostolic authority akin to the American Mike Bickel and the Kansas City false prophets, and not least of all Rick Joyner and Cindy Jacobs where pretend prophets can in God's name predict time-specific events that fail to happen with utter imputing, and still be revered as "prophets." The third component of what they are trying to restore is Kingdom Now theology uniting hyper-Calvinistic Reconstructionism with the Latter Rain/Manifest Sons heresies of certain ultra-Pentecostals in the tradition of the late William Branham.

The Restoration Movement is therefore committed to restoring three things that never existed to begin with within scriptural Christianity anymore than have the unscriptural notions of its American first cousin the New Apostolic Reformation of Peter Wagner. In order to hold sacrosanct what is not scriptural, Scripture itself can no longer be held sacred in their quantum leap.

There is, however, at least one further ingredient that is essential for their quantum leap cum paradigm shift to take further root, permeating the church and ultimately predominating as its cardinal belief. This is a new eschatology where events prophesied by Jesus must be ignored with the aim of preventing them from ever transpiring. In this "new think," scriptural Christians heeding the warnings of Jesus to be alert for signs of His return are criminalized for not seeing an alternative "Kingdom Now" scenario that is, in fact, based on an interfaith universalist view of salvation, much of it built on the global P.E.A.C.E. plan of Rick Warren that is at fundamental odds with the divine peace plan of Jesus found in Isaiah 52 and Ephesians 6, that depends upon the preaching of the scriptural Gospel. Thus we see Warren arguing that his plan can work together with Hindus, unbelieving Jews, Muslims, Buddhists, or *any* "people of faith." At the same time in Great Britain, Stephen Chalke teaches that Hindus and Muslims can be "born again" and "saved" the same as Christians due to the truths found in these religions. Such notions are not original but have earlier precedents in the writings of Peter Kreeft and Colin Chapman.

In this new eschatology the denial of God's capacity to know the future voiced by Clark Pinnoch and John Sanders is a pre-requisite. Scripturally, however, if God does not know the future then He is not God. In this "new think" the outcome ultimately depends not on the sovereign foreknowledge of God or on the final plan of divine redemption as outlined in Scripture, but it rather depends upon us, armed with our own peace plans in order to achieve God's "dream." The very concept of God having to dream of what He would like to see take place itself demeans the divine status of God as eternal, omniscient, and omnipotent. It is not simply a false eschatology; it is de. facto blasphemy.

In the Olivet Discourse Jesus commanded in the imperative that His disciples prayerfully and carefully watch for the signs of His impending return (Mt. 24:42). In order to demolish this command, Rick Warren instructs his followers to ignore end-time prophecy as a "diversion." He does this by employing a translocational hermeneutic where he erases Acts 1:6 and replaces it with Matthew 24:3. The result of this is that instead of Jesus answering the question of the restoration of Israel actually asked by the Apostles in Acts 1, informing them that the timing of this is not their concern but evangelism is, Warren shifts the verses between books making it seem as if, when asked what the signs of His return would be, Jesus said, "Don't worry about it; it's none of your affair." By his "cut-and-paste" shifting of biblical verses Warren makes the Scriptures say not what God said, but anything that Warren wants God to have said!

His second device is to proof-text his theological arguments, supporting them not by exegesis but by finding whichever paraphrase of the Bible closest suits what He wants the Bible to say, with no regard for what it actually does say in the original languages or original autographs. With the help of the renegade mistranslation known as *The Message* by Eugene Peterson, Warren has effectively rewritten the Word of God as the word of Rick Warren. Yet relatively few seem to even notice it, and fewer still seem to care. In Laodicea he is "entitled to his opinion." Indeed, in Laodicea everyone has "the right to their opinion." This is once more what the very name of the church means. In an odd sense the root of this strangely surfaced over one hundred years ago during what is sometimes called "The Second Great Awakening" attributed to Charles Finney. Finney, a virtual Pelagian heretic, denied original sin even though he admitted everyone has sin. The scriptural Gospel teaches that we are born with a fallen nature due to the sin of Adam, therefore we must be born again and receive a new nature from Jesus, the "last Adam." Finney denied the spiritual nature of man as sinful, and toyed with the eternal nature of God. Although it was not what Finney taught directly, the "cheap grace" and "easy believism" from which the seeker-sensitive and seeker-friendly models of a compromised gospel and of a pseudo-evangelism requiring neither repentance nor discipleship had their seminal influence, began with Finney. Finney's borderline Pelagianism was as dangerous, unbalanced, and unscriptural on one extreme as hyper-Calvinism is on the other. Yet Finney was the harbinger of Evangelical "new think" just as Bultmann (and, arguably, Feurbach) were the harbingers of liberal Protestant and higher critical "new think."

Just as higher critical "new think" was the by-product of the spirit of the age or *zeitgeist* of philosophical Rationalism from which it "emerged," so to the "Emergent new think" is the by-product from the *zeitgeist* of New Age. In the quantum world the tangible becomes illusional and the absolute becomes delusional in the thinking of those subscribing to it. It all comes down to a matter of "imagination." This is what we have seen repeatedly in everything from Yonggi Cho's *Fourth Dimension* to Brian McLaren's *Generous Orthodoxy* which is in fact nothing more than a disingenuous heterodoxy pointing the way to Babylon the Great in tandem with the ecumenical seduction that fits it like a glove.

Human imagination not the illumination of Scripture by the Holy Spirit, but a counterfeit of it. In the Emergent Church however, and among the followers of McLaren dancing to the tune of Satan, Christianity is not about answers to eternal questions, or about ultimate truth; it's about what someone thinks works for them. Once you have imagined a new meaning of Scripture concocted from within yourself, the gate is opened wide for the guidance of the Holy Spirit to be counterfeited by the guidance of a familiar spirit–a demonic spirit guide. Those professing to have had such bogus revelations are nothing more than New Age "ascended masters" pretending to be prophets of God. Among these are Rick Joyner, Todd Bentley, Kim Clement , and others like them. The propulsion for this trend did not originate with McLaren however, but with Mike Bickel's support of the Kansas City false prophets, and promoters of this kind of deception such as Bill Johnson. The travesty of Jack Deere's apologetic for the Manifest Sons distortion of Joel's Army is taken to its natural conclusions by the ideas of McLaren (whether McLaren realizes it or not). What we have in essence is not merely a satanically deceived pied piper leading rats into a deluge, but more accurately a Judas goat leading the sheep of Christ into the slaughterhouse of Satan.

A Consumerist World View

Instamatic discipleship, experiential theology, propositional truth. What is the new world view? The Emergent Church. I call it the "*Sub*-mergent Church." In the new world view, the new economy, if it is anything it is consumerist.

In the United States are TV channels with no programming, no shows, just commercials. "Phone in now 1-800-S-U-C-K-E-R! Give us your Visa number, your American Express number! And this hideous piece of junk you would never purchase otherwise can be yours! As an added bonus we'll throw in another hideous piece of junk! Call now!"

Name it and claim it! Blab it and grab it! A consumerist world view.

How does someone recontextualize the unchanging Gospel of Jesus Christ, how do they recontextualize the unalterable doctrines of the Word of God for a consumerist society with a consumerist world view? That is a fair question. Only instead of recontextualizing the Gospel for a consumerist society we get Kenny and Benny and we redefine the Gospel as a consumerist religion. "Name it and claim it! You're a King's Kid! Blab it and grab it! We take Visa. And for a love offering of just $1,000 we'll send you an imitation pair of earrings that look just like Joyce's. Your friends won't be able to tell the difference on Sunday"

They call it "Faith-Prosperity."

It is no coincidence that the suave-styled male televangelists resemble con-artists, and their female accomplices resemble geriatric Barbie dolls so gaudy that the secular world justifiably mocks them. When Jim Bakker was portrayed as a religious con-artist in the character of Elmer Gantry, his late wife Tammy Faye Bakker would come out holding a microphone and crying, causing waves of black mascara to flood down her face, reducing her in appearance to a cross between the bride of Frankenstein and Miss Piggy. The world mocked and we cannot blame them. If the church had mocked, perhaps Bakker would not have wound up in jail.

A consumerist world view results in a consumerist Christianity (if you want to call it "Christian"). Forget about "the love of money is the root of all kinds of evil" (1 Ti. 6:10); if someone chases it they will lose their faith. Never mind that if they are out chasing it they do not have any faith. The worship of mammon masquerades as the worship of God, faith in faith calling itself "faith in Jesus." In truth, it is the sin of covetousness, but they call it "faith." Instead of recontextualizing the Gospel for a consumerist society they redefine it as a consumerist religion.

A Multi-Faith, Multi-Cultural World View

We live in a multi-faith, multi-cultural society. What they do not tell you when they promote an Islamic preacher like they had at Bill Hybel's church, or they had at Mr. Schuller's place, is that not a single Islamic country in the world gives Christians the freedom they get in America. It is a "religion of peace and tolerance."

Our present government, the present president, lets them build mosques all over the United States funded by Saudi Arabian Wahab, but not one church can be built in Saudi Arabia. They know it is a lie, but if politicians could not lie they would not have anything to say.

God does, in fact, have an agenda for multi-faith multi-culturalism: His is a one faith multi-culture. *We are one in Christ.* But instead of having God's agenda for a multi-faith, multi-cultural society they have to find a way to make the Gospel palatable. So they will get Peter Kreeft, author of *Ecumenical Jihad.* "We must have ecumenical union with Islam to save society," says Peter Kreeft, a Protestant convert to Roman Catholicism.

"Oh, yes! This is a wonderful book!" says Chuck Colson—a man who used to be a liar and a deceiver for the Nixon White House during the Watergate scandals who has now adopted his formidable prowess that sent him to federal prison and is serving the Vatican.

"Great idea!" says J.I. Packer.

Rick Joyner spoke in a synagogue but did not mention the Lord Jesus, the Jewish Messiah.

When someone gets in bed with the pope they are, with the pope, in bed with the Dalai Lama. It is not guilt by association; I do not believe in guilt by association. The Word of God does not teach guilt by association, but it absolutely teaches guilt by *cooperation*.

There are Evangelicals in the ecumenical and interfaith movements. Richard Mouw from Fuller Theological Cemetery is in it, as well as guys like Ravi Zacharias, who is now compromising with Mormonism. Packer, Zacharias and Mouw are not liberal Protestants; these are people who claim to be Evangelicals—born again.

Bill Hybels claims to be a Christian. He had a Muslim preacher in his pulpit in Chicago explaining Islam after September 11. Please find me a mosque that will let me explain the Gospel to Muslims. I am afraid there is none to be found. Robert Schuller had the Muslim Grand Mufti of Damascus in his Crystal Cathedral, with Schuller saying he would not object to his grandchildren becoming Muslim, a religion that teaches Jesus Christ is not the Son of God and that Mohammed is a greater prophet than Christ. Such pronouncements are openly hostile to the true Gospel and are the joy of Satan's heart. This is the same Schuller who referred to the pope as "the Holy Father," as did the former Archbishop of Canterbury George Carey. The New Testament containing the words of Jesus in Matthew 23:9 no longer appear to be in Schuller's library, but the Quran rejecting that God even has a Son seems to be.

A Programmatic World View

The new world view is a programmatic society. Get the right software package for your computer and your hardware will do what you want it to. Just get the right software package, just get the right program, and it will all happen for you. What you need is the right sales strategy, the right marketing strategy. Get the right strategy, the right approach to management, and you will grow says the new world view. It is a matter of getting the right program for your computer, of getting the right management philosophy for your company. It is a programmatic society.

Central to a programmatic world view is its obsession with power. What horse power was to the industrial era of hot rods, where cars could deliver more speed than one could legally drive, computer speed and gigabyte has become to the high tech era.

So, too, many are captivated by an obsession, not with The Holy Spirit Himself who is the source of spiritual power (*dunamas*), but with power for power's sake. We witness this in Laodicean churches from the counterfeit revivals of Toronto, to Todd Bentley's Lakeland characterization of The Holy Spirit as "Bam!", to the choral chanting of "More power! More Lord!" It is not more of The Lord's Spirit being sought with His derivative power as the bi-product, but a quest for and focus on the power itself. Jesus directly rebuked this fixation with power (Luke 10:17-20). People seek a newer program capable of delivering more power often for power's sake.

How do we recontextualize the Gospel of Jesus Christ in its eternal, unchanging essence for a society whose world view is programmatic? It is a good and necessary question. The problem is that instead of recontextualizing the Gospel for a programmatic society, they are redefining the Gospel as programmatic. Get an *Alpha Course*, get *Purpose Driven*, get with the program—*40 Days of Purpose*. Once they get the program, the hardware will do what they want. It is no longer, "Get God's vision for your church"; it is no longer, "Let's have a prayer meeting and seek the Lord." It is, "Let's have a church meeting and be 'seeker friendly'." Sheep are to be led, not driven. But they redefine the Gospel as a programmatic religion.

267

The Dilemma of Laodicea

The dynamo of this unscriptural thinking has been C. Peter Wagner, who once occupied the Donald McGavern chair at Fuller Seminary. It was from that chair the concept developed that by studying a revival in one area it could be replicated in another by a programmed formula. No real place was given to a sovereign outpouring of the Holy Spirit. And more irrationally, Wager's ecclesiology was ecumenical. In actual fact the large Pentecostal church growth throughout Latin America that Wagner's devotees studied constituted an *exodus* from Roman Catholicism, not an acceptance of it. Not only did Wagner factor out the sovereignty of God from his equation, he factored in the wrong variables, not even correctly identifying the characteristics of the revivals being studied which are *not* ecumenical in nature. Unfortunately, ecumenical influences have been exported to Latin America from the USA and Europe. The multiple aspects of the new world view dovetail, overlap, and co-operate synergistically. Concurrent with a progammatic world view, for instance, is the media-driven world view where packaging again trumps substance.

One example of how a scriptural philosophy of missions and evangelism is usurped instead of facilitated by the elements of emerging world views was seen in the Mel Gibson Hollywood film, *The Passion of The Christ*, foolishly heralded by one Evangelical leader after another as a powerful evangelistic tool with many proclaiming Mel Gibson to be a saved Christian.

The film, in fact, was the Hollywood interpretation of a book by a Roman Catholic mystic, which book was loaded with scriptural and historical inaccuracies and heavily punctuated with poetic license alien to the actual Gospel narratives.

Paleo pathology has proven that the Roman nails would have to have been driven through the radius (wrist) to support hanging body weight, but the film had the Roman nails being driven through the metacarpal (palm) in support of the Roman Catholic dogma of stigmata. In truth, it was a Roman Catholic film and not a scripturally Evangelical one, and Gibson is Roman Catholic not an Evangelical.

Interviewed on America's ABC TV by Dianne Sawyer on Ash Wednesday for the film's premier, Gibson insisted he was not an anti-Semite and refused to discuss his father having been a holocaust denier. Gibson stated categorically that one did not need to be a believer in Jesus Christ to have salvation or go to heaven. So while thousands of Evangelical preachers were claiming the film was Evangelistic, and many that Gibson was a saved Christian, Gibson himself rejected the fundamental substance of the Gospel on national prime-time TV.

The Dilemma of Laodicea

Following the commercial success of the film (in large part made possible by Evangelical church and youth groups being bused to see the film) Gibson was interviewed in Australia by *The Sydney Morning Herald*. He was asked what impact making the film had on his own life. His direct reply was "I don't have to answer questions like this anymore; I have a hell of a lot more money than I use to have."

Gibson bluntly admitted the film was about making money like any other Hollywood film.

Shortly afterwards, Gibson was arrested early in the morning driving drunk out of his mind near Malibu Beach in California, cursing the Jews as responsible for all of the world's troubles. Not long after that "Saint Mel" left his wife and children, and divorced her in order to quickly re-marry a younger woman Hollywood style.

Not long after this, in mid 2010, he split with her with a recording being released in court proceedings where he shouts about her "being raped by a gang of niggers."

Gibson is a racist, an anti-Semite, and a liar who abandoned his family to go off with another woman. He flatly rejected the scriptural Gospel and admitted with his statement that, because of *The Passion* film, he has "a hell of a lot more money than I use to have," that his motives for making the film were financial.

Yet again, one senior Evangelical leader after another publicly lacked not only wisdom and discernment, but plain doctrinal knowledge of God's Word that reveals the film to be inaccurate, flawed in its historical and cultural content, and promotional not of the scriptural Gospel, but of mysticism. Anxious to get a quick fix to spiritual decline, and deluded by progammatic and media-driven world views, they were gullible enough to look to Hollywood for evangelistic leadership. What is most startling is that those singing the praises of Gibson were a chorus of Evangelical America's most visible shepherds parading the sheep into the clutches of a Hollywood wolf.

This was not the first time that Evangelical leaders were sucked in and conned by a Hollywood film star.

No one made a bigger fool out of Evangelical America than Ronald Reagan when he lied to them over the abortion issue to gain organized Evangelical support for the Republican Party as an alternative to the Democratic Party. This was replayed in the later Bush era. The late Jerry Falwell led an effort of the so-called "Moral Majority" to redeem America morally, as if that could be achieved by electing the correct politicians. Once more, a quick-fix program was to be the salvation.

There is no New Testament basis to align the cause of the Gospel with any political party or ideology; we are only to pray for those in power and be a moral influence by the preaching of the Gospel.

In the end Ronald Reagan did nothing to reverse abortion, but instead advanced it by appointing a pro-abortion judge, Sandra day O'Connor, to the US Supreme Court. It was O'Connor who wrote the court's decision ordering the Ten Commandments out of the courts in a decision regarding the Alabama Judicial Building. It was the Republican Supreme Court of Earl Warren that ordered God out of the classroom, the Republican Supreme Court of Warren Berger that ordered God out of the maternity ward with Roe v Wade, and it was a pro-abortion Reagan Republican Supreme Court Justice who ordered God out of the court room. Reagan was a Freemason and relied highly on the advice of his wife who consulted with Jean Dixon and fortune tellers, and was an occult practitioner. Reagan deceived Evangelical America.

The Epistle of John teaches clearly that denial of The Father-Son relationship is "antichrist." The Quran has precisely this same teaching that "God has no Son" ("Allah is not begotten and does not beget"). Yet, George W. Bush placed a Koran in the White House in order to honor Islam after the September 11 attacks, and began celebrating Ramadan at the White House. Once more, Laodicea looks for a program–a media program, a political program, a Hollywood program, or any program to solve its problem of a decline in Christianity in the post-modern World.

A Psychologized World View

If the new world view is anything at all, in modern Western society it is psychologized. Psychology is a pseudo-science because apart from bio-psychology, neural psychology, and psychiatric medicine (and even that stuff is corrupted by non-quantitative psychology), it is non-quantitative; it is pseudo-science. It is also pseudo-religion—the religion of man.

Biblically we are a box within a box, within a box. "Know ye not you are a temple of the Holy Spirit?" (1 Co. 6:19). We are three-dimensional. We have a body (Greek "*soma*," Hebrew "*guph*"), we have a soul (Greek "*psuche*," Hebrew "*nephesh*"), and we have a spirit (Greek "*pnuema*," Hebrew "*ruah*"). We are three-dimensional because we are made in the image and likeness of a triune God. Psychology, both Jungian and Freudian in its adjuncts, however, says we are two-dimensional, that we are simply monkeys with better DNA.

Even before I was saved I never believed there was any empirical evidence for Darwinism. I found it an implausible proposition. When I was a youth in college I went to a lecture about protein synthesis. Proteins are extremely long molecules, and at one time before super computers, if you figured out the structural formula for one protein (it did not matter what it was) you got the Nobel Prize automatically. But it is necessary to get right down to the level of atomic covalence. String the right number of amino acids together (there are twenty of them) to eventually get one peptide, and then the right peptides together in the right sequence to get a polypeptide, and then the right sequence of polypeptides together to get a polypeptide chain in order to synthesize one protein (and for that one protein there must be an equally complex coenzyme). And I am supposed to believe this happened by chance!?

There is not a program in the world that does not require a pre-existing intelligence to write the program. This is infinitely more complicated than any program humanly possible to create, and I am supposed to believe, "But that happened by chance." If there is one zero or one digit out of sequence in a software program it does not work. That happened once and over 20 million telephones went out in the Northeast of the United States for 6 hours. If there is one genetic mismatch the result is a hemophiliac. It is infinitely more complicated than anything anyone invented, and it could never happen by chance. ·

I could not believe that a code could exist without a pre-existing intelligence. However, I realized I was wrong. Now I understand there *is* empirical evidence for Darwin. Anybody who believes that recombinant nucleic acids transmutate across the gene's barrier in a natural environment *must* be related to a baboon. I know of no other plausible explanation. When I am wrong I have to admit it.

The Bible says we are three-dimensional; psychology says we are two-dimensional. It confuses the soul with the spirit. So does Eastern religion like that espoused by Yonggi Cho who has said, "Your subconscious imagination is your spirit."

And the visualization thing? It is shamanism, mystical Buddhism, Hinduism. Psychology is pseudo-science; it is non-quantitative. It has corrupted education; it has corrupted marketing; it has corrupted psychiatric medicine; it has corrupted everything it can. It is the religion of man; it is not even a real science.

God breathed on Adam. (Gen. 2:7). Adam became a living soul. What people are in terms of their consciousness, intellect, emotion, etc., is a product of what we are physically—organically, with what we are spiritually. Mental illness never originates in the mind. There is something *chemically* wrong with someone, such as hyperthyroidism or a reaction to a drug, or there is something *spiritually* wrong with them. Or both. But mental illness never originates in the mind. The whole thing is a lie, but we live in a psychologized society. "Christian psychology" is an oxymoron, emphasize the "moron."

Bill Gothard psychologized the Christian youth of America in terms of self-esteem. If I were the only person who sinned, God would have had to become a man and go to the cross just for me. When I was first saved I thought "personal Savior" meant I had to personally accept Jesus Christ; that is *half* of what it means. What it means is that if I were the only person alive and sinned, He would have come down and been nailed to the cross just for me. If that is the value the God of the universe places on you and on me, what is this issue of self-esteem? We are not called to have self-esteem, we are called to crucify our selves. Self-esteem is the diametric opposite of the Gospel message.

But as the youth were psychologized by Bill Gothard, the women of Christian America were psychologized by James Dobson (another ecumenical figure), then the pastors of America were psychologized by Robert Schuller, and lastly the men of Christian America were psychologized by Promise Keepers. So twisted was Promise Keepers (an ecumenical organization founded by Bill McCartney who not long prior had been a drunk and had little chance to grow in his professed faith) they massively distributed tens of thousands of copies of Robert Hicks' book *The Masculine Journey* bearing the Promise Keepers' seal of approval and logo.

When challenged about *The Masculine Journey* which became their tome, the Promise Keepers published an 8-1/2 page defense before finally being forced to distance themselves from it. The book's association with Jesus as a phallic male maintained that Jesus Christ was tempted to engage in sex with other men. The book taught that when someone's child came home intoxicated, or under the influence of drugs, or lost their virginity outside of marriage, instead of responding as Christian parents normally would we should "see it as a rite of passage, shake their hand, and congratulate the next generation for being human." The author maintained that this was not placing a benediction on sin, but it is logically impossible to interpret it otherwise.

The companion workbook of Hicks' *Masculine Journey* for Promise Keepers' men's fellowships called upon Christian men to allow other Christian men in the groups to question them about details of sexual intimacy with their wives. In the thinking of any scripturally-based Christian, far from being "men of integrity," the Promise Keepers seem to be for blasphemers, condoners of immorality, and filthy perverts who respected neither Jesus, their wives, nor their families. The Gnostic hermeneutics used by various Promise Keepers Bible teachers spiritualized biblical text out of context to the point of being laughable, assigning the Word of God their own definition.

Promise Keepers' leader James Ryle even taught that the Beatles were God's prophets and had a prophetic anointing. Having attempted to share Christ with both John Lennon and George Harrison it is my own testimony that both held to a New Age spirituality. George Harrison was a professed Hindu and John Lennon subscribed to a kind of pantheistic humanism, although he seemed to have a clearer understanding of the scriptural Gospel. George Harrison's idea of Christianity was the Liverpool Irish Catholicism into which he was born, and which he and his second wife Olivia, a Mexican-American, rejected. These were certainly not Christian prophets.

Promise Keepers however, found its essence not in any doctrinal theology but in psychology. A close version of the same became briefly prominent in Australia and New Zealand with Cole Springer who likewise substituted anecdotal motivational psychology while employing Christian jargon for a scriptural definition of ministry.

Instead of exegetical preaching there were anecdotes, stories, and a few verses out of context. This was a Tony Robbins using scriptural terminology but not scriptural theology. The problem is the adherents of such foolishness are too ignorant of the Word of God to know the difference. These are not preachers; these are motivational speakers. I once heard Springer at a meeting in Australia ramble on about the verse, "The joy of the Lord is my strength." He spoke about how his holiday house was destroyed and he laughed it off. The entire time he did not mention Jesus Christ once, and his emphasis from this verse was not on the Lord but rather on the joy.

One can laugh off the destruction of their holiday home by a disaster (particularly if it is insured), but how can one laugh off a tragedy such as a loss of a child or some other anguishing disaster? This is the theology of clowns and it will fail any man if his faith is really tested. The false teachers who propound such nonsense have deluded themselves into thinking they are something other than the theological frauds they actually are.

Motivational psychology says, "Maximize the positive, minimize the negative! Visualize your ambition, your aim—make it a reality in your own mind!"

Some guy comes out wearing a suit and a Benny Hinn haircut and says, "Once you make it a reality in your mind, you'll make it a reality in the minds of others! You'll get that investment capital! You'll get that venture capital! Don't exercise the negative; emphasize the positive!"

Of course, when the Dow Jones goes through the basement during the next business cycle, one realizes the only person it worked for was the motivational speaker.

So this comes to church now. "The Lord gave me a vision of this church, hallelujah! We're going to see ten thousand people! Don't tell me how many single parents we have in our church, don't tell me about the unemployment in our community! That's negative and in the name of Jesus, I don't receive it. We have a positive faith confession!"

These are motivational speakers using motivational psychology; they are not expounding the Word of God. It is a lot of hype. We have a psychologized society so we have a psychologized church. Instead of recontextualizing the Christian message for a psychologized society, we psychologize Christianity.

A Synergistic Impact

These things have a synergistic impact; they compound each other as in physics. The sum becomes greater than the individual components when they are put into practical application.

The Bible tells us how to deal with past hurts, but "I was abused as a child." Reckon yourself dead (Rom. 6:11). That abused child is dead; you are a new creation (Gal. 6:15).

"Get a shovel and dig up the corpse" is the advice of Ruth Carter-Stapleton a proponent of inner healing. Instead of reckoning the old creation dead, dig it up and live in it again and ask Jesus to bring healing into it. If somebody has polio and they die, they no longer have polio. If somebody was an abused child and they are dead, they are no longer an abused child.

Twelve Step programs for Christians? Their fellowship becomes based on their old sin. "My name is Jack, I'm a recovering alcoholic." "My name is Jill, I'm a recovering addict." Well, my name is Jacob and I am *not* a *recovering* cocaine addict, I am *born again*; I am a *new creation*!

A New Age World View

In 1968 the Maharishi Mahesh Yogi came to London and gave a series of lectures at the University of North Wales in Britain where I sometimes speak. It was attended by the Beatles, the Rolling Stones, and various Hollywood film stars—the pop icons of my generation. And in 1968 the New Age Movement was born. That same year the charismatic movement kicked off big time. Both of these movements declared publicly and openly they were going to spiritually revolutionize the Western world. The charismatics said they were going to revolutionize it for Christ; New Age said they were going to revolutionize it along the lines of Eastern metaphysical religion. I have to ask, in the last 40 years has society become more Christian or more New Age? The only thing that has failed more miserably than the charismatic movement has been its leaders. ***Nothing*** has failed the cause of Christ more decisively than the charismatic movement other than its leaders. This is not to say that some people were not saved, but it is to say, "Saved into what?" Lunatic asylums with a cross on the roof? New Age has won.

Christ will not be defeated, but the church has been. The Lord of glory will trample Satan in defeat. This is not promised to the church, it is promised to the Lord. It is the ***seed*** of the woman who crushes Satan's head, not the woman (Gen. 3:15). Do not listen to Kevin Connor and these Kingdom Now proponents; their false doctrines are not only false, but nuts.

When witnessing to New Agers it is amazing because they are Gnostic. There is a rebirth of Gnosticism in the Western world, and it is New Age based on Eastern religion (Isaiah 5 warns about it).

This is the third time in the history of the church where Eastern religion has invaded the Western world. The first time was with the post-Nicean fathers—Origen and such. The second time was when Medieval Roman Catholicism was influenced by Islam and Hinduism brought back by the Crusades into Europe.

When witnessing to a New Ager one has to be careful of the terms because they are witnessing to a Gnostic. Gnostics will use the same terms we do, but mean something different by them. For instance, in Roman Catholicism their Gnosticism is known as *Sensus Plenior*. Tell them we are saved by grace and the Jesuit will say, "Oh, yes! We're saved by grace!" So the Protestant and the Jesuit theologians shake hands and agree the Reformation was a mistake, we are all saved by grace. "Grace" in Hebrew is "*hesed*"—God's covenant mercy. In Greek it is "*charism*"—"gift." In English it is "undeserved favor." But in Catholicism? "An ethereal substance earned by the sacraments." We can all agree we are "saved by grace" when there are two different definitions of grace.

New Agers are the same. You saw "the light"? They saw "the light"—the cosmic illumination of the inner self. You were "born again"? They were "born again"—reincarnated. You believe in "sin"? They believe in "sin"—negative energy. You believe in "the Spirit"? They believe in "the Spirit"—the *zeitgeist*, the spirit of the age. They use the same terms we use, but believe something different by them. People do not understand this. All these Gnostics will use the same terms that mean something different. There are all kinds of Gnosticism but the most prevalent today is New Age.

How do we recontextualize the Gospel for New Age? Well, they did not; they redefined the Gospel as New Age: Kundalini Yoga, Toronto, Pensacola —all with the blessings of theocrats like Thomas Trask. (I met him only once, briefly; in my view he was as phony as a $3 bill. Please tell him I said so.)

A Politically Correct World View

We live in a society that is politically correct. (I long for the days when "PC" meant only "personal computer.") In a politically correct society what some think is needed is a politically correct church. So what if the Bible says the blood of Christ cleanses from *all* sin (1 Jn. 1:7)? We have to let Catholic people believe they are going to atone in Purgatory for their own. It is not politically correct to tell them the truth.

Where did the Lord Jesus ever compromise the truth for the sake of political correctness? "But we *love* people!"

He loved the woman at the well. That is why as soon as she began with her false doctrine He said, "Lady, you do not know what you are talking about; salvation comes from the Jews" (Jn. 4:22).

He loved that Syro-Phoenician woman and her little girl; that is why He said, "I cannot give the children's bread to dogs" (Mk. 7:27). "I would like to help you and your little girl but your religion is not fit for human consumption; it is dog food." Mormonism is "dog food"; Roman Catholicism is "dog food"; Talmudic Judaism is "dog food"; Jehovah's Witnesses is "dog food"; Islam would have to improve substantially before it could even be considered "dog food."

But we cannot say that; it is not politically correct. It may be theologically correct, but we have to have a politically correct church where love is compromised. Always remember Philippians 1:9:

> And this I pray, that your love may abound still more and more in real knowledge and all discernment.

If there is no knowledge of the Word of God and no discernment they do not have love; they have frothy, emotional stupidity camouflaged as love. It is a cheap substitute that only someone who is biblically ignorant and/or demonically deceived can possibly believe is love. Jesus never compromised truth in the name of love. On the contrary, *because* He loved people He told the truth. If I did not love people I would not care what they believe in.

The Dilemma of Laodicea

If someone walked into a physician's office puffing on a cigarette and coughing, what kind of physician would say, "It is not politically correct to offend smokers"? Would they offer, "Do you have enough matches?" "Do you want an ash tray?" "Let me go out and buy you a carton of Marlboroughs." What physician would say things like that? *No* physician would say such things.

A physician would say, "We've got to get you a chest x-ray. Please put those things away before they put you in your grave ahead of your time." Otherwise he should not *be* a physician. On the same merit, if a preacher will not say, "Get out of that heathen Roman church," they should not be a preacher.

A Feminist World View

We live in a society that is feministic. The "Marian Agenda" dovetails with the feminist agenda if you understand it. (That is why Catholic families are so often matriarchal.) What happens in a feminist society, a feminist world view? Ordain the women.

Nobody says women cannot teach other women to a limited degree (Titus 2:3-5), but the Bible does say that Joyce Meyer has no biblical right to be doing what she is doing. A husband is the head of the wife as Christ is the head of the church (Eph. 5:23). That is what "head covering" really means; it was a cultural emblem (1 Co. 11:7).

Because of the fall of man, men have become insensitive, women have become hypersensitive. When a husband and wife pray together it is usually the wife who hears from the Lord first. When a husband and wife get saved it is usually the wife who gets saved first. If the husband gets saved first the wife usually becomes a Christian. Not always, but usually. When the boot is on the other foot I know some very godly ladies, sisters in faith with unbelieving husbands who grieve every day. Women are more sensitive. It is easier for them to hear from the Lord, easier for them to get saved. Men are reliant on female sensitivity. But anything God intends for good, the world, the flesh, and the devil will use for evil. So while it is easier for women to hear the voice of the Holy Spirit, it is also easier for women to hear the voice of a counterfeit spirit. They are more vulnerable to spiritual seduction. The serpent beguiled the woman (Gen. 3:13). Leadership being male is not based on bigger musculature or orthomusculature; male leadership is based on protection. That is what God says.

Who needs God when you have Joyce? A feminist world view, a feminized church. The ladies wear the trousers, the men sing soprano.

A Pan-Sexual World View

We live in a pan-sexual society: gay, straight, bi. When homosexuals have specifically reduced longevity by 25-30 years, how can I as a Christian love people and not hate a lifestyle that is going to kill them 25-30 years before their time? I am not a Darwinist, but if I were, Darwinism dictates that homosexuals are genetically inferior. If they are born that way they are genetically inferior according to the principles of the Darwinistic approach to biomedical science. Why? Because it is non-reproductive. They cannot have children, so that is why they want to adopt children and artificially inseminate; they want other people's children. Darwinism says that if they were born that way they are medically inferior; there is something wrong with them as a birth defect.

Now I do not believe they were born that way. Unless they became a homosexual or lesbian in a penal institution, find me one single homosexual that does not have an absent or weak father figure, or lesbian who does not have an absent or weak mother figure. It is a direct consequence of the divorce rate. That in turn relates to delinquency and a lot of other things such as the proliferation of AIDS.

Society is pan-sexual, therefore they have to ordain homosexuals says the United Methodists, says the Church of England, says the Presbyterians. Homosexual ordination, same-sex matrimony—these are Christians called to be "salt" and "light" (Mt. 5:13-16). How do they recontextualize the Gospel for a pan-sexual society? One thing is for sure: it should not be redefined into a pan-sexual religion. We again refer to Rick Warren's appearance on *Larry King Live* where he backtracks, going against California's Proposition 8 and the refusal on *Larry King Live* of Joel Osteen to affirm the plainly stated teaching of both Testaments concerning homosexuality and lesbianism.

A Media-Driven World View

We live in a media-driven society. As Andy Warhol said, in the future everybody will be famous for 15 minutes. You can have your own show on the Internet! It is a media-driven society, therefore we have a media-driven church.

It becomes about teleproduction, not substance; presentation and style are the aim, not theological or doctrinal content. Hype easily replaces anointing and glitz eclipses God's glory. It is the Jim Bakker Show, starring the bride of Frankenstein! Every time she cried that mascara ran down her face and she looked like the bride of Frankenstein.

Then there was the other tragic figure Jimmy Swaggart who liked to publicly hang people for doing the kinds of things he was into himself.

The Dilemma of Laodicea

A media-driven society, a media-driven church. They are paying their tithe to an idiot box. It is a production; it is a show; it is all about media.

A No-Fault World View

We live in a "no-fault" society. There are states with no-fault insurance. So what if someone was drunk out of their mind when they ran a little kid over? There is no-fault divorce. So what if she went out and cheated on her husband and had an affair with the postman? It is not her fault. We live in a no-fault society with a no-fault world view. We are all victims. "I was a sexually abused child; that is why I did it to another little child." Because someone was a victim himself, this justifies victimizing someone else? "I am sick; it is not my fault." So we have a no-fault Christianity and Rick Warren says, "Don't preach repentance, we have to be seeker sensitive." The Bible is not "seeker sensitive," it is "sin insensitive"—repent!

Where Are We Now?

Once again we find the church in a fast-transforming world with a paradigm shift where the world view has changed radically and continues at an even more exponential pace. Instead of recontextualizing the Gospel for a consumerist world view we turn Christianity into a consumerist religion courtesy of Paul Crouch (who paid $425,000 in a hush clause legal settlement demanding silence about charges of homosexuality), Kenneth and Gloria Copeland, John Avanzini, Benny Hinn, Jerry Seville, Rod Parsely, Mike Murdoch, Joyce Meyer, multiple divorcee Paula White, Todd Bentley, and a host of other money preachers ranging from heretical hype-artists to out-and-out freaks. Their doctrines are not derived from Scripture, but when examined exegetically are the products of their own opinion.

In an instamatic society with an instamatic world view we have invented an instamatic church with instamatic spirituality acquired by unbiblical deliverance ministries, financial contributions, and having a heretical false prophet lay hands on someone.

In a new world view rife with feminism we see the ordination of women.

In a pan-sexual world view we see the ordination of homosexuals and lesbians.

In a new programmatic world view we see a church-growth movement capable of delivering only transfer growth because it is based purely on the programs of marketing psychology.

In a politically correct world view we see a church that is politically correct to the point of being scripturally wrong concerning the apportionment of culpability for sin.

In the new psychologized world view we have a psychologized church that confuses the spirit with the soul.

With a media-driven world view we have a media-driven church activated by performance, not genuine anointing. When the church uses entertainment to draw people it must inevitably use entertainment to keep them, but in the end the church can only lose, because the secular world will always put on a better show. And so the show goes on.

The multi-faith/multi-cultural world view of a multi-faith/multi-cultural society has produced an ecumenical and interfaith church where the fundamental doctrinal tenets of Scripture are willingly sacrificed in a quest for unity with those who do not believe these tenets and where the proponents of this betrayal, such as Chuck Colson, J.I. Packer, and others are heralded as "Christian leaders."

Not least of all, and perhaps above all, we have an emergent world view that is not only New Age but Post-Modern. As a result, under the inspiration of Satan some in our ranks have invented the Emergent Church.

He Is At the Door

This is the new world view. We have the challenge to seek God for His wisdom on how to recontextualize the Gospel for the new world view. But instead we are redefining the Gospel. We should be recontextualizing, but we are redefining. We are turning it into something it is not, something God never intended. How do we do it? We are making big mistakes. We are getting as wrong or worse than Augustine and Aquinas ever were. Anything the Reformers did in their errors we have compounded ten-fold. But Jesus says, "*I stand at the door and knock*" (Rev. 3:20).

"Hey, Laodicea! Let Me in! You are getting it wrong, Laodicea! You are redefining the Gospel; you are not recontextualizing! Let me in, Laodicea! You are running on people's opinions instead of on My Word! Laodicea! You are running on people's opinions instead of by My Spirit! It is not *My* wisdom but yours! Let Me in, Laodicea! I can show you what to do! I showed Paul what to do when he had a new world view to contend with! I showed George Whitfield what to do when he had a new world view to contend with! I showed John Wesley what to do! Let Me in, Laodicea! Let Me in, Laodicea!"

"*He who has an ear, let him hear.*" God bless.

Index

Index

Index

Index

Index

T